Our Romantic Niagara

Dedication

This book is dedicated to Albert H. Tiplin as a tribute to his unique contribution to the knowledge of the geology of the Niagara River and the Falls, and in recognition of the countless hours he spent in observation, research, teaching and writing about "Our Romantic Niagara".

10,2

Tiplin, Albert H. (Albert Henry), 1908-
   Our romantic Niagara: a geological history of the river and the falls

Includes index.
Bibliography: p.211
ISBN 0-9690457-2-7 (bound) –
ISBN 0-9690457-3-5 (pbk.)

   1. Geology--Niagara River (N.Y. and Ont.).
2. Geology--Niagara Falls (N.Y. and Ont.).   I. Seibel, George A. (George Alfred)   II. Seibel, Olive M. (Olive Marguerite)   III. Title.

QE191.T46 1988   557.13'51   C88-090202-7

Book Design and Layout
George A. Seibel

Typesetting and Finished Layout
Just Your Type, Niagara Falls, Ontario

Printed and Bound in Canada by
The Ainsworth Group Inc., Kitchener, Ontario

Our Romantic Niagara

A Geological History of the River and the Falls

BY

Albert H. Tiplin, B.A., M.A.

WITH ADDITIONAL MATERIAL BY

George A. Seibel

Niagara Parks Historian and
City of Niagara Falls Historian

Olive M. Seibel, B.A.

Editor

Published by
The Niagara Falls Heritage Foundation
1988

Reprinted by the Niagara Parks Commission
1990

Patrons

The Niagara Parks Commission

Kiwanis Club of Stamford,
in memoriam W. Paul Branscombe and Winston C. Fischer

Niagara Falls Review
R.D. Gale family – Bob, Ida, Keith, Barb, Dave and Bob Jr.

Maid of the Mist Steamboat Co. Ltd.
Walker Brothers Quarries Ltd.

Eckert, James F.

Tustin, Alan and Agnes

Acres International Limited
Carr, Bruce and Shirley
Cooper, G.F.
Grice, Jim and Elizabeth
Kitney, Connie Dunn
Minolta Tower Centre

Montgomery Brothers
Moriyama and Teshima,
 Architects and Planners
Olsen-Sottile Insurance Brokers
Rosberg, Gerald M.

Aceti, Michael and Rita
Ainslie, Dr. Robert
Allison, Mary Ann Miller
Anstruther, John and Kathy
Anstruther, Kenneth J.
Anstruther, Robert A.
Badger, H.C.
Bailey, George
Bald, Isabelle, Gospel
 and General Book Shoppe
Ball, Mr. and Mrs. Edwin J.
Barratt, Bill
Biggar, Robert and Annie
Branscombe, Anne-Louise
Bratley, John T.
Briggs, Mr. and Mrs. John
Burns, Wayne
Calaguiro, Albert and
 Carmella (Cupolo)
Campbell, Robert
Campbell's Historical
 Museum, C.S. Campbell
Collins, Bruce
Coombe, Bob and
 Marion (Dell)
Copeland, Rob
Cote, James and Helen
Cox, Bernice and Harry
Cropp, Alfred
Damato, Charles
Dewar, Mr. and Mrs. W.E.
Duns, G.A., B.Comm., CA
Feren, Mirree
Frantz, Ed
Frum, Barbara
Gauld, Rankin
Gould, Gwen
Groves, Gary A.
Haeck, Christel

Haine, Kathleen
Hall, Jack R.
Hardwicke, Helen Brooks
Harris, Gertrude
Hetherington, Carol
Hopkins, John B.
Hosking, Sheila J.
Istok, Joe and Sachiko
Janvary, Paisley and Zoli
Johnson, Mildred and Carl
Johnson, Gordon G.
Karafiloff, Ned
Keppy, Myrna
Kerr, Shirley (English)
Kewley, Dave
King, Donald C.
Kudlac, Theodore A.
Lowe, Ed
Lundy's Lane Historical
 Museum
Mackenzie, David
Mackenzie, Rod and June
MacQueen, John and Vera
Major, Joseph C.
Malloch, Dr. W. Bruce
Mason, Walter E.
Matthews and Cameron Ltd.,
 Ontario Land Surveyors
Matthews, Ruth (Agnew),
 Harold, Ray
Maxwell, Margaret (Stevens)
McDowell, Ruth
McKay, Mr. and Mrs. Kenneth
McMillan, Yvonne
Merritt, Dr. Richard
Miller, James Rysdale
Minov, Nicholas
Monroe, Mrs. G.F.
Montgomery, R.P.

Mottershead, Harry
 and Audrey
Nagy, John G.
Neal, Art
Newman, Bill
Niagara Falls Museum
Nicholson, Rob, M.P.
Oatley, Eugene R.
Pearson, Janet (Grindall)
Pierce, Ruth
Pope, V.W.
Prentice, Mr. and
 Mrs. F. John
Proctor and Redfern Group,
 The, (David Schram)
Quance, Richard A.
Robinson, Philip S.
Robinson, Val
Robinson, W.A. Lorne
Russell, Elaine (Grindall)
Saks Hardware
Salisbury, E.L.
Seibel, George
 and Olive (Haine)
Simons, Gerald F.
Smith, Florence and Jim
Stephenson, Jack and Milly
Sunstrum, Dennis
Titley, Colin and Candis
Underhill, Gordon and Mary
VanSlyke, Dorothy
Walker, John and Doreen
Watson, Eric H.
West, Allan C.
Weston, Alfred and Patricia
Williams, David and Valerie
Wilson, Edith (Biller)
Wreggitt, Ronald and Rita
Young, Roger

Preface

"Albert Tiplin deserves to be recognized for the time he spent in research and observation, and for his written record of the geology of the Niagara River". These are the words of an eminent geologist who is familiar with our river and gorge, and who read Al Tiplin's complete series of newspaper columns.

It is more than fifty years since these columns – almost seventy of them – first appeared, weekly, in the Niagara Falls Evening Review. I was one of the many who were introduced, through these columns, to the fascinating story of Our Romantic Niagara. This book contains most of the columns, arranged in order by geological period. It progresses upriver from the birthplace of the Falls. Sometimes there is repetition of information. Originally this served to refresh the memory of readers because the columns were written at different times.

Readers are reminded that Al Tiplin wrote, using geological knowledge available fifty years ago. Because there have been advances in geological science since that time, the geologist who was our adviser, suggested areas where present knowledge made Al Tiplin's conclusions obsolete. We attempted to make necessary corrections.

"N.B." in this book, always indicates explanatory material which has been added to the original Tiplin columns. In other places, brackets are used to insert present day names for bridges, power facilities, etcetera.

There are no footnotes because Al Tiplin did not provide them in his columns. The bibliography, however, includes many of his references, as well as current references consulted during the writing of chapters listed under my name. Those who are interested in further study, should consult the more recent books on the subject.

Photographs are important in this book and because of Mrs. Tiplin's persistent searching, we were able to include many of her husband's original photos. For other photos I am grateful to: the New York Power Authority, Paul J. Pasquarello, Chief, Photographic and Reproduction Services, and Tom Robbins, for his painstaking printing of the photos used; Ontario Hydro, Eileen Pilby, Photo Librarian, A.T. Jakubick, Civil Research Department, Manfred Erhardt, Acting Environment Specialist; Golder Associates; National Gallery of Canada, Ottawa; Coutts Library Services Ltd., Mark Hopkins; Herbert C. Force; Ken James; Barry Virgilio, Conservation Educator, Schoellkopf Geology Museum; Amon Carter Museum, Fort Worth, Texas; Helga Studios; Wunderlich and Company Inc., of New York City; Niagara Mohawk Power Corporation; Frank O. Seed, who formerly granted permission for use of his copyrighted photographs; Niagara Falls Ontario Fire Department, Deputy Chief John Shapton and fireman Paul Hibbard. I drew on the picture collections of both the Niagara Falls, Ontario and the Niagara Falls, New

York, Public Libraries. I appreciate receiving permission from the Niagara Parks Commission to reprint pictures from Ontario's Niagara Parks, 100 Years.

I appreciate receiving permission to reprint and quote material from: Geological Survey of Canada Sector, Energy Mines and Resources, Ottawa; U.S. Army Corps of Engineers, Buffalo District; Royal Ontario Museum; Acres International; valuable information was supplied by Ivan Lloyd, Ontario Hydro Corporate Relations Officer, Western Region, as well as from Ontario Hydro Reports and Publications supplied by Peter Maitland; Environment Canada Water Management Branch, Burlington, Ontario; Dario Violanti, Senior Engineer, Niagara Frontier State Parks; Robert D. Barnett, Historical Technologist, provided the information on the Niagara Falls Park and River Railway Powerhouse; Robert B. MacMullin allowed me to use his treatise and photos of the Whirlpool Reversal Phenomenon; Schoellkopf Geology Museum for L.S. Bernstein's graphic account of the collapse of the gorge wall on the Schoellkopf Power Plant; Harold Moynihan shared his reminiscences of the fish traps; John Morley, Director of Horticulture, Niagara Parks; Dave LeMasters, Niagara Parks Naturalist and Dave Gillis of Niagara Parks Engineering helped in many ways. George Bailey, Niagara Parks Director of Public Relations, took hundreds of photographs, and provided encouragement and advice.

My work was made easier by the staff of the Reference Department of the Niagara Falls, Ontario, Public Library. Inge Saczkowski researched the story of "Old Mother Hubbard". John Burtniak of Brock University, Christel Haeck of the St. Catharines Public Library, and Donald Loker, Local History Consultant at the Niagara Falls, New York, Public Library, shared their extensive knowledge of the area. Dwight Whalen first made me aware of Scott Ensminger's work on the Hubbard Point Caves and Mr. Ensminger allowed his work to be reproduced in this book.

Several of Al Tiplin's former students worked on this book. Helen Stanley transcribed the newspaper columns onto typewritten manuscript pages; Astrid Akkerman reproduced Al Tiplin's original sketches; Doreen Gervais typeset the book; Dorothy Van Slyke, Chief Librarian of the Niagara Falls, Ontario, Public Library, was our third pair of eyes for editing and proofreading. The index is the result of her expertise in reworking the information provided until it reached its most concise form.

Notwithstanding all of the help mentioned above, it would not have been possible to publish a book of this quality without the financial support provided by the patrons who responded in such a heartwarming and generous manner. Many wrote or called to say how glad they were to be able to show their appreciation for the benefits they had received from Mr. Tiplin, as they still call him.

I am most grateful for the support given by Pamela V. Walker, Chairman, and Dennis W. Schafer, General Manager, of The Niagara Parks Commission, to my request for a grant-in-aid from the Commission toward the publication of this book. The generous contribution made by the Kiwanis Club of Stamford and the donation of advertising space by Gordon Murray, publisher of the Niagara Falls Review is also acknowledged.

I appreciate the support and encouragement of my fellow board members of the Niagara Falls Heritage Foundation: Robert C. Coombe, John A. Sampson, William R. Sauder and Robert F. Smith.

This book has been a joint effort with my wife Olive, also a former Tiplin student, assisting as editor, rewrite specialist and proofreader. However, in spite of all the assistance I have received, I accept full responsibility for the content of this book. My goal was to put A.H. Tiplin's work on record and to add to the knowledge of Our Romantic Niagara.

George A. Seibel, Chairman
Niagara Falls Heritage Foundation

March 1988

Table of Contents

N.B. in this volume indicates explanatory or other material added to Albert Tiplin's original text.

Formation of the Sediment Beds

"There rolls the deep where grew the tree,
O Earth what changes hast thou seen!
There where the long street roars, hath been
The stillness of the central sea.
The hills are shadows and they flow
From form to form and nothing stands;
They melt like mists, the solid lands
Like clouds they shape themselves and go."

Although the science of geology was a mere infant when Alfred Lord Tennyson wrote these lines, the great poet had a very clear conception of the main imports to be cherished from a study of rocks. Plainly the "eternal hills" of other poets and the psalms are not so eternal; at least geology teaches us not to use the word "eternal" lightly, or if we do so use it, to be aware of its possible relative time value.

The light areas on the map represent dry land during the Silurian Period of the Palaeozoic Era; that was the age when all the rocks were formed in the Great Lakes Basin, except for those south of Lake Superior and in small areas at the southeast end of Lake Ontario. In the unshaded regions on the map which are above water today there appears in the rocks no trace of fossil life such as we have found in the Niagara District layers. But everywhere that the map shows a shaded area on the continent, due to borings and valley or gorge cuts, it is known that sea life very similar to our Niagara varieties flourished. In some spots these rocks are at the surface because the layers which once overlaid them have since been worn away and deposited anew and in different form in other later seas or oceans. Notably these appear exposed in a band about 48 kilometres (30 miles) wide along the south shore of Lake Ontario, through Buffalo and our own district, extending in the same narrow band from Hamilton to Georgian Bay. Outcroppings can be seen inside the Arctic Circle on many of the islands there, in South Africa, China, Russia, England, Ireland, Scotland, and Scandinavia, all with the same sort of fossils.

Early in Palaeozoic time the main outlines and mountain masses of the North American continent with which we are all so familiar, slowly began to form. There were many interruptions by encroaching arms of the sea; these very interruptions may be looked upon as favouring the growth of our land mass, in as much as they deposited great layers of rock which caused the land to grow into its present form. In Europe, for instance the maximum depth of the deposits laid down in this age is estimated to be 30,480 metres (100,000 feet). In the

1

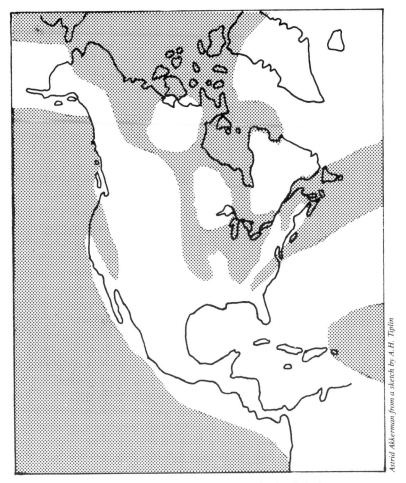

The light areas on the map represent dry land during the Silurian Period of the Palaeozoic Era. The Palaeozoic Era was the geological era containing the oldest forms of highly organized life, reptiles and seed-bearing plants, dating back from 500 million to 350 million years. Niagara District sedimentary deposits, mostly sandstone, shale and marine limestone, were laid down in the Silurian period, which dates back 430 million to 390 million years. This is the third period in geological time during the Palaeozoic Era.

Appalachian mountain region they are as much as 7,620 metres (25,000 feet). The general character of the life in these rocks shows that they were formed by shallow water in the neighbourhood of land. The great thickness of the layers shows that extensive wearing down of the rocks which were above water must have taken place. It is certain that the waters were shallow because the type of life which then existed had not yet learned to live on land at all, and not in deep water. This was characteristic at least of the early part of this age but in the latter part, some 400 million years later, plant life had developed with the swamp ferns as high as our modern trees. Insects, dragon flies of giant size, and true fishes which could live in deep water also evolved. Indeed the next period of this age, called Devonian, was marked by plant life venturing from the shallow shore to swamp land.

During this long age the shape of the continental mass changed greatly about six definite times, periods represented by slight but significant advances in the forms of life, and their various abilities.

The map shown, taken from a standard geology text (of the 1930's), represents roughly the way our continent was when invaded by the sea in the period when most of our rocks in this district were laid down. First were deposited the Clinton series of shales and limestones. Then came the Lockport (with the Rochester shale preceding it in New York State) and Guelph stages.

But let us try to see the Silurian Period of this age in general fashion. When the Palaeozoic Era began, the land area of the continent seems to have been fairly level. This means that the land must have been above water for a great time, long enough for it to have been all worn fairly smooth by rains, gases in the air, and the earlier glacial period which, surprisingly enough, seems to have afflicted the land even long before this distant age. Then the land slowly submerged again, this lowering being merely a phenomenon in connection with some vigorous mountain building going on in some part of the earth. The sea encroached from the east and north, the part flowing in from the New York region westward to ours being called the Medina Sea or the Appalachian Gulf. It was similar to the Mediterranean Sea in Europe today.

It is quite probable that in the early existence of this Appalachian Gulf the waters were very saline; no deposits of salt were formed, but as we said before, salt water from these layers is encountered in drilling. If this period was salt, then quite likely the climate was quite dry and thus favoured the concentration of minerals in the waters.

The life of the Silurian Period both in our hemisphere and in Europe was very similar. This was natural for it is evident that there existed a path of migration between the two continents by way of the Arctic at least; and quite possibly Labrador, Greenland and Scandinavia were joined by a land bridge.

The first rocks in this district laid down by the Appalachian Gulf were the Medina. These were shallow water deposits derived from the only land masses which were nearby – the Appalachian highlands (not yet mountainous) on the southeast. These deposits, as the water deepened more and more, gradually overlapped the previous layers of the preceding period, and forming farther north as the shoreline advanced in that direction, came to rest on the earliest volcanic crystalline rocks of Laurentia. It is known that the early rocks of this period were formed in shallow water where waves vibrating shoreward could leave ripple and wave marks on the sand. Indeed in the Niagara District, some of the ripples are from .30 to .45 metres (one foot to one and a half feet) apart. Life was not abundant in this gulf, possibly because the water was too salty.

Later, as the waters deepened with the continued submersion of the land, in the Niagara District at least, they became purer and thick with delicate, lace-like colonies of coral forms called bryozoans. The presence of these early plant-like animals always meant deposition of limestone. For short periods the destruction of coral reefs and shells followed; thus were the calcareous shales laid down which separate the Clinton from the Niagara Limestone layers along the gorge. In all of these layers both of shale and limestone, frequent cross-bedding is indicative of shallow water.

The Mediterranean-like sea of the time was quite prolific; in it lived jointed "sea weeds" which were really coral, as their true plant nature is still a matter of doubt; also crinoids or sea-lilies which were animals too; these fragile creatures were easily broken by the waves when death claimed them; thus it needs rare luck to find a complete one outlined in the rock. They may have been very numerous in the rocks such as are at the end of the Three Sisters Islands and Goat Island – those massive tough layers which strangely have so many holes in them. It is thought that the holes were in many cases formed by these crinoids being dissolved out after fossilization had taken place. Goat Island once may have been the site of beds of coral sand which fostered heads of coral and other kindred organisms.

Later the rich Mediterranean-like sea (this word meaning "between the lands") with its abundant life became a comparatively dead sea devoid of life, salty, surrounded by arid desert lands.

But after the reign of the arm of the sea which formed the Salina rock salt beds, fresh water followed, staying for a long time. Dry climate and then wet alternated, until permanent elevation above the ocean was attained at the end of the Palaeozoic Age so that this district remained dry until the melting waters of the glacier flooded it perhaps only 150,000 years ago.

4

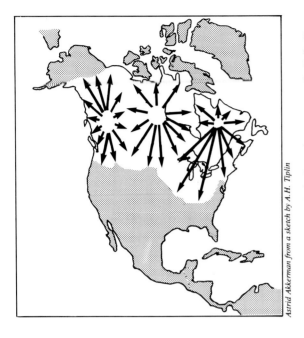

Astrid Akkerman from a sketch by A.H. Tiplin

This map of ancient Arctic Canada was produced by the Canadian Government Department of Mines. The arrows point out main outflowings of thick ice from three main sources of glaciation occurring throughout a recent geological age at several different periods. Cause of such ice growth is not yet known.

During the Pleistocene (glacial) Epoch, much of Canada and the United States was subject to four ice ages, interspersed with warm inter-glacial intervals. All evidence of earlier ice ages was removed during the last (Wisconsin) glacial advance. Wisconsin glaciation consisted of an early advance of ice – Early Wisconsin; a major retreat of ice, then another advance – Middle Wisconsin – about 42,000 to 20,000 years ago; then the last advance – Late Wisconsin – which retreated from this area about 12,000 years ago. This glacial map represents present knowledge of the path of the Late Wisconsin glacier. (Terasmae – Colossal Cataract 1981).

Geological Survey of Canada

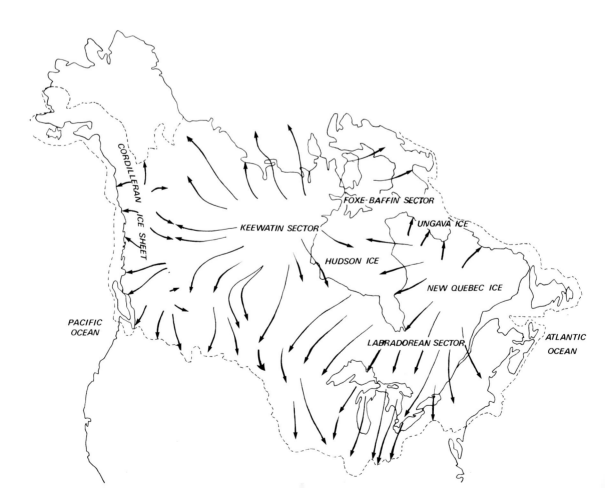

Ice Age Footprints

Are there traces of an icy age? Yes, the following, and yet more besides had I room to tell and picture them all. Why should there not be such in plenty here, since this is, of all places in the world, perhaps entirely unique in presenting to our view a variety of evidence that is usually all too rare or so disjointed as to be nearly meaningless. Such evidence, layered, and obligingly pigeon-holed in gorge and valley of different date as it is in the Niagara District sheds the clearest light yet on other previously puzzling features scattered about the Great Lakes region. For example, if a reader were to come upon a geologist at work in the Chicago River outlet at the bend of Lake Michigan, it would not be at all unusual to ask him if he were at the moment studying the geology of the Niagara Gorge. Such are the distant and various influences which have wrought and left this spot as it is!

In the same quarry which held the other footprints of that distant and uncomfortable age, the striae, (furrows in rocks caused by glacial movement) are other markings much larger and at first glance strangely familiar to one who has held communion with our Niagara Gorge. What is so familiar about these long ridges which run the opposite to the glacial striae, or very nearly so? Where has such met the eye of the local history enthusiast before? Hum-mocks so uniform in curvature that it is no wonder the French, with their flair for the artistic and the precise, imaginative word, have called such formations "roches moutonnées" because they do seem like sheep in a row? They are formed by the polishing action of the small particles of rock embedded in the base of the glacier. Why they are in waves or ridges I cannot say more than that such forms are found quite commonly wherever glaciers have sojourned. Glaciers are still mysterious and are the object of present intensive study nearly everywhere in the world. However, I can warn the reader from personal experience not to be too sceptical regarding the high polish such formations receive. Earlier in the Spring when the surface here was all little pools of water and quagmires of sticky red clay I had occasion to jump for drier footing. The expected and usual two-point landing turned into a broader one-point landing with surprising suddeness, and the landing-field was nearly my camera.

Seriously, to "return to our muttons" as the French say when they refuse to have the subject of conversation changed, such formations do occur more in the beaten path of the average tourist to the Falls. Let the reader go to the waters at the east end of Goat Island and the Sister Islands. In much larger form he will see the mutton rocks forming the ledges

N.W.

A.H. Tiplin

These strangely polished, carved ridges (glacial striae) are called "roches moutonnées" or "sheep's rocks" and are characteristic of glacial country. The ridges pictured here run diagonally across the bottom of the picture, toward the northwest and they are from a Port Colborne quarry. There are others in Walker Brothers Quarries and Queenston Quarries.

of the rapids above the Falls. These I am quite sure are not the true type of these ridges; these were formed by the cutting of an ancient stream; later, they were polished by the glacier. It may be objected that perhaps the ice carried down by the river every winter and spring caused this polished and rounded surface; such was undoubtedly the case to some slight degree, for the glacial striae have been obliterated here. But these same ridges are smooth and rounded where they are exposed on the land to one side of the river.

It is not yet known why glacial ages occur. There are, of course, several theories, none of which is absurd. The most likely are connected with astronomy and the cycles of momentum which affect our globe. Briefly we may take note of each one without commenting on any of them:

1. Our Sun is a variable star which is not constant in its output of light, heat and actinic rays – in short, in its production of the electro-magnetic rays. Sun-spots, which are being counted by the students of the astronomy classes throughout a year are proof of this. These are known to go in 11 year cycles; they are storms like tornadoes on the gaseous surface of the Sun but they are not centrifugal eddies of air as they are on Earth but gigantic eddies of magnetic forces. In the long run they cause our climate to be damp. The moot question is – do they occur in cycles of a much more enormous scale (say, 100,000 years) with corresponding more extreme climatic changes?

2. Our Solar System (Sun, Moon, and all the nine worlds which go about the Sun) may have recently, with fair regularity, run into some dark clouds which can be observed in space with a telescope. These masses are so thick that they can obscure

the powerful light rays from giant stars which are on the far side away from us. They have been measured as many billions of miles across. If the Earth were to accompany the Sun through such a mist for a long time, the heat of our luminary would be appreciably lessened, causing a steady growth in all the snowfields on Earth.

3. At distant periods of time, figured by some astronomers as roughly every 100,000 years, the Earth's path around the Sun is irregular, so that at such times it could be as much as 14,000,000 miles farther from the Sun than it is now at any time of the year. Strangely enough, some geologists have from evidence considered such a period of 100,000 years as fairly close for the interval between Glacial Ages, although at the same time recognizing that such a figure could only be provisional.

4. The levels of the various lands are constantly but slowly changing. Suppose such a change caused the Gulf Stream to flow across the Isthmus of Panama to the Pacific when it was submerged?

5. The relations of the quantities of gases making up the air envelope of the Earth are not always stable. There is now about 2 percent or less of carbon dioxide gas in the air in most places on Earth at sea-level. This gas is able to absorb the heat of the Sun more than the other common gases; moreover being heavy it would hold this heat close to Earth's surface. Extensive and luxuriant vegetation growths, jungles for example, in the presence of sunlight use this gas and produce oxygen which does not absorb the Sun's heat nearly as much. Thus a warm cycle of climate would inevitably bring on its own cold spell because a warm, tropical climate would also have rich foliage which would use up the heavy gas. The only catch to this idea is that Nature has provided a balance. These same plants, when there is darkness, use up oxygen and give off carbon dioxide just as we humans do all the time. In the final analysis then, the effect of this theory would depend on something which affected the length of the daylight hours apportioned to the thickly forested part of the world. This is too long-range for me to comment upon. N.B. The foregoing hypotheses are based on knowledge current on the subject in the 1930's.

On the map presented here which I have adapted for my use from a report of the Ontario Department of Mines, one can easily locate three main sources of the ice which covered Canada. A fourth is not indicated here because it is still almost wholly in existence today – the Greenland Continental Ice-sheet. Each of these distributing centres is a high plateau upon which winter snows could collect to great depths if the climate of the world were to become on the average only a few degrees lower – snows which like some today on the tops of many mountain ranges could not appreciably be melted by the summer's heat. Slowly then, pushed on to slightly lower land by the increasing snows behind, these snow ice fields could influence the climate as they spread over more and more of the lowlands – influence it so that the sources which gave them momentum were greatly enlarged. Such ice streams are like rivers in many respects – they eat out the land wherever it is low, carrying with them, held fast in the mass of ice and snow, rocks, sand, gravel, and clay. They enlarge any valley they may pass down, smooth the tops of any elevations they have the energy to climb, undercut what they cannot climb, and then when it is time for them to rest – when either they have reached the ocean, or are forced to melt by some miraculous climatic change – then they give up their burden, enriching some stretches of country with fine sand and clay, making other places wastes of barren gravel and boulders.

What is in the bottom of the glacier, a confused mass of ice, stones, sand, clay, settles as a fairly flat sheet of soil upon the country beneath the glacier when the ice melts – undisturbed except for the streams of water which may at points issue from the ice. Such is known as the ground moraine. This may be observed over all our district wherever the ground is fairly flat. At the foot or end of the glacier, after one of its advances made after a cycle of severe winters, when the final retreat for the total mass is sounded, lies abandoned the terminal moraine which is usually a ridge or heap – Lundy's Lane Ridge, and smaller ridges to the south. Part of all this – the ground moraine, terminal moraine, and encased drift in the ice near the top – is swirled into heaps by the streams from under the ice and forms a kame – Goat Island, St. Davids Ravine Gravel Pits, Stamford itself, Fairview Cemetery and the "Plains of Abraham" (the football field of Stamford Collegiate). These areas will be discussed in later chapters.

Owing to some vagary of Nature's thermostat, the second ice age, called the Wisconsin, came to a stubborn end in this district at least. The change in climate was not enough to make it give up its frigid grip entirely so that it would melt back nearly to its home in the highlands of Canada. It was forced to retreat, but not very far north of Midland or North Bay it halted. Then for a while there seems to have been a temporary balance between so much cold and the new heat, for the glacier remained more or less in the adjacent northland influencing the land to the south by releasing great floods of ice strewn waters when the seasonal thaws came. Thus the inter-glacial deltas near Toronto, and in fact under the city itself, were deposited; these today form the remarkable laminated cliffs of Scarborough.

But in the Niagara District the distant ice was working changes also. We mentioned before that the ancestors of Lake Erie and also of the more western lakes were formed by the melting of the second glacial age. A southern extension of its far flung water empire seems to have been left as a threat of third advance in the embryo basin of the present Lake Erie. This ancient body too was impelled by gravity to fall from the cuesta or step-land into the lowland of the Ontario basin. At least one of its outlets was in the Niagara District near the side of the Whirlpool, and its course was roughly northwest through the region of the present St. Davids Valley which it formed. This gorge had the same work performed on it by the inter-glacial river as our younger, better known Niagara River is still performing.

After a warm spell of possibly four thousand years, snow in the north became the main order of the weatherman. More snow fell in the winter season than the short summer could melt away. As this layered snow field became deeper and thicker through the centuries, its own pressure rendered it plastic so that it slowly began to flow as a semi-solid river down the valleys in the highlands to the inviting lowlands where it could at last find rest. It is said that if a barrel of molasses becomes smashed, even in freezing weather, the mass becomes plastic and slowly flattens out until it is as level as the floor. So the ice came, possibly at the rate of only a few feet a day, from the Labrador highlands moving ever southwesterly in a mass thick enough to carve polished grooves in hard limestone and granite as the modern stone-cutter shapes the flutings on a pillar. St. Davids channel became choked by the silt deposited by the ice-filled waters which heralded its advance.

But this ice age in turn had its day and was forced to relinquish the southern lands to the increasing heat which portended the modern period – an era which we do not yet know as even ephemerally permanent. Some experts, if there can be men skilled in such an investigation, are of the opinion that this warmer time of ours is merely another inter-glacial stage; that the ice will at some future date threaten again Man's best works, perhaps even his existence. Others believe that this last retreat is the final one; that the whole earth will become tropical or temperate as it was several times before so that coal could again be formed even in the Antarctic; and they hold that the ice will not come again for perhaps millions and millions of years, for there have been times before in the story of the Earth when ice ages were long eons apart; indeed one of the earliest rock-floors of the Earth bears traces of an ice-burden almost before any life forms appeared on this planet. But such considerations, while they speak of eternity and of a Power omniscient, and omnipotent, remind us of our mortality and confuse our consciousness.

We have read how the new glacial lakes formed by the melting of this last ice age found the surface of the country scarred with ridges and trenches of debris and gravel, hummocks of debris, and barriers which seemed to be laid down everywhere in the path of water trying to hurry back to its mother, the ocean. And it is now an old story how these bodies of water and their interconnecting streams underwent various changes which left their traces in the contours of the land or in the rock foundations of the country itself as the rivers performed the duty of emptying their sources to lower and lower levels, until both the rivers and the lakes evidently cognizant of that law of nature by which everything on a grand scale is harmonious and full of meaning, became the loveliest, most inspiring setting for a homeland that one may see the world over.

Our Home
on the Steps

The most prominent and most puzzling feature of our topography in the Niagara District is the Niagara Escarpment. It begins at Watertown, N.Y. and extends along the south shore of Lake Ontario, through Lewiston-Queenston, continuing northwest through the Bruce Peninsula up to Manitoulin Island, a distance of 1609 kilometres (1000 miles). This weathered edge of a very ancient sea-bottom is a focal point for all eyes.

It is not generally realized that we in the Niagara area live in a great plain which runs east and west, and extends from the rocks of the Laurentians (Canadian Shield) about 161 kilometres (100 miles) north of Toronto (which is near Lake Ontario at Kingston) south to the Allegheny Plateau which forms the foothills of the Adirondack and Appalachian Mountains. This plain, to view things in a much larger scale, is merely part of the lowland in which even Lake Superior and the other Great Lakes lie. North and south of these Great Lakes there are highlands.

About 600 millions of years ago the region now forming these lowlands, which was then granite, basalt and other rocks, was submerged beneath the early oceans. The northern edge of these oceans lapped against the Laurentian Highland (Canadian Shield). Their waves, aided by the rains and suns

of countless centuries gradually eroded the rocks in the form of sands, muds and carbonate sediments which formed the bottoms of these oceans. These turned to rock in various layers, dated fairly well with different forms of sea-life which turned obligingly to fossils when they were not eaten by other creatures or did not otherwise disappear. Map I shows how this region must have looked at the end of the Silurian Period of the Palaeozoic Era, about 450 million years ago. (Present knowledge: The sediments which formed the rock layers came from the rising mountains to the southeast).

The top layer, the Salina, has since that time weathered back from where it lay on the granite rocks north of Toronto to about the latitude of Buffalo, New York. It is not found in the Niagara Region proper. The Lockport Limestone layer, of course, starts at Queenston. Just below the Heights there, the Queenston Shale layer appears brightest in all its rust-red glory and it underlies Lake Ontario. Those layers not labelled below this familiar one were laid down in the period before the Silurian which was witness to the formation of all the rocks in the Niagara Region – a period lasting about 75 million years, from 435 million years ago to about 390 million years ago.

After the rocks of the Silurian age there were

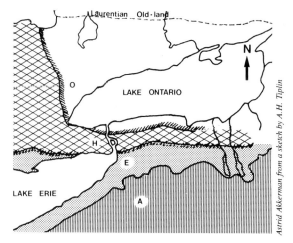

This map shows Our Home on the Steps, that is, plateaus or cuestas, with their fringes of worn rock: A – Allegheny Plateau on the horizon; E – Erie Plain with Onondaga Escarpment; H – Huron Plain with Niagara Escarpment; O – Ontario basin fringing the crystalline rocks to the north, the lowest and most weathered lowland.

those of many periods in the rest of the world's time down to today. Map I shows the present tilt of the Silurian and lower layers in this district. This scale is exaggerated vertically a great deal in order to show the slope in a small space. Perhaps this tilting, about 3 metres (20 feet to a mile), was made between the Silurian Period and the next one – the Devonian or Age of the Fishes. At any rate, there is another escarpment of rock layers beginning under the University of Buffalo, and another higher one about 64 kilometres (40 miles) south of Buffalo – a very high and uneven one leading into the Carboniferous Age layers of Pennsylvania which produced the coal and perhaps the oil which are now being so eagerly used. These appear in Map I. A glance here will show that we live on the second lowest layer of a series of steps or plateaus coming down from the Allegheny Highlands to the Ontario Basin where the Laurentian Plateau (Canadian Shield) is more or less skirted by the lake as it flows eastward toward the ocean. As a matter of fact, from Brock's Monument on a clear day and with fairly powerful binoculars one can see the white cliffs of Scarborough 16 kilometres (10 miles) east of Toronto. Only a short distance to the north of that the crystalline rocks of the Laurentian Highlands (Canadian Shield), or old lands, emerge from beneath their blankets of Palaeozoic layered rocks.

Weathering has greatly eroded the ancient Palaeozoic ocean bottoms which used to fringe the northern crystalline rocks. On a south to north axis, reading left to right: P – Portage Escarpment; O – Onondaga Escarpment; F – Falls of Niagara; N – Niagara Escarpment. Scale: 1 centimetre equals 19 kilometres (one inch equals 30 miles).

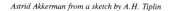

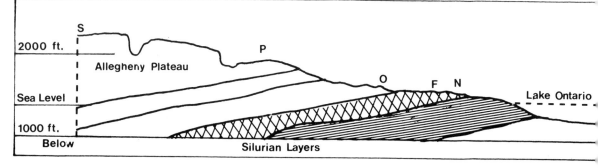

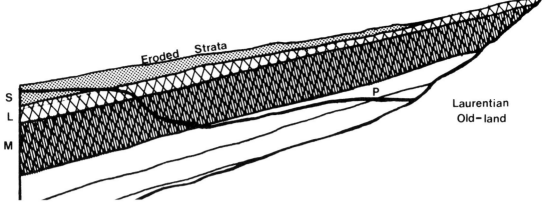

The ancient ocean bottoms shown in position before millions of years of erosion could remove the strata to the level of "P" – the present surface of the Ontario Plain, with the deepest part filled by the Lake. (Vertical scale much exaggerated). S – Salina rock; M – Medina rock; L – Lockport limestone.

MAP II

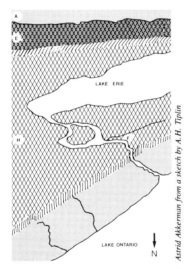

This map of cuesta topography shows the lowlands and their eroded edges – our escarpment.
O – Ontario Plain; H – Huron Plain; E – Erie Plain; A – Allegheny Plain.

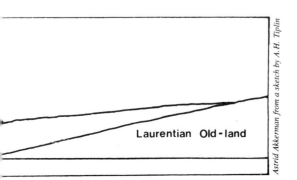

From that distant Silurian Period all down through the Mezozoic Era which was characterized by giant reptiles and through the long Cenozoic Era until this last part of it in which we, the mammals, partake of a place in the sun – all this time these gorge rocks have been wearing away from the Laurentian Shield, and all this time no further building has taken place in this lowland unless we count as building the spreading of debris by the glacier. During the Mezozoic and Cenozoic era, then, this section of North America was above sea-level. Ever since it has been undergoing erosion. Naturally, the edges of the rock layers as they rested against the Laurentian crystalline rocks to the north, or on top of the Silurian beds near Buffalo, or on top of these Genesee and Hamilton and Cayuga shales and limestones farther south yet near Gowanda or Salamanca, New York, would tend to decay and weather back from their original limits. The blankets of rock would also as naturally tend to retreat in distinct sections wherever there existed a thick hard limestone or sandstone on top of a deep mass of soft shale, or very thin limestones. Once this dissection and eroding back started, it would proceed more rapidly. For then lowlands would be formed, rivers would run in all directions toward the lowest layers as towards a basin which promised them an outlet to the sea. So the softer layers continually broke away, being less resistant to the weather, while the upper harder layers of any section of beds became more or less prominent cliffs or escarpments which even today are slowly retreating southward.

Today the escarpment, which really made our cataract and which is still its real and ultimate reason for being, is still after many millions of years, eroding southward.

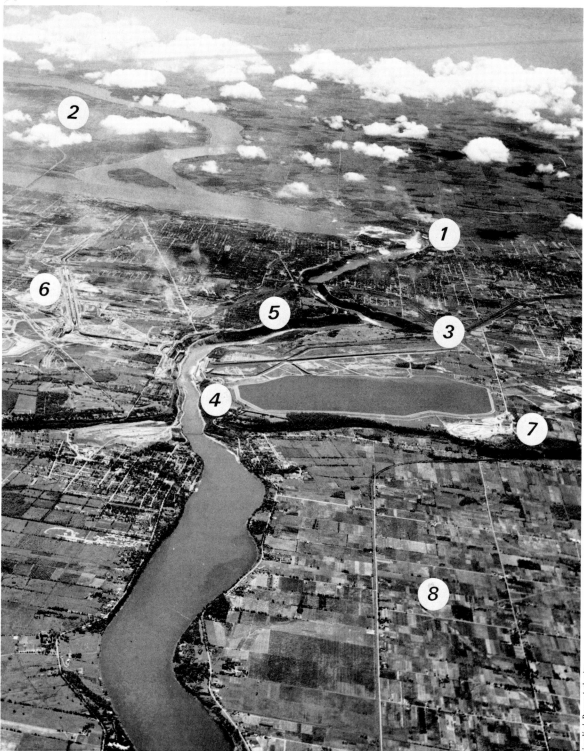

The Niagara Escarpment shows in this 1960 picture as the dark tree line running across the centre. No. 1 is the Horseshoe Falls; No. 2 is Grand Island; No. 3 is the Whirlpool and the point where the twin tunnels come out of the ground at the edge of the Whirlpool-St. Davids Buried Gorge. The water then goes through an open cut canal to the Sir Adam Beck Generating Stations at No. 4; No. 5 is the Niagara Glen; No. 6, the State of New York Niagara Power project under construction with the cut and cover conduits not yet covered; No. 7, the white area to the left is the Queenston Quarry and to the right and above the number the light areas are sandpits; No. 8 is the fertile Ontario plain, the Niagara fruitlands.

The Former Lake Bed

"Once upon a time" all the upper lakes were united in one, called Lake Warren for convenience. This was formed by the melting ice from the glacier front when it rested somewhere north of North Bay District, during its retreat. So great was the flood for many centuries that it formed a beach near here at Fonthill. Here the gravels of this ancient inland sea are 242 metres (793 feet) above sea level (present sea level). This glacial lake was rather east of our main great lakes; it exited from Lake Huron high over Lake Erie territory and into the Ontario basin. Its beach was the last and lowest of the gravel margins formed by this ancient lake. One has to cross this gravel ridge in travelling north to North Bay or south to Ohio. The plain of the lowest beach was between 122 and 153 metres (400 and 500 feet) above that of the later glacial lake in the district, Lake Iroquois (present Lake Ontario).

As these backed-up waters removed gravel and drift deposits in the old valleys and in new low places uncovered by the glacier as it retreated, the water level was slowly lowered by the outlets leading eastward to the ocean and three lakes were formed; one lake covered more or less the territory of present Lakes Huron, Michigan and Superior; the second was a small Lake Erie, and the third a smaller Lake Ontario at nearly the same level as Lake Erie. Soon afterwards the upper lake of the two emptied its waters into the lower at five or six different places over the Niagara Escarpment; the Niagara River was perhaps the chief outlet and started to flow over the escarpment edge at the point shown in the second picture. At this time the lake plain from Queenston to Niagara-on-the-Lake was covered with a Lake Ontario whose waters lapped within 11 metres (35 feet) of the average level of Queenston Heights. So our Falls was this high in the beginning.

At various points along the lake there are visible today, wave-cut shores or beach deposits marking the stages of descent toward the level of the glacial waters of this ancient Lake Ontario. For instance, as the ice to the north abandoned the land to the light of day which it had not seen for tens of thousands of years, and as the ice waters pouring from the ice at its southern edge removed more and more of the glacial drift, which was blocking the outlets to the ocean, the waters of Lake Ontario began to become shallower. This lowering of the level was not due only to the above causes. Most important, no doubt, was the rising of the northern crust in the Great Lakes region to somewhere near its former preglacial high level. This reflex action to the weight of the 0.8 kilometre (half mile) or more thickness of the glacier, naturally caused a faster outpouring, especially along the outlet of the St. Lawrence and Mohawk-Hudson valleys.

A.H. Tiplin

Roy Terrace is located at No. 1 in this photograph taken in 1937. No. 2, Lewiston-Queenston Suspension Bridge; No. 3, one of the lake boats, probably the "Cayuga", at Queenston dock.

These various stages of short or longer pauses in the descent of the waters are as follows:

1. Roy Terrace: 87 metres (287 feet) above present lake level, mentioned above.
2. Eldridge Terrace: 61 metres (200 feet) above present lake level. It is prominent above the Lewiston end of the former Lewiston-Queenston Suspension Bridge.
3. Bell Terrace: 53 metres (174 feet) Kings Highway No. 8 (York Road) in Canada and the Ridge Road in the U.S.A.
4. Iroquois Beach: 43 metres (137 feet) noticeable in the village of Queenston.
5. Unnamed beach: 23 metres (75 feet) visible in the village of Queenston.
6. Further lowering of the Lake to 56 metres (183 feet) below the present level, or to such a low level that the Niagara River, which had been flowing during all these lake changes, was enabled to cut a channel at the same depth, 56 metres (183 feet) below the present lake level near the spot pictured in the second photo. The present Niagara River has that surprising depth of its channel to bed rock. Of course, much of this is taken up by silt and gravel deposits now. The distance from Queenston to the lakeshore was 19 kilometres (12 miles) compared to 11.2 kilometres (7 miles) today.
7. The tilting of the land in the St. Lawrence region caused the lake to back up again at a fairly recent date. It rose higher than it is now. The fall again to the modern level was caused by the St. Lawrence channel being deepened by the steady rush of waters. When the lake level fell again this last time, the Medina Sandstones and Shales were exposed so that the third falls began to cut back through the gorge forming Foster's Flats at Niagara Glen. Why the previous lowering to a great depth as mentioned above in Stage 6 did not cut through the Medina rocks I cannot say. It is likely that these changes occurred before the Falls cut back to the Glen, so that the great subsidence did not cut these layers back somewhat from Queenston: the cutting back was continued in our modern day about 7,000 to 8,000 years ago when the Falls were at the Glen, only after a pause in the erosion caused by the succeeding flooding up of the lake valleys and rivers.

What the future holds for this fertile lake bed is hard to say. The reputable scientists claim that there is still a tilting of the eastern side of our continent taking place, a continuation of the reflex crustal rising since the ice burden has been removed. If this is so, then the outlet of the Great Lakes at the St. Lawrence is gradually becoming more shallow, causing the waters to slowly back up. Moreover, the upward tilting of the lake basins at their eastern sides would be causing a downward tilting of the lake basins at the western sides. Such actions might be counteracted by the Great Lakes outlet waters cutting through the bed of the St. Lawrence faster than the tilting could raise it. Such a phenomenon is shown at the Delaware water-gap on one of the routes to New York City where the river has succeeded in cutting its way through slowly rising mountains while maintaining its proper level.

Fine homes and fertile farmland now occupy the area on the Niagara Parkway north of Queenston where the

restless glacial melt waters of our present lower lake were 87.5 metres (287 feet) higher than now.

The Lower Niagara River as seen from the Lewiston-Queenston Bridge. The 11.2 kilometre (7 mile) stretch of the river to Lake Ontario was once 19 kilometres (12 miles) long. Artpark, built on top of the spoil area

for the Niagara Power project, is visible centre right, along with the cable towers of the former Lewiston-Queenston Suspension Bridge.

A.H. Tiplin

This terrace of Medina Whirlpool Sandstone over Ordovician Red Shale laid down in the Palaeozoic Era about 430 million years ago, became an ancient beach when the Falls of Niagara were near the Niagara Glen. Named Bell Terrace after the geologist who first realized its geological significance, this ridge runs 1126 kilometres (700 miles) along the south side of Lake Ontario. Ridge Road, U.S. 104, runs east along this ridge to Watertown, N.Y. York Road and Kings Highway No. 8 run west along this ridge on the Canadian side to Hamilton. No. 1, present day site of New York State Artpark; No. 2, Lewiston, N.Y.

A.H. Tiplin

Glacial Lakes
Lundy and Iroquois

When the ice of the Glacial Age had melted finally out of the region adjacent to the Great Lakes the land was revealed depressed by its enormous weight. The glacier was in places, especially in Northern Canada as much as 3 kilometres (2 miles) thick. The Glacial Age is also called the Pleistocene Period or the Quaternary Era. Geologists are always miserly as possible with dates. So it is after looking at many writings dealing with this period all over the world, that I venture to give some approximate figure. The end of the Pleistocene Period, marked by the beginning of the ice-retreat which in itself was a very gradual thing, was, at a conservative estimate 12,000 years ago.

As the ice moved back towards its birthplace, just east of Hudson Bay in Labrador, with maddening slowness, the land naturally began to rise, for the crust rocks are elastic when bent over large sections. The old streams were set to work clearing out the glacial debris in their valleys. At least one stream, however, did not start just where its ancestor had

York Road, formerly Kings Highway 8A, above Queenston Village, is on the continuation of Bell Terrace on the Canadian side. The terrace extends with varying widths into Hamilton. William Lyon Mackenzie's restored home is in the centre.

been; the Whirlpool – St. Davids Buried Gorge, a stream existing before the coming of the last wave of ice, was never re-opened. This task that the reborn streams had to do is not yet fully completed. In fact, scientists all agree that the changing of the drainage systems of a region is the most striking effect usually made upon a country by an ice invasion.

This ancient lake which occupied the Lake Ontario basin was called by another name; it would be much more correct historically to say "is called". The name geologists gave the large body of fresh water formed by the melting ice was Lake Lundy. The lake comprised the area now covered by most of the Great Lakes, and in its embrace present day Lake Ontario and Lake Erie were one. After the waters of this Lake Lundy fell, due to the rising of the land, these two lakes became separated and a new lake was formed in the basin of Lake Ontario. This was larger in extent than the present lake and was named Glacial Lake Iroquois, after the Iroquois Indian tribes that lived in a fairly recent period of history along the beaches and high terraces which the lake had abandoned. Lake Iroquois waters were held back by an ice barrier which lay across the St. Lawrence Valley. The outlet of this lake was at Rome, N.Y. through the Mohawk Valley, to a marine estuary in the valley of the Hudson River.

The surface of Lake Iroquois was considerably lower at first than when it made the great Iroquois Beach. There are traces of this older and former beach below the present one which appears in the picture showing William Lyon Mackenzie's home at Queenston. But this marking of the lower Lake Iroquois terrace is only sporadic: I have never attempted to take a picture of it. During its early history came an event which covered it with the waters that were giving it shape and form. There was a further uplift of land at the northeast so that the outlet of the lake was raised and the waters were backed up on its western shores and the first and lower beach was submerged.

There began to form what is one of the best known and best developed old shore lines in the Great Lakes region. It is composed of sandy gravel with pebbles well-rounded, mostly of hard, dark red sandstone. The surface of the country between the earlier beach, which is unmarked in the Niagara District, and the later Iroquois Beach shows very strong evidence of having been submerged at one time. Nearly all of it is stony or sandy and in certain parts it is even covered with many boulders. By the way, this brings to mind a certain picnic along the present Lake Ontario beach somewhere between Port Weller and McNab. My companions and I tried swimming there; to get out to deep water we had to wade; several sat down and crawled out disgusted by the thickly packed and slippery boulders which were all but invisible under the water for more than 30 metres (100 feet) from shore.

The height of the Escarpment which is the greatest at Lewiston is 76 metres (250 feet). Throughout its great length from Hamilton to near Watertown, New York, it is from 183 to 189 metres (600 to 620 feet) above sea level. Almost 5 kilometres (3 miles) west of Lewiston, looking in the direction which the picture here indicates, the escarpment is so steep that it rises about 73 metres (240 feet) in 0.4 kilometres (a quarter mile). From there on eastward, it is in parts, with the terrace separating the two sections from 159 to 165 metres (520 to 540 feet) above sea level.

This terrace, the Bell Terrace, so named after the scientist who first realized the significance of this beach (Ridge Road), runs on the Canadian side with varying widths right into Hamilton and along the stretch is known as York Road and Kings Highway No. 8. For some 1126 kilometres (700 miles) it has

been traced along both sides of the lake. This ridge, whose suitability for a road was recognized by military authorities early in pioneer days, has varying heights. For instance starting at the eastern end, Watertown is 147 metres (483 feet) above the present lake level; Rochester 57.6 metres (189 feet);

Major-General Sir Isaac Brock was fatally wounded while leading a charge up the slope of Bell Terrace, in a valiant attempt to recapture the Redan Battery on the Heights. Brock's cenotaph, at the bottom of Bell Terrace, is in the foreground and Brock's Monument stands on the Heights above.

George A. Seibel

Pleistocene gravel bed north of Lewiston landing. It is clean gravel with coarse and fine layers alternating.

Niagara River 42 metres (137 feet); while Hamilton is only 35 metres (116 feet). Thus the extent of the ancient uplift and of the rising of the rock crust of the earth in this eastern part of North America is easily noticed. After all it is strange even to the most casual observer to come across a gravel beach 147 metres (483 feet) above the level of the only body of water nearby. This beach is sometimes close to the Escarpment, sometimes more than four miles north of it – a low but well-marked twisting ridge 3 to 9 metres (10 to 30 feet) above the general surface of the surrounding country. Since it forms a good highway, the country along it is thickly settled.

It may be wondered how it can be determined just what the probable date was when this beach was formed. Surely if this can be found out clearly, and since it is known that the falls, formed by the union of two smaller falls at Niagara Glen, began to be followed in its backward cutting by a lower and a third falls cutting through Foster's Flats as soon as this Iroquois water level dropped to expose the next rock layer underneath, then we shall be quite sure of the age of the falls and gorge. Such a piece of good luck did befall the scientists who were trying to solve this very problem which was of such interest not only to nearby residents but to visitors and scientists from all parts of Europe.

At a point north of Lewiston, New York, opposite Queenston Landing, there appears one of the most remarkable sections of Pleistocene gravel in this whole region. It is clean gravel with coarse and fine layers alternating; there are some stones 20 to 30 centimetres (8 to 12 inches) in diameter. There exist there individual gravel beds running to 12 metres (40 feet) deep. In some places it is even deeper and hasn't been measured. This gravel deposit extends northwestward along the bank for 0.8 km (one-half mile) or more thinning out in that direction. A considerable part of it is now hard conglomerate rock, that is, rock formed of various masses and textures of gravel cemented together. To one looking for it from the surface before excavations had been made, the surface appears only stony and sandy, and would be considered merely a surf-worn plain lying in front of Iroquois Beach. There is a similar but smaller bed on the Canadian side. The ridge of Iroquois Beach runs west through the village of Lewiston and comes to the bank of the river at the gravel pits where it overlies the coarse and steeply inclined beds with their southeast slope. The beach is easily distinguishable by the fine grain gravel or coarse sand. The important point is that there, in the coarse gravel pit at a depth of 5.4 to 6 metres (18 to 20 feet), were found the bones of a mastodon. This find shows the pits to have been formed just before the Iroquois Age. This primitive type of elephant, of a simpler type than the mammoth is said to have roamed these parts from 100,000 to 30,000 years ago. The one found was of a later type; that is of a type dating near the 30,000 year minimum. N.B. Recent radio carbon dating places the age of the Lake Iroquois shoreline at 12,000 ± 450 years in 1950. The disappearance of the mammoth is placed at from 10,000 to 11,000 years ago.

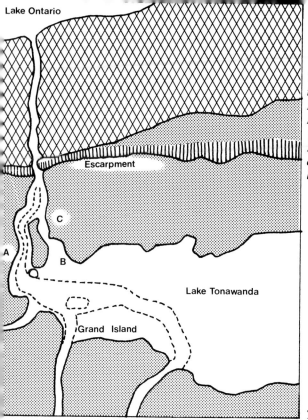

Lake Ontario

Escarpment

C

A

B

Lake Tonawanda

Grand Island

Astrid Akkerman from a sketch by A.H. Tiplin

This map was drawn from information contained in the United States Geological Survey of 1913. Ancient Lake Tonawanda shows as merely an enlarged Niagara River which spilled over the 644 kilometres (400 mile) escarpment at five main points – Holley, Medina, Gasport, Lockport and Lewiston in present day New York State. The Lewiston outlet prevailed to become the only outlet – our Niagara River.

The Oneida Community Silver Co. (the present site of Maple Leaf Village) once stood on this slope, A on the map. This was the bank of the Niagara River before the deep gorge was cut in the centre of the river (about 4,000 years ago) when the cataract was cutting through the highest limestone ridge, Hubbard Point at the foot of Eastwood Crescent.

A.H. Tiplin

Lake Tonawanda

Before a period of fifty thousand years ago the ice front filled the basin of present day Lake Ontario which, prior to the glacial age, was merely a broad valley with a fairly deep canyon in the centre, and, pressing high over the Niagara Escarpment, held its own icy waters in check to the south. These waters formed a large glacial lake similar to the smaller lakes to be found today in the Rocky Mountain District. Geologists have called this Lake Lundy.

As the ice slowly retreated, a lower outlet was found by the dammed up waters at Rome, New York, which resulted in a rapid draining of Lake Lundy. For a long while, the waters were held high enough so that the Niagara Escarpment was covered by a large lake which it is convenient to regard as present Lake Erie and Lake Ontario joined into one. But upon a further retreat of the ice front, the waters separated and the two modern lakes became distinct even though slightly different in outline from their present form. Lake Erie was much expanded so that its eastern branch was quite large, extending to very near Rochester, New York, with the outlet used being the same as the former one carved by the cold waters of the former Lake Lundy, and following the Mohawk River Valley to the Hudson River. As the ice burden was slowly lifting, the land in the Hudson and St. Lawrence valleys was just as slow-

ly elevating to somewhat the level it had had before the glacier's advent. This turned the waters of the small adjoining lake called Tonawanda back to find another outlet or outlets. It found them in present New York State – at Holley, Medina, Gasport, Lockport and Lewiston.

Near Rochester the depth of water does not seem to have been more than 1.2 metres (four feet) on the average, nor did this level last for long, as may be judged by the small beach terrace it had time to build up. The main spillway was Lewiston, and when the waters of this extended Lake Erie found their way over the escarpment there, the Falls of Niagara were born. Naturally with Lake Erie so swollen, the Niagara River was much higher than it is now, and therefore much broader. Near the Goat Island region, which was then of course submerged, the greatest depth was from 9 to 12 metres (30 to 40 feet).

There is a part of Niagara Falls, New York which is rather low in elevation. Beginning near the mark "B" on the map, the engineers for the Schoellkopf Power Company found it convenient to take advantage of this when they made the cut to divert water for the power plant. Their canal was similar to our Hydro Electric Power canal in speed of the current, but was much shorter. It started at Port Day on the

Hotel Niagara in Niagara Falls, N.Y. stands at point B on the map, the south end of an ancient island, around which were the waters of Lake Tonawanda.

U.S. side of the Upper River and at first took advantage of the low ground which formed the eastern branch of the Lewiston Spillway but later in its course through the modern city, it had to cut across the higher part which forms the large island on the map to the south of which the modern Goat Island is situated. The railway builders found this natural depression convenient for their tracks across the city. A regular maze of tracks followed this depression nearly all the way to the point "C". Indeed, one line went past the Niagara University here, cutting under the highway skirting the gorge, wending its adventurous way along the edge of the cliff, descending all the way to Lewiston. (Note: All these railway lines have since been abandoned).

There is a very distinct rise upon which the Niagara Hotel, shown in photo II, stands so prominently. This hotel forming a landmark visible from Queen Victoria Park is on the south end of the elevation in the city around which even the deep waters of the Lewiston Spillway found it easier to go. On the map, this would be in line between "A" and "B".

On the Canadian side, Maple Leaf Village (the former site of the Oneida Community Silver Co.) shown in photo III, standing on the same slope,

marks the west bank of the west head of the same spillway. Clifton Hill might be said to be partly formed by this ancient terrace. But Clifton Hill, all the way up, is the side of the Niagara Falls Terminal Moraine which forms one of several resting places of the glacier during the course of its retreat. More familiarly, this is called Lundy's Lane Ridge. The Spillway terrace is merely an extension on the side of this mighty deposit.

The disappearance of this broad inter-glacial river known as the St. Davids River, and its shrinking into the more modest stream (Niagara River) we find so grand, was caused by the ice front retreating still more as the milleniums wore on and Time began to belong more relatively to the human race. As the country became clear of ice farther north, the upper lakes began to pour their waters down the depressed Nipissing-Ottawa system to the St. Lawrence. Thus the drawing of the waters away from the Erie basin caused a corresponding smaller flow in the formerly much extended Niagara River so that Lake Tonawanda was drained. Grand Island and the Three Sister Islands appeared above the water current, and the eastern part of Niagara Falls, New York and the area we know as Queen Victoria Park, were left high and dry.

Birthplace of the Falls

Let us imagine… It is in the beginning of the era called the Dawn of the Conscious Brain. Scattered nomadically over Europe and Asia, possibly Africa too, creatures almost human by modern standards, but more hairy and beetle-browed, with clumsy, shambling gait, very short but very powerful in build, are beginning to leave crude tools and ornaments, lost in piles of well-cleaned bones and shells, on the floors of caves, or mere rock shelters. Sometimes too, in smaller niches in rocky country, these creatures, in reverence mingled with fear and hope, arrange the bodies or bones of their kin; nor do they slip away from the awesome task without leaving behind, in nearly every case, some laboriously made tools and utensils, for use in some dim land whose existence their sorrow and nameless fear taught them to imagine. Furs and skins of animals these higher animals held at a premium; even in Africa fur-bearing animals are plentiful, but are only to be made proud possessions by the skill of a well-flung rock, a close-up, desperate thrust of a stick hardened and burnt to a point in fire, or by the craft of a well-concealed pit where the animal can be stoned to death or choked by a noose. But such animals are becoming scarcer; unaccountably the climate in all tropical and temperate zones is becoming milder; the animals that keep the tribe warm are each decade to be caught farther north; storms are less violent and sudden, and even to a dim brain noticeably less frequent; marshes are drying up in as quickly as one generation, short as generations are in these days. So after the last of the four glacial ages, embryonic civilization has moved slowly northward from the latitude of Spain to the lowlands of Germany, from Arabia to the steppes of Siberia. The ancestors of time to come did not unconsciously follow the retreating ice in Asia; strangely, eastern Asia was not visited by the green-white sliding ice monster.

In America no creatures of this higher type are present. Only mastodons, mammoths, sabre-toothed tigers, giant wolves, and animals of more or less familiar type roam the thick forests which have sprung up after the glacier has begun to retreat; at first, the cold-resisting evergreens alone draw up life in the damp, new soil which is being deposited each spring in diverse amounts by the floods drawn out of the northern ice by the direct summer rays of the sun. Then trees so sensitive to the seasons that they partially die when it becomes cold each year, timidly interspersed their varied forms amid the monotone of firs.

Thus, as we stand at Hall Point shown in the photo, no other witness of similar form is present

23

A.H. Tiplin

At Hall Point, No. 1, the waters of a larger Lake Erie about 12,000 years ago, began to cascade over the Niagara Escarpment on to Eldridge Terrace, No. 2, into a larger Lake Iroquois 11 metres (35 feet) below. This 1915 photograph shows the Lewiston-Queenston Suspension Bridge No. 3; the stone cable towers of this bridge No. 4; the right-of-way of the Niagara Great Gorge Railway No. 5; the tunnel through the escarpment and the right-of-way of the Rochester, Watertown and Onondaga Railway which operated between 1888 and 1938, No. 6.

at the important event about to take place. In the Escarpment edge before us, both to right and left for many miles, there appears no gorge or outlet of stream. The Falls are not yet born. No human eye, other than ours of spirit form, is destined to see their birth. As we hover here, and glance behind us, it is not hard to see how the event is to take place. About 11 kilometres (7 miles) back to the south we can see beneath the waters of Lake Tonawanda two islands; no, three – present day Grand Island, Navy Island, and a very small one, Goat Island, fated to become world-famous. From this region a high bluff of material left by the recent glacier cramps the waters into a wide arm which extends to within a few rods of the escarpment edge here but has not yet found a pathway over. It hovers shimmering there as though conscious of its sleeping power, of its sinuous strength which can make dust of its barrier and of its very bed if it once even for a little time can leap to join its brother below. That reminds us – we look down at our feet at a great body of water only 11 metres (35 feet) below the top of the escarpment where we are, Lake Iroquois swollen by the Spring

flood from the glacier. A mounting torrent which is already spilling into this lake at four small outlets at present day Lockport, Gasport, Medina and Holley, New York. Such tiny flows are giving the tide pouring into Lake Tonawanda from ancestral Lake Erie coming through the Port Huron outlet from the Upper Lakes, temporary relief. But the channels which take this much overflow are shallow, tiny arms groping for exit. Another yet is needed. The flood mounts higher even as we stand here, the shimmering wide arm near us, developing a slender finger, thrusts it tentatively through the soft barrier of reddish soil, the base of which for many days now it has been dissolving and nibbling away.

Surprised at its easy conquest, the slender finger beckons to the stream behind and quickly cascades down the sloping front of the escarpment to mingle with the reservoir below. Such a small beginning, only a cascade of 11 metres (35 feet) about to the bottom of that first indentation (Eldridge Terrace) shown in the picture. But see – gravity lends weight to the first invitation of the probing waters and draws on the flood.

In a surprisingly short time the top of the cascade is many metres (feet) wide and having eaten down through glacial material only a few metres (feet) thick, has even formed a rim over which it is beginning to fall. But the edge is quite fragile, being composed of thick-bedded limestone. Evidently, in view of the powerful currents already eddying down the long arm, now the Niagara River, drawn as if by a magnet to the tiny fall, this rock is doomed to swift incision for some time until a small gorge is formed which can ensure its continued growth into our famous scenic gorge – the Niagara Gorge.

We've been looking at the origin of the Falls at Hall Point on the American side of the Niagara River. Now I want to draw the reader's attention to the same event from a different viewpoint – Queenston Heights on the Canadian side of the River.

Leading up to Queenston Heights Park from the village below is the steep, winding Niagara Parkway presenting many a tempting view of the Lower river. Before this Parkway enters the park proper, it makes a curve to the right. If the reader some day will stop at the paved parking space about half-way along the curve, at the ornamental stone entranceway leading to Brock's Monument, he will be at the birthplace of the Falls. If he then goes to the other side of the road and crosses a small stretch of grass towards the railing which adds safety to the park, he will find himself on the beach terrace of glacial Lake Iroquois, called Roy Terrace, about 152 metres (500 feet) inside the escarpment edge. Of course it would hardly be possible to say that such a flat represented the shore of an early lake at such a high level above the present waters if this were the only one which existed at this level.

The old beach line may be seen farther west near St. Davids, faintly once again between St. Catharines and the last mentioned village, prominently at Decew Falls, 21 kilometres (13 miles) west, where it is 27 kilometres (17 miles) west, about 85 metres (287 feet) above the present lake level. I am sure the reader is already asking himself why the beach line is not at the same height all along the escarpment. Surely the old lake-bottom below the escarpment has not sunk? The truth is that the escarpment has been tilting so that it is high in the east and low in the west, the same sloping changing the tilt of the whole land.

A.H. Tiplin

Roy Terrace, on the Niagara Parkway leading to Queenston village, slopes 11 to 13 metres (35 to 42 feet) from the top of the escarpment. This terrace corresponds with Eldridge Terrace on the U.S. side of the gorge. Here the Falls of Niagara began about 12,000 years ago.

Roy Terrace as seen from the U.S. side. The Terrace is just to the left of the top of the gully. Brock's Monument is in the distance.

A.H. Tiplin

George Bailey

Eldridge Terrace shown here, 11 metres (35 feet) from the top of the escarpment, marks the height of the waters of Lake Iroquois, into which the Falls of Niagara first fell, about 12,000 years ago.

At the time the Falls had its start, the glacial mass, as discussed in previous chapters, slowly retreating, was to all evidence somewhere not far northeast of the Trent Valley district, still covering the Lake Nipissing-Ottawa River line with the climate steadily growing milder; the conditions which had given birth to the monster ceased to impel it any longer down from the centre of the Labrador Peninsula. Great floods of icy waters, similar to our Great Lakes in spring movements of thin ice, began to fill the valleys southward to a higher level each warmer spring as thousands of years rolled by. The waters of the valleys in which the Great Lakes now lie moved as they do now, into Lake Erie via Port Huron. Lake Erie spilled over the Niagara Escarpment in five separate places, as we have said before. With about 25 percent of its present volume, it began to make the first stage of the Gorge, tumbling in an infant cataract or rapids only 11 metres (35 feet) from the highest point of land to the left of the picture, to the old shore line of Roy Terrace. An absurdly small beginning for our mighty Falls!

N.B. In 1937 when this article was written, the volume of water going over the Falls, after calculating the amount diverted above the Falls for electric power generation, was approximately 4248 m³/sec (150,000 cfs). This means that at the first stage of the Gorge mentioned above, the volume was only 1062 m³/sec (37,500 cfs).

The old shore line of Roy Terrace is just where the slope of the escarpment would end if the river had not eaten it away. It seems to me that if the Falls in its beginning had been one drop over the thin capping of Lockport Limestone here to approximately the level of the present river bed, the scouring action would have been enough to clear the river channel below to a greater depth, or at least to a more uniform depth than it is. Hence I am inclined to think that the thin capping formed a small falls which quickly ate back before the waters could wash away the glacial debris and the talus slope at the foot of the escarpment, and that then the waters cascaded over the Clinton rock layers below. But this could not have happened in this stage of the gorge while the lake was as high as Roy Terrace because the Clinton layers were below the surface of the lake. But this stage of the gorge is a short one – 609 metres (2,000 feet), extending only half way back to the Sir Adam Beck Generating Station No. 1 and the Floral Clock at Smeaton Ravine.

As the glacier, retreating while the Falls ate back this much, left a new channel open to the north, the Trent Valley system, the upper lake waters left Port Huron exit in time and for many centuries coursed to the ocean by the newly opened path. Thus Lake Erie was lowered, as well as Lake Ontario. The Falls, finding a greater drop to the lowered Lake Ontario, also discovered a new power of deeper erosion, and scoured deeper into the river bed. Thus the depths in the river near this point are as follows and are already partly explained: south of the former bridge, near Smeaton Ravine, 21 metres (69 feet); going northward, 36.5 metres (120 feet); 42 metres (138 feet); 46 metres (150 feet) where the level was lowered and the Falls could scour more deeply; 30 metres (99 feet) at the former Lewiston-Queenston Suspension bridge site where the slope of the escarpment tempered the drop of the first and second Falls; and then most surprising of all, 56 metres (182 feet) deep in the broad part of the river between the two villages, Lewiston and Queenston (as explained in a previous chapter, *Former Lake Bed*).

Five Stages
of the Gorge

The Great Lakes and the rivers connecting them are unique in the world because of their size, and the way they are joined together. Really they are misnamed; if they were in a smaller country the chances are they would be given their proper title of "seas". They are characteristic of a surface which has been glacially disturbed – they are linked together so as to form one huge waterway; in this, the rivers, however short, are the true runway of the water, while the lakes are merely reservoirs which serve to equalize the flow. The mighty water drainage system of ours flows from northern Minnesota to the Atlantic Ocean via the St. Lawrence. Since the Falls of Niagara form one of the steps down from high land to near ocean level, anything which affects the volume of the lake reservoirs must intimately affect the cataract. Due to the glacier and the crustal upheavals during its retreat this lake system has suffered five significant changes; each has a different outlet from the stage before and after it. And of course, the volume of the Niagara River changed with each change of outlet. There were two periods when Lake Erie waters alone cut the gorge. Since the flow then would be about one-seventh of the normal flow today, the gorge cut during this period is naturally small.

As the ice barrier melted back to the north farther and farther, the one great lake formed by its waters began to find various outlets to sea level. The water level was lowered until the great body, single before, began to break into distinct parts. One part was the so-called Lake Algonquin; this at first was not much larger than Lake Huron today, with very little assistance from Lakes Michigan or Superior. Later it came to comprise these also.

When the water level fell sufficiently to bring the Niagara Escarpment above water, a divide was formed in the larger lake mass so that there existed more separate lakes – Lake Algonquin, ancestral Lake Erie (sometimes) and Lake Iroquois (Lake Ontario). Then the Falls of Niagara were born.

The history of the Great Lakes and the Falls of Niagara can be divided into five stages:

Stage I – Lewiston Branch Gorge
(Lewiston Spillway Gorge)
Stage II – Old Narrow Gorge
(Erie Gorge)
Stage III – Lower Great Gorge
Stage IV – Whirlpool Rapids Gorge
Stage V – Upper Great Gorge

In Stage I the volume potentially available then for the Niagara River was probably greater than at

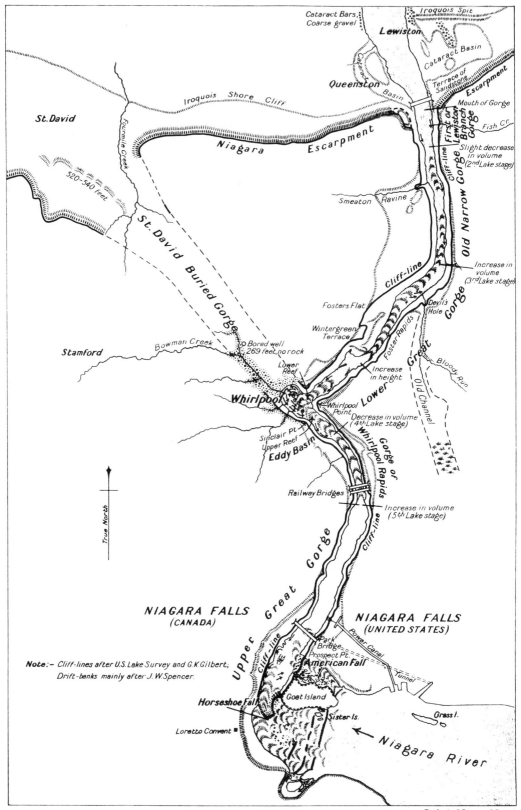

Iroquois Spit

Cataract Bars, Coarse gravel

Lewiston

Cataract Basin

Terrace of Sandstone

Queenston

Mouth of Gorge

Niagara Escarpment

Fish Cr.

Iroquois Shore Cliff

First or Lewiston Branch Gorge

Slight decrease in volume (2nd Lake stage)

St. David

Niagara Escarpment

Fourmile Creek

520-540 feet

Smeaton Ravine

Cliff-line

Old Narrow Gorge

St. David Buried Gorge

Increase in volume (3rd Lake stage)

Fosters Flat

Devil's Hole

Great Gorge

Wintergreen Terrace

Foster Rapids

Bowman Creek

Bored well 269 feet, no rock

Lower Reef

Bloody Run

Stamford

Old Channel

Increase in height

Whirlpool

Whirlpool Point

Decrease in volume (4th Lake stage)

Sinclair Pt.

Upper Reef

Lower Great Gorge

Eddy Basin

Gorge of Whirlpool Rapids

Railway Bridges

Increase in volume (5th Lake stage)

Cliff-line

Upper Great Gorge

NIAGARA FALLS
(CANADA)

NIAGARA FALLS
(UNITED STATES)

Park Bridge

Power Canal

Cliff-line

Prospect Pt.

Note:– Cliff-lines after U.S. Lake Survey and G.K.Gilbert;
Drift-banks mainly after J.W.Spencer.

American Fall

Tunnel

Horseshoe Fall

Goat Island

Sister Is.

Grass I.

Loretto Convent

Niagara River

Geological Survey of Canada

This map produced by the Geological Survey of Canada in 1913 reflects much of present day knowledge of the Niagara Gorge. One point of contention to geologists is the Eddy Basin located south of the entrance to the Whirlpool. Here the gorge widens for a short distance indicating a dramatic increase in the volume of water going over the inter-glacial St. Davids falls. The ledge of Whirlpool Sandstone, visible elsewhere in this area at low water, is missing in the Eddy Basin and reappears where the Whirlpool Rapids begin. The hypothesis put forward in this book for the Fourth Stage of the Gorge presumes that the Eddy Basin was cut by the falls of the inter-glacial river and was part of this river gorge when the glacier filled it with debris about 22,800 years ago.

When the present Falls broke through at Whirlpool Point, the rushing water quickly eroded the Whirlpool, Whirlpool Eddy and Whirlpool Rapids Gorge back to a point south of the Railway Arch Bridge where it found the rim of the inter-glacial falls and began to erode the Fifth Stage of the Gorge, the Upper Great Gorge.

by its tremendous burden, so that the land near the ice margin would not only be choked by the rushing waters from the ice front but would also be lowest. This second stage comes back as far as Niagara University on the American side and the bend in the river there – 1.8 kilometres (1.125 miles). It is remarkable for its straightness and uniformity of width. Both Stages I and II are choked with wide

The Five Stages of the Gorge: I – Lewiston Branch Gorge (Lewiston Spillway Gorge); II – Old Narrow Gorge (Erie Gorge); III – Lower Great Gorge; IV – Whirlpool Rapids Gorge; V – Upper Great Gorge. The dotted line shows the present River; the lines outside that area denote the high bank of the river through Stages I to V.

present. But since it was formed during the existence of Lake Tonawanda, which really was an expanded part of the Niagara River at the Erie end, it did not have all the flow going over the escarpment. In the chapter on Lake Tonawanda and the Lewiston Spillway we pointed out the names and locations of the various other outlets, four in number. The Falls had to share in this division of work to the extent that it diverted about 25 percent of the total flow available at that time. During this time the gorge section near Lewiston-Queenston (Stage I) was formed. The gorge here, from the top of the bank to the bottom of the river is nearly 152 metres (500 feet) deep.

Stage II is called the Old Narrow Gorge or Erie Gorge. This was undoubtedly the longest in forming because it represents the work done by a falls which had only the meagre discharge of a small ancestral Lake Erie to give it power. By that time Lake Algonquin was much larger. The ice margin had retreated so that an outlet at Kirkfield through the Trent Valley was used by the mass of the waters. This stage of lake history is shown in Map II. The ice it will be noticed, is still over the Ottawa River District. We may at first wonder why the waters would then take such an outlet when they do not naturally do so now. Let us remember that as the ice retreated it must have uncovered a land depressed

Astrid Akkerman from a sketch by A.H. Tiplin

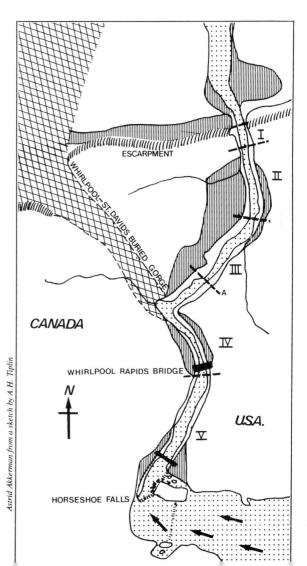

talus slopes of eroded and weathered rock. This alone is an indication of great age. It must be confessed, however, that the accumulation of such a pile is considerably helped by the great mass of soft Rochester and Clinton Shales which are exposed in the old part of the gorge. It will be remembered that these are not so well exposed in the younger parts or the more southerly parts of the gorge because of the southward dip of the rock layers. These layers by the way, are remarkably uniform, so level and uniform in most places as not to enter the question of why the gorge is of different widths at all. Indeed the flatness and even thickness of the rock layers of the Niagara District are so marked that I believe they are the most important topographical characteristic.

Stage III saw the waters of the glacier and the upper lakes again coming through the Port Huron outlet, as it did in the first stage. This time, however, there was a small and temporary flow at Chicago due to an unprecedented melting of the glacier which then seemed to be retreating in real earnest. Thousands of years later Chicago engineers took advantage of the natural channel made by this early flow to locate their drainage canal. The waters of Lake Iroquois were at this time backed up because the outlet at Rome, N.Y., was raised by the reflex tilting of the earth's crust. Lake Iroquois was then

about 38 metres (125 feet) higher than the waters of present Lake Ontario. Lake Tonawanda was still in existence at this time. This is evident by the alcove cut back at the Devil's Hole.

During this Stage III the flow therefore had its eroding power greatly curtailed by the flooding in of the lake waters, thus making its thundering waters fall a less effective distance. The flow was more spread out here than at any other part of the gorge except the modern division. This seems to have been caused by the extreme flatness and level character of the surface limestone, especially near Niagara Glen. The level characteristic will be noted if we refer to Wintergreen Flats at Niagara Glen. At Cripps Eddy at the southwest end of the Glen, Lake Iroquois was lowered to near present level either by a lowering of the crust once again at its outlet along the Mohawk Valley through Oneida Lake to the Hudson (a lowering which did occur, but whose time is not exactly known), or by a deepening of its channel there so that such water poured away to the

The Falls of Niagara had only a fraction of their usual flow during cutting of Old Erie Gorge, Stage II on the map. This period is much the longest in the history of the Falls. A – Lake Algonquin; M – Mohawk Valley; T – Trent Valley; I – Lake Iroquois.

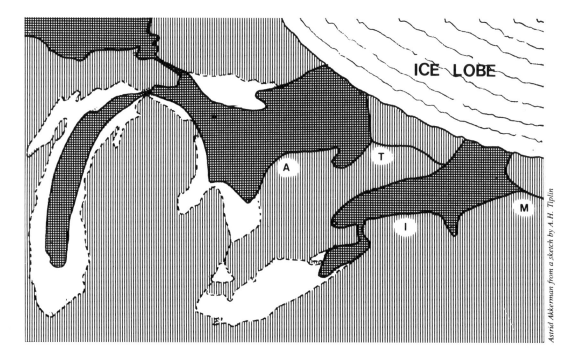

ICE LOBE

A

T

I

M

Astrid Akkerman from a sketch by A.H. Tiplin

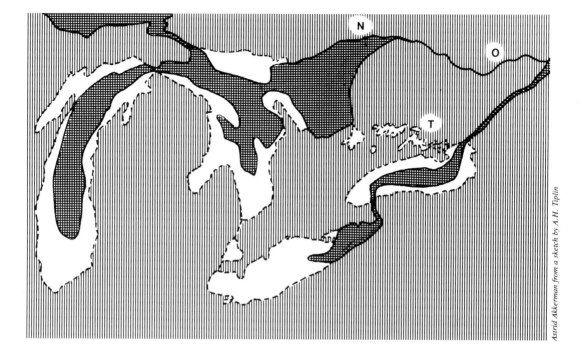

Astrid Akkerman from a sketch by A.H. Tiplin

ocean. (The ice was still in the St. Lawrence on a line across the present lake basin between Belleville, Ontario and Watertown, N.Y.).

Once this lowering took place in the Niagara River, the gorge at the Glen became much wider and deeper in about 91 metres (a few hundred yards) of cutting back with its new stronger power of erosion given by the higher fall of water. Lake Iroquois may even have attained a low level as much as 31 metres (100 feet) below present Lake Ontario level, according to some experts. At any rate, the river below the Glen was lowered enough to allow the falls and rapids which must have existed just below it to undercut the various layers which are now exposed at the Glen. At the same time Foster's Flats was cut by a third and lower falls starting near Queenston and cutting back through the softer Medina Sandstone layers. This third seems to have overtaken the main falls at the Whirlpool.

The ice now disappeared from the St. Lawrence valley; slowly the masses of gravel and glacial debris were cleaned out by the pressing of the waters eastward on their way to the ocean, and the Thousand Island district became the scene of discharge for Lake Iroquois. But just to the east as

This map shows the Great Lakes in the period just before the present level of flow began. Again the Falls of Niagara cut a narrow section of gorge – the Whirlpool Rapids Gorge Stage IV. N – Nipissing Outlet; O – Ottawa River; T – Trent Valley.

shown on Map III, the upper waters were using the Lake Nipissing-Mattawa system to the Ottawa River. Down this course flowed most of the upper lake waters through North Bay; the Falls of Niagara once again had to get along with a pittance.

When the region to the north of the Ottawa and North Bay district was finally relieved of the pressure of the ice, it rose again. Soon the Nipissing outlet became too high for the waters of the lakes, and under the urging of the tilting land the water found the lowest outlet which it had used twice before in Stage I and Stage III through the Niagara River when the falls was just south of the Whirlpool Rapids Bridge site. From here the falls cut the Upper Great Gorge, even larger than the Lower Great Gorge near the Niagara Glen (Stage III).

The history of the famous Falls and gorge of Niagara in its five stages is therefore the history of the Great Lakes.

Charles Mason Dow

The Old Narrow (Erie) Gorge, c. 1900. Smeaton Ravine is the slash in the gorge wall to the left. Both sides of the gorge are now occupied by the Sir Adam Beck Generating Stations, the Robert Moses Power Plant and the Lewiston-Queenston Bridge. The tracks of the Niagara Gorge Railway are visible on the U.S. side in the centre.

This photo taken in 1987 shows the same section of the gorge as in the photo above. Ontario Hydro's Sir Adam Beck Generating Stations are on the left. New York Power Authority's Robert Moses Generating Station is at centre right.

George A. Seibel

Smeaton Ravine

Travelling from Niagara Falls towards Queenston on our scenic Niagara Parkway motorists are confronted with two curves before reaching Queenston Heights. The first is around the dead end of the Whirlpool; the second is just north of the Sir Adam Beck Generating Station Number 1. Most motorists are so engrossed in making the turn and preparing to make the turn into the Floral Clock parking area that they do not realize they are skirting the edge of a ravine very important geologically, Smeaton Ravine, part of the Old Narrow Gorge, or Erie Gorge.

This side gorge is not now important for the drainage of the local terrain as most of its drainage area is cut off by the Ontario Hydro Pump Storage Reservoir and the Ontario Hydro canals bringing water to the generating stations. The side of the gorge where Sir Adam Beck Generating Station Number 1 now stands was once an island like Goat Island and like a former island at Wintergreen Flats at the Niagara Glen. Now only a little water leaps down in a falls and a rapids, and then only in wet weather. From the edge of the Niagara Gorge side this smaller gorge had cut back about 152 metres (500 feet) when it was abruptly drained by the main falls, which was then just behind and to the south, annexing the slightly higher waters of this ancient "American" Falls. This, eventually will be the fate of the present Goat Island and American Falls.

The evidence for the former height of Lake Ontario is easy to read here once the observer grasps the general idea. Here conclusive evidence is provided of the varying heights of Lake Iroquois (Lake Ontario). The little water there now drops 26 to 27 metres (85 to 90 feet) over the Lockport Limestone which is so characteristic of the whole gorge, to a ledge of Rochester Shale which still remains intact at the bottom of the cliff.

Most of the cliff is of this finely-layered Rochester or Niagara Shale, grey in colour. The evidence here is this ledge which has not been eaten by falling waters either now or in the long past years when the flow must have been quite large to carve a gorge 152 metres (500 feet) long and 46 metres (150 feet) wide. There is only one substance which would have prevented such a ledge from wearing away under the pounding of the falling torrent – more water at a higher level than the ledge.

The rocks of the cliff evidently failed to withstand erosion of the water for 26 metres (85 feet) or so; then since their nature remains the same there is no reason why they should suddenly have been able to resist. Therefore, the ancestral Lake Ontario waters must have been high enough to act as a shock ab-

Smeaton Ravine is the dark streak in the gorge bank in the right of the picture. The break in the layer of Whirlpool Sandstone indicates the bottom of the ravine.

sorber to protect the Clinton Limestone layer ledge, which is at the same height above Lake Ontario as Roy Terrace at Queenston Heights, where the waters of ancestral Lake Erie first met the other lake with a drop of about 11 metres (35 feet).

But the drop here at Smeaton Ravine is greater because the Lockport Limestone is thicker than at Queenston and the land is a little higher at the gorge edge. But the levels at the bottom of this first drop and the floor of Roy Terrace are the same. Hence the falls reached here in one small step.

There used to be a cable farther north along the gorge to assist in getting safely down past the Clinton Limestone layer. I discovered it after I had succeeded in walking down the 2.4 to 3 metres (8 to 10 feet) thickness of this layer with the help of a short cable which finally casts one off to make a drop to a pointed mound of clay talus which is very steep. In any case one would have to drop from the cable to get below the Clinton layer because it is undercut very much. However, making use of the safe cable was difficult enough for a person with

camera equipment! This locale was ideal for a picture, with the moss under the spuming water, the red of the Medina Shales, the greys and whites of the fallen rocks below these shales, and the luxuriant foliage bending over many twisting waterfalls. All these would delight a painter's or a photographer's heart, if such can be satisfied in this world.

The secondary stream here was not drained before the waters of Lake Ontario suddenly, geologically speaking, sank to about 61 metres (200 feet) below the present surface. Then this Clinton Limestone layer, which is 73 metres (240 feet) above the present surface of the modern lake, was exposed. Thus the second layer which forms the Falls gorge was the top of a second falls in this side-gorge, but there was a drop of a mere 12 metres (40 feet).

To a falls of this height the Medina Shales and the underlying Clinton Shales and the thin-bedded limestones would offer no resistance at any point along the gorge for nearly 37 metres (120 feet). But once again the lake level cushioned the falls so that today we find a drop of 12 metres (40 feet) over the Clinton layer and then a rapids to the roadway below.

To put this important fact in another way: if the water had been lower than 12 metres (40 feet) below the second limestone layer, the falls once started here would not have degenerated into rapids. These rapids began to form while the lake level slowly descended to the level of Bell Terrace (York Road) at Queenston which is 53 metres (174 feet) above the present lake level. This slightly higher level endured for some time; evidence for this is the erosion of the second falls and rapids some 61 metres (200 feet) back inside the gorge proper.

Thus came the last great lowering of the lake to considerably below the present level, causing exposure of the Medina Sandstones and the beginning of the third falls in the main gorge which did not catch up with the other two until they were in the vicinity of the Whirlpool and causing a slight fall in the Smeaton Gorge and an eating back since then of some 15 metres (50 feet).

Thus does this small and little known ravine, the Smeaton Ravine which is now merely an obstacle in a scenic highway, definitely disclose how Nature's forces worked in the Great Lakes Region and in our Romantic Gorge many thousands of years ago during the long Old Narrow Gorge or Erie Gorge stage of the Cataract.

Niagara Glen Terraces

The Niagara Glen is a geologist's paradise and Cupid's playground! This mass of shattered gigantic boulders is incorrectly called a glen because it occurs on one side of the river only. The true glen should encompass both sides of a stream. The people on the American side of our historic river, perhaps realizing this, have traced out the paths for a nature trail and picnic area among the piled rocks on their steep side. Their venture was successful. From its vantage point you can spot nearly anyone in the Glen if there are not too many leaves on the trees. And from these cramped picnic grounds you may more clearly see the three main rock ledges which used to break the now spectacular drop of our Falls into three falls.

At the far left top of the picture, if this were the sort of perfect picture I should like always to show you, you may see the snack bar and gift shop which serve the swarms of visitors to this gorgeous spot. The mighty rock layer on which this stands is of gray, fine-textured limestone formed over 400 million years ago by the chemical reaction of minute animal-bodies with the calcium in the warm waters of an ancient ocean. This great sea, which we know was salty because the same type of microscopic bodies are at work in the salty waters of the earth today, once covered most of our continent except the Rocky and Appalachian mountains. It was but the successor, different in form, extent and perhaps in temperature, of many seas which had covered the same regions millions of years before the approximate date mentioned above. It was in turn replaced slowly by seas which covered this district much nearer our own time. Each ocean had deposited at its bottom, layers of mud, sand, and tiny bits of worn-out coral and powdered shells. These in time, under pressure of the great depths of waters, hardened into rock layers of various qualities. Here where so many tourists and natives gaze and walk are several of these ancient, solidified ocean beds.

The topmost one, on the average at this point nearly 24 metres (80 feet) thick, is called Lockport Limestone. The section here which houses the picnic grounds and shelter (if memory serves me well there used to be two charming open-walled log huts), from which the steep rustic wooden steps led down, is called Wintergreen Flats. This very hard layer was undercut a great deal by the soft, tearing teeth of the river a little more than 7,000 years ago. So fierce were the turbulent waters here that the frayed edges of this limestone at one particular spot in the path along its base, present a striking picture of the stern of a ship in an ancient and mystic fleet about to weigh anchor. This band of rock is the top

Niagara Glen Terraces: No. 1, overhanging ledge of Wintergreen Flats; No. 2, Wilson Terrace, the level of the second falls; No. 3, Foster's Flats the third falls; No. 4, Cripps Eddy; No. 5, Glen Rapids. Photo circa 1937.

of the escarpment edge at Queenston; its long-wearing qualities really keep our Falls as waterfalls and prevent them from degenerating into rapids; it forms a great dominating ledge from far beyond Hamilton to the westward, and yet at Watertown, N.Y. near the source of the St. Lawrence River, it is twice as thick as it is here.

The second layer is rather lighter in colour and is coarser in parts. The thousands of broken rocks which smother it form a terrace sloping down from the Lockport Limestone above. This ancient bat-

tlefield of Nature's forces is named Wilson Terrace in honour of James Wilson, the first Superintendent of Queen Victoria Niagara Falls Park, the man who first thought of making the Glen into a natural, wild park. The rocks which underlie this terrace as its floor are named Clinton Limestone and Thorold Sandstone. Their broken blocks are to be seen in the Foster's Flats terrace below this one, and even partly submerged in the waters of the rapids. Indeed there would be no rapids if these limestone giants did not here obstruct the progress of the river.

Whirlpool Sandstone, white, yellow and reddish in colour, very coarse in texture, forms the floor of the red paths and all the lowest paths of the Glen. This is the same layer which strikes the eye so strongly at Lewiston just on top of a brilliant red layer

New York State Power Authority

This 1963 air view shows the Niagara Glen Terraces. No. 1, Wintergreen Flats and Terrace; No. 2, Wilson Terrace; No. 3, Foster's Flats; No. 4, a dried out Cripps Eddy; No. 5, the abandoned crest of the Wintergreen Flats waterfall and the dry gorge; No. 6, Ontario Hydro access road to the Sir Adam Beck Generating Stations; No. 7, Niagara Parks Whirlpool Golf Course; No. 8, abandoned roadbed of the Niagara Gorge Railway, now a nature trail.

of Queenston Shale. Close to the point from which the picture was taken, near the Whirlpool, this layer disappears under the waters, being tilted as all the other bands of rock are so that they are high at Queenston but low at Fort Erie. It is because these layers are sloped backwards that the height of the Falls will decrease greatly after the waters gnaw back through the high ledges of the rapids above the Falls.

The famous potholes and caves (discussed in a later chapter) are in this lower terrace called Foster's Flats. It is about 11 metres (35 feet) above the water at this end of the Glen, yet affords a thrilling close-up of the towering waves in the 40 kilometre (25 mile) per hour rapids.

N.B. The Niagara Glen was originally called Foster's Flats. According to a report in the Niagara Parks Archives, dated May 22, 1887: "Twenty or thirty years ago a man named Foster built a saw mill on these flats at the edge of the river and having, it is said, a license from the Crown, cut and removed heavy timbers growing there, floating them down the Niagara River to Queenston. That license expired and there are no traces of the mill at the present day". The Queen Victoria Niagara Falls Park Commission, the forerunner of The Niagara Parks Commission, acquired the property in 1894.

New York State Power Authority

Stage III the Lower Great Gorge from the Niagara Glen to the bend in the River at Niagara University. This 1958 photo shows: No. 1, Wilson Terrace in the Niagara Glen; No. 2, Whirlpool Sandstone layer and Foster's Flats above; No. 3, Ontario Hydro access road to Sir Adam Beck Generating Station construction site; No. 4, rock scaling for the Niagara Power Project.

Wintergreen Flats

To my mind there is no scenery to compare with the Glen in breathtaking beauty and convenience of access anywhere east of the Mississippi or north of the Mason-Dixon Line. There are only two possible competitors for preference: that Grand Canyon of the East, Letchworth Park, which is about 113 kilometres (70 miles) due south from Buffalo; and Watkins Glen, which is farther south-east and justly world famous.

Perhaps I am prejudiced in favour of the Glen below the Whirlpool because I saw it first, and first impressions, as people say, are wont to be lasting. Photographers surely find much more variety of subject here, and parents, I have noticed, find there are an amazing number of niches and caves in which to lose wandering offspring. Other places hem one in with ladders and restrictive paths.

But to a geologist the traces of things that happened here in the most distant past are some of the most priceless treasures of his science. Here can be detected the times of crustal movements, these mysterious breathings and spasms of the Earth's bosom, which have long ago determined the levels of the Great Lakes and even the heights of the mountain ranges near our region, and which are even now working in their slow, serene way towards some distant end, which, if continued at the present rate, must surely change the scenery of the Niagara District and others nearby.

From the Whirlpool to just past the bend at Niagara University is the part of the river called Lower Great Gorge. It is the third section of the channel counting back from the beginning at Lewiston-Queenston. This part does not include the Whirlpool itself, but from that to the lower end of Foster's Flats it is about 3 kilometres (2 miles). As the Falls cut back from Queenston to near the side of Niagara University its progress was slow because its volume was only about one-seventh of what it was to become at the Niagara Glen. The water-level of ancestral Lake Ontario, which at Queenston was very high – within 11 metres (35 feet) of the top of the Lockport Limestone layer there, had gradually dropped to a considerably lower level during the long time required to cut back to the approximate position at the southern end of the Niagara Glen as shown in Map I. Here the waters of ancestral Lake Ontario (Lake Iroquois) began to back up again as the land in the immediate north slowly rose or rebounded when relieved of the burden of its ice barrier, the glacier. Just previously, the great outpouring of the Upper Lakes was through Trent Valley as we have shown in a map in a previous chapter. Now the uplift became too great for the waters any longer to use this northern channel and the waters began to find their way through the lower Port Huron exit which had been used once before, long ago.

At the same time as these floods, which up to now formed the main and upper cataract, made their mighty flow felt over the Lockport Limestone layer, the outlet of Lake Iroquois was raised. Due to this same northern uplift, the glacial debris in the bed of the St. Lawrence River was raised, so that comparatively little water from Lake Iroquois could flow on to the ocean.

At Rome, N.Y. the beach formed by the backed-up waters of Lake Iroquois, can now be seen 37 metres (123 feet) higher than the level of present-day Lake Ontario. Below the Niagara Escarpment at Queenston it is 42 metres (137 feet). In the gorge here at the Glen, there is every reason to believe that the waters rose nearly to the same height; the result was that the cataract at its beginning fell into deep water and therefore had its erosive power lessened with regard to the Clinton Limestone and shale beneath. This high water is marked in Part I of the diagram.

I have not attempted to show the water falling, in order to lessen the markings on an already complicated sketch. It will be noticed that the waters everywhere in falling over a rock ledge ate backwards into the soft shale beneath the edge over which they leaped. The lack of erosive power due to the cushioning by the high water level in the gorge below the early cataract is no doubt the main reason why the early gorge was shallow. In fact the falls had not pierced the second of the three layers of hard rock through which it now is constantly eroding. There was also at least one other reason why the gorge here was shallow. Although the flow of water, now that the strength of the upper Inland Seas had been added, was seven times greater, still it is easily seen that the Lockport Limestone layer here is very thick, compact and moreover very flat and even, thus allowing no point along the crest of the falls at which the waters pulled by gravity could chance to concentrate their forces and eat back more quickly. The increased stream then was forced to fall over the rim in a comparatively even sheet of water such as is now true along the top of the American

By the time the falls had reached this point – Wintergreen Point – the outlet of Lake Iroquois became blocked when the land there rebounded after being relieved of the crushing weight of the glacier, so that comparatively little water could flow from Lake Iroquois to the ocean. The lake water backed up into the river, decreasing the height of the falls and reducing its erosive power.

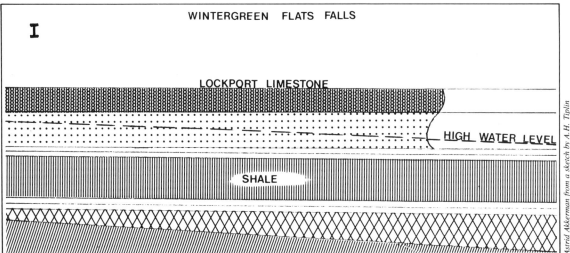

WINTERGREEN FLATS FALLS

I

LOCKPORT LIMESTONE

HIGH WATER LEVEL

SHALE

Astrid Akkerman from a sketch by A.H. Tiplin

II

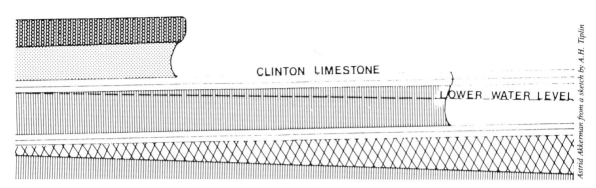

CLINTON LIMESTONE

LOWER WATER LEVEL

Astrid Akkerman from a sketch by A.H. Tiplin

When the falls reached the point called Cripps Eddy, the level of Lake Iroquois fell 30.5 metres (100 feet) when a further tilting of the land at its outlet allowed the water to rush out via the St. Lawrence channel. A second falls then began at Lewiston-Queenston, and having less resistant rock to erode, soon eroded back to the Glen. Wilson Terrace was the crest of this falls.

Falls. (N.B. This is true now also of the Horseshoe Falls since remedial work in 1954.) These two important conditions seem to have held sway until the cataract had eaten back from the bend at Niagara University to the back of the Niagara Glen, near Cripps Eddy. By estimating how quickly it is likely that the Falls ate back here it is possible to do more than conjecture the length of time that Lake Iroquois existed at the high level.

Until Cripps Eddy was reached, Lake Iroquois continued to be at the same high level shown in Part I. But then the level of the old lake fell at least 30.5 metres (100 feet). This brought the level down to almost the present one. Then the Falls was 30.5 metres (100 feet) higher. The reason for this lowering and for another subsequent one was discussed in the chapter *Former Lake Bed,* when we looked at the Iroquois Beach at Lewiston-Queenston. By that time the scouring power of the falls was much greater and the gorge top which guided the waters seems to have become a bit narrower, thus concentrating the water. These two new conditions were responsible for a narrower, deeper gorge made at a more rapid rate. Part II of the diagram shows the lower level and the formation of a second falls from Clinton Limestone beds. Doubtless the force of the upper cataract falling directly on the thin limestone beds below, 2.4 to 3 metres (8 to 10 feet) thick at this point, always compact but offering little resistance

to the thudding forces of a good-sized cataract, soon weakened these rocks. When this second falls did form, it quickly eroded back to the higher one and caught up with it, forming one large descent over the very thick Lockport Limestone layer.

The projecting ledge of Lockport Limestone, the first terrace at Niagara Glen, is known as Wintergreen Flats; the half-smothered Clinton rocks form Wilson Terrace; the lowest layer, Medina Sandstone, which in Part III of the diagram is not eroded back, is known as Foster's Flats. I have attempted to show this in shadow-graph, and have labelled the three outstanding layers of rocks which are responsible for the features at the Glen as "A", "B", and "C".

Wintergreen Flats was then the floor of the Upper falls. Wilson Terrace was the floor of the second or middle falls, while in Part II Foster's Flats is still covered with the waters of the river. These last flats are remnant of the old river bottom underlaid by Medina Sandstone and Queenston Red Shale. When the top falls had cut back to the southern end of the Glen, it was overtaken by the middle falls at Wilson Point, an eastward projecting part of the Clinton layer. Meanwhile, due to the slope of the rocks as one may see in parts of the diagram, the Medina Sandstone being higher, the gorge towards the south was more exposed and formed the third cataract. This did not overtake the other two falls because of rocks which forced it to form slopes underwater at the Whirlpool. But it is likely that when the united upper and middle falls were at the Whirlpool region, this third cataract, about 11 metres (35 feet) high, was cutting through the former river bottom and forming Foster's Flats. The appearance of this third or lower falls was no doubt due to the slope of the rock layers and merely helped by a further lower-

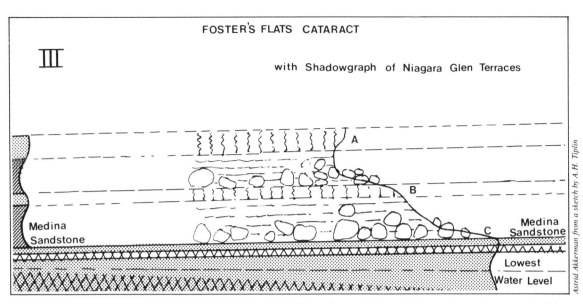

A

B

C

Medina
Sandstone

Medina
Sandstone

Lowest
Water Level

Astrid Akkerman from a sketch by A.H. Tiplin

When the top falls had cut back to the southern end of the Glen – Cripps Eddy – it was overcome by the second or middle falls. Then a further lowering of the lake to modern levels, caused a third or lower falls to fall over the Medina Whirlpool Sandstone layer. Having a less resistant Queenston Shale to erode, it quickly eroded back along what is now the Foster's Flats level. It did not catch up with the other two falls, now combined, until almost at the Whirlpool.

ing of the lake level which probably was of comparatively short duration. This appears in Part III.

The red Queenston Shales underlying the heavy grey sandstone of the Medina Formation are a feature of the Glen walks near the river edge. These gradually disappear at the Glen; due to the slope, they leave the light and do not appear again to the south in this Niagara region. But at Lewiston-Queenston, they are very high and startlingly bright.

The slope of the rock layers from the mouth of the gorge to the Whirlpool Rapids Bridge is about 7.9 metres to 1.6 kilometres (26 feet to the mile). The distance from the mouth of the gorge to the northern or lower end of Foster's Flats is about 3.2 kilometres (2 miles). Therefore, if the Medina Sandstones and the Queenston Red Shales go under the waters at the Glen, they must be 19.8 metres (65 feet) above the river at Queenston. This is allowing .8 kilometre (one-half mile) for the length of Foster's Flats.

Those not used to walking will agree that the distance is all of that, especially when they are thinking of the steep paths and ladder-steps to the precipice of this ancient upper falls.

The steel stairway built down the Wintergreen Terrace cliff in 1986.

George A. Seibel

Niagara Parks Archives

The Niagara Glen and Wintergreen Terrace from the U.S. side. The "Stern of the Great Eastern" is just to the right of centre and farther right is the abandoned crest of the falls and the dry gorge below. The rock ledges of Foster's Flats show all along the bottom of the picture.

The Niagara Glen from the U.S. In this view from the 1960's, the rock overhang along Wintergreen Flats can be seen. The "Stern of the Great Eastern" is visible at the far right. Some of the paths and stairways are visible through the leafless trees, and the picnic shelter, the scene of so many cookouts during the 1920's to 1970's, is at lower right. It was destroyed in a fire set by vandals in 1970.

George Bailey

NIAGARA GLEN, CANADA.

This postcard view from the early 1900's shows the pathway in the Glen under the Wintergreen Terrace overhang. The extent of the overhang goes beyond the end of the picture at the left. It was this overhang which was blasted off for safety reasons in 1959 – almost sixty years after this picture was taken.

The scaled cliffs of Wintergreen Terrace, with the pathway now open to the sunlight. The indentation under the first layer of limestone is the location of the fossilized coral reef.

Wintergreen Flats – Ancient Goat Island

They say history repeats itself; I suppose any occurrences which are dependent upon the nature of man or upon the nature of the physical world are bound to come again. At least it is so in the science of geology, that handbook which attempts to explain the unchanging laws of nature. That most majestic of all islands, Goat Island, although not at all unique in its formation, is pre-eminent in the stupendous scale of its setting and environment; Goat Island, however, had a predecessor several thousands of years ago, born of the same parents – water and rock.

Let us go to the Niagara Glen. As we leave the parking lot in front of the snack bar, steps down a 3.7 to 4.6 metres (12 to 15 feet) slope face us. This same descent we notice, follows all along the back of the well-kept level grounds on which are benches, small summer houses and a picnic shelter. It was once the bank of the wider ancient river. A drop-off into sheer space which seems imminent if we approach the edge, draws us like a magnet. We follow the rustic railing to a point where only space is on the left and right and ahead. This is the top of the ship's formation, which is known as "The Stern of the Great Eastern". The Great Eastern was a famous

iron steamship of the 1890's.

Composed of Lockport Limestone such as forms the edge of the Falls today, this formation is really the remnant of a small "Goat" Island. There were at one time three stairways down into the Niagara Glen. The third, and the one which to my mind afforded some of the loveliest views, collapsed due to a natural scaling of rock from the edge of this ancient "Goat" Island. Weather and frost finally managed to force away from the mother cliff a mere trifle of 19.7 tonnes (20 tons) or so. (N.B. This stairway location abandoned in 1937 is now the location of the new steel stairs).

All that side of the Wintergreen Flats from the location of the third stairway to the projecting point seems to have been the edge of a side falls of small volume which flooded over and around this table of rock long ago. The spot marked "A" on the accompanying map shows the location of this point when the gorge at this spot was being cut by the first falls from the Lockport Limestone layer to the Clinton Limestone layer below.

The heavy dotted lines represent the deep gorge now formed by the three successive falls from the three layers of rock. The first or upper falls was very

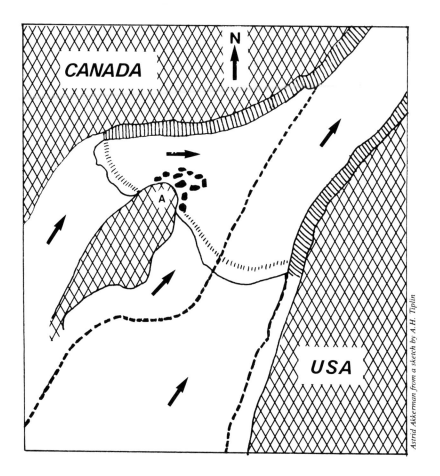

Astrid Akkerman from a sketch by A.H. Tiplin

This map shows the position of the divided falls when it reached the present Niagara Glen area. The heavy dotted line shows the gorge, formed by the three successive cataracts from three different layers of rock, through which the river flows today. The east falls on the right was to erode back faster than its branch falls, eventually cutting off the flow of water through this channel and drying off the western falls. This dried-off river bed is now the Wintergreen Flats picnic area. The American Falls will some day suffer the same fate as befell this western branch falls.

broad, if we include the side fall which was drained away by the main one as it cut back. It was not more than the distance separating the first two rock layers 36.5 metres (120 feet). The second or middle falls was about the same height but not the same great breadth as the first falls. It caught up with the upper falls at Wilson Point just south of the location of the falls pictured here and near Cripps Eddy

formed a single falls over 61 metres (200 feet) high. In so doing it undercut the western side of the gorge beneath the ledge of the first falls. Thus the visitor will usually find that if he stands on the edge of Wintergreen Flats he has some rock overhang to support him, but under that is only air for as far under his feet as he dares to look. Much of this undercutting is still going on by the quieter forces of chemical action of air, water and the prying force of frost. In fact the Niagara Parks Commission has closed one of the best walks along the north side of the Wintergreen ledge because of the danger from falling rock.

It is true, although unfortunately not many parents realize it, that the Niagara Parks Commission is at times quite discouraged by the vandalism committed by rowdies in this public park. Such benches as I have mentioned above which used to afford restful contemplation of the many vistas here, were often smashed on the rocks of the terrace below; some of those on the lower path were thrown in the river. Is it possible that there are some citizens like these among us?

N.B. There is no mention in the Niagara Parks Commission Annual Reports of rock scaling being done at the Glen. However, in 1959, it was reported "... at the Niagara Glen a new barrier fence along the edge of the escarpment was built, replacing a

This is the dry crest of the western branch of the first falls at the Glen. It was abandoned when the main eastern falls which flowed on the other side of the island which existed then off Wintergreen Point, cut into its bed at Cripps Eddy. This cut off the flow of water, drying up the river bed, which was higher than its eastern branch. The former river bed is now the Wintergreen Flats picnic area at the Glen.

A.H. Tiplin

wooden fence there. The new fence has stone piers with cedar log rails". This indicates that the old fence had to be removed for some reason, probably for the scaling. The rustic picnic shelter and the last of the covered arbours were burned by vandals in the early 1970's and not rebuilt.

Today, to counteract the vandalism to picnic tables placed on the Wintergreen Flats, they have been chained to cement pads, so that they cannot be thrown over the bank on to the rocks below. During the late 1970's a chain link fence was built around the top of the stairways, with a gate that can be locked, to limit access to the Glen if necessary. The aerosol spray paint cans are a further hazard and there is a constant program carried out by the Glen's caretakers to obliterate the graffiti which appear from time to time on the rocks. Vandalism has always been a problem at the Niagara Glen.

This undercut rock promontory jutting out at the northern end of Wintergreen Flats was named "Stern of the Great Eastern" in honour of the world famous British iron steamship, which was scrapped in 1888, at the time the Niagara Glen was opened. The "Great Eastern" launched in 1858 was the largest ship built to that time. She became a famous passenger liner. Cyrus Field who had tried unsuccessfully in 1857 and 1858 to lay a trans-Atlantic cable, to carry messages from North America to England, chartered the "Great Eastern" and successfully laid the cable in 1866. Photo circa 1937.

"Stern of the Great Eastern" after scaling, looking upwards from Wilson Terrace.

Wilson Terrace

I hope none of my readers has missed the pleasure of a walk beneath the cliff edge at Niagara Glen. The first picture shows one of the paths, perhaps the one which will be already the favourite of three similar ones. And yet that could hardly be so; the lowest path, along Foster's Flats is more colourful with its red walks, and red cliff streaked with grey and green and white on the one side, while on the other hand is the river, green or leaden, with white plumes. But the lowest path does not afford such far-reaching vistas as this second under Wilson Terrace ledge even if the latter does lack the varied colouring. As for the top path under Wintergreen Flats, that is so undercut and has a cliff towering so high that one can hardly take it all in as familiarly as the lower one which is smaller and more on our own scale.

In the second path the undercutting by the weather and the frost is still going on. I call to witness the large rock attempting to bar the pathway and forlornly surveying the mother rock it has been slowly but surely forced to desert. If it is wondering what next is to happen to it, I think we can tell it. No doubt the workmen who care for the park will lever it down the hill to come to rest with its many larger

and smaller fellows who preceded it. This wearing is now slow. Once there were terrible currents here doing the same work much more quickly.

In ancient days, possibly 6,000 or 7,000 years ago, the first falls, tumbling over Wintergreen Flats above, set the resistant rock pictured here and formed it into a floor similar to the floor which must doubtless exist now. The Wilson Terrace above is strewn with huge monoliths and boulders jumbled on the smooth rock layer. Such must be the present picture at the river bottom today all along the river.

Then came a second falls trying to catch up to the first, tumbling over the very same kind of rock layer. Both falls were equal in height – about 36 metres (120 feet). It could not have been otherwise because both layers are separated from each other and the one below by that distance of soft material. Very near the point shown in the second picture it did catch up and then the falls was one drop of over 61 metres (200 feet).

The combined falls, eating back through a channel nearly as wide as from this point to the American side, used the Medina Red Shale and Sandstone layer as a floor. Then the level of Lake Iroquois was lowered, so that a third fall was formed over the lowest ledge of rock at Lewiston-Queenston. This quickly eroded back, cutting into Foster's Flats soon after it began, and then finding that its rock edge was tilting southwards caught up with the upper and middle falls, with which it then combined somewhere near the Whirlpool at a later date.

But just before this lowering of the waters took place the combined falls cut back to near Fisherman's Eddy or Cripps Eddy. The undercutting below Wilson Terrace shown in the first picture had not yet taken place. In fact the channel which had been cut did not suddenly veer off westward as the Clinton layer does here. Near the Eddy, while the river channel was still much larger than the present one, rushing through Foster's Flats, the Huron

Wilson Terrace, a shelf of rock supporting 20 metres (65 feet) of talus debris from Wintergreen Terrace. The cliffs were undermined by the ancient Niagara River, shortly after its volume increased from 15 percent of the present river flow (5664 m³/sec – 200,000 cfs) to slightly more than its present volume.

waters began to flow again into Lake Erie with the upper lake floods. Such an increase in volume, shortly followed by a lowering of the Lake Iroquois waters, caused a much more mighty falls than the present one. The channel was suddenly widened; the waters, similar to those at the base of the falls today, hurrying to escape from the large basin thus formed and now visible as Cripps Eddy at the Glen head, met the narrower channel at Wilson Point and naturally quickly undercut it in the manner shown in the picture.

It is not to be supposed that the ancient river in this manner described performed all the widening visible here. The same process is still continuing but Nature is now compelled to work with weaker tools. However, this last year or two (1937-38) she has been so vigorous as to claw away enough debris to nearly obscure the path in the second picture, and to cause the Niagara Parks Commissioners concern for the safety of visitors. N.B. The teetering rock referred to has long since been toppled into the flats below. The path referred to has been blocked off for some time.

George Bailey

George Bailey

Wilson Terrace from above. Just below the tree line top right, the second falls caught up with the first falls and they became one.

The smooth rock layer of Wilson Terrace is strewn with huge monoliths and boulders fallen from Wintergreen Terrace above. This leaning rock, stopped in its fall by a much smaller boulder, is a fine example of the erratic way in which rocks fall.

George Bailey

George Bailey

This huge monolith of Lockport Limestone, once part of the ancient river bed, fell from Wintergreen Terrace thousands of years ago, and landed in an almost perpendicular position. It stands partially buried, and the exposed portion of this boulder wall is 5 metres high, 27 metres long, 6 metres thick (17 feet high, 90 feet long, 20 feet thick).

The "Rock of Ages", a flower pot shaped piece of limestone which dropped into the gorge on the U.S. side many hundreds of years ago, landing in an almost perpendicular position. The watermarks on the rocks along the river bank show the height of the summer flow through the Glen.

Cripps Eddy

Some time in early spring I was standing on a dry rock about 15 centimetres (6 inches) above water at the edge of the Whirlpool. Looking back to the ice jam on shore I made sure of the settings on the camera and took the picture. Hardly had I tripped the shutter when I felt an icy cold near the ankles. In a moment the waters receded below the level they had attained when I jumped to the rock in all good faith. Since then I have tried to explain the breathing action of the Whirlpool which I had heard of before but had not experienced.

I knew of the tide-like action at Cripps Eddy and included that in my study too. Three pupils of Stamford Collegiate and myself, about a month ago posted our lookouts in the following manner: one at the north side of the Whirlpool; one directly across it but far enough up the gorge to be visible from the end of the Glen, that is, practically under the Aero Car's south station. This man had a large newspaper to use as a flag; another on the rocks near the rapids at the Glen, looking up-stream with binoculars at the flag; myself observing the spot pictured here with watch, notebook and pencil listening for the shout of the man with the binoculars which was to indicate high "tide" at the Whirlpool. The idea was to trace any connection between the two either for low or high "tide".

Our signal system worked very well. I calculate that it took not more than five seconds to send word of high water at the Whirlpool to Cripps Eddy. In all, we checked twenty successive high waters. After all that, our work merely established the fact that the high swell at the Whirlpool was not followed at any definite interval by high waters at Cripps Eddy at the Glen. This is what I had hoped to establish; I did not think that they would be simultaneous.

On several occasions, for some time, I sat on top of the gorge in that area watching the currents, the boils, and the smaller, fleeting whirlpools. I believe that the topography of the river bottom is such that these boils and swirls are formed irregularly. There seems to be no surface feature which would cause regular medium high waters at the Glen and Whirlpool followed at more rare intervals of three to five minutes by very high water. I believe if these "tides" are to be explained by the current action such an explanation will have to come from an hydraulic engineer with an intimate knowledge of water-knock, water frictions, etc. The secret lies in the Whirlpool, I think, unless it is merely coincidence that the amount of swell at both Whirlpool and Glen are the same to within an inch or so.

To introduce this fascinating subject to our readers, or to refresh the memories of many of them,

I took these pictures. I waited for a low "tide" which would uncover the small rocks. I took the picture when I thought I had a low "tide". Then I waited for the following high "tide". This meant fast work with the camera. I did not use a tripod, and therefore the reader can see I did not quite succeed in the quick work required because I did not cover quite the same territory in the second picture. The water in the high "tide" picture is about 63.5 centimetres (25 inches) deep. This is slightly higher than usual. But imagine my chagrin, when just as my camera was empty, there came an overflow which completely uncovered the rocks and then a high flow which came about 8 centimetres (3 inches) higher than the one pictured here; in fact it nearly swamped me.

I have checked the height on different days when the wind has been from several directions. Wind pressure on the waters in the Whirlpool seems to have no connection with "tides" below the Glen. The swell is about 8 to 15 centimetres (3 to 5 inches) at Pebbly Beach. I could find none near Lewiston-Queenston Bridge, although I sat at the fishing cabin for an hour. There is none at the Queenston Dock. N.B. In the 1920's and 1930's there were fish traps set out in the river below the Lewiston-Queenston Suspension Bridge. They were suspended from 5.5 to 6 metres (18 to 20 feet) 30 centimetres by 30 centimetres (12 inch by 12 inch) timbers. The trap, made of fishnet was set in the current and fish caught in the shore current directed into the trap by the cone-shaped entrance. The fisherman sat in a hut on the shore, and waited for the sound of the bell, which rang whenever fish pushed against the downriver side of the trap, as they tried to escape. The trap was then hauled up with a windlass, the fish removed, stored in boxes and sold either to people who came to the trap for fish, or to customers in town.

Before the last major diversion of water for electric power generation at the Robert Moses Power Plant in 1962, there was a "tidal" action at Cripps Eddy. Here "low tide" leaves the rock between the shore and the big rock island almost out of water.

A.H. Tiplin

A.H. Tiplin

This is "high tide". Anyone who crossed to the island rock at "low tide" could be quite certain of being marooned within a minute.

A.H. Tiplin

The "tide" going out at Cripps Eddy. Photo circa 1937.

Cripps Eddy circa 1970. The rock around which the "tide" used to swirl is shown high and dry since 1962 when water was diverted for the Robert Moses Generating Station.

When water was diverted for electric power generation in 1954 for the Sir Adam Beck Generating Station No. 2 and in 1962 for the Robert Moses Generating Station, the river's flow was reduced and Cripps Eddy dried up.

Foster's Flats
Sandwaves
Potholes and Fossils

The water-edge path along the Glen is most beautiful in the early summer season when the green of the leaf is so tender and delicate. In direct contrast are the Medina Red Shales streaked with green. Then, as if these were not enough, the blue of the sky, the spume of swirling water, and the white, yellow, rust and red of coarse-grained scintillating sandstone form a wondrous couch of colour for the winding paths which invite us not to hurry. There is not a better place along the gorge for the amateur or professional colour-photographer. All the symphony of the spectrum is here.

And to lend a deeper, persistent note to that harmony which comes from the inner self in response to beauty, there are objects on this pathway which remind us, even in this age veneered with the practical and the mechanical, of timeless mystery. The rocks themselves if closely examined show practically no fossils, however tiny, which might assure us of ancient life in the days when the rocks were made. But the setting was right for life to develop from whatever early forms it had then attained. That is to say, if the scientists are correct when they assert that all life started in the shallow parts of warm seas, we may be fairly sure that such conditions did maintain them; the proof is at the Glen.

At least the evidence for the shallow seas can be seen along the Foster's Flats pathway. As for proving that these seas were warm, that is more difficult. Let the reader walk from Cripps Eddy northward to the spring which has its exit through the Medina Sandstone and Shale. If he will continually watch the water's edge so that no rock of good size projecting from the water at a sharp angle can escape his notice, he will not miss seeing one with very plain and large ripple marks.

When the reader has spotted the slab resting on end in the river at the Glen, he will no doubt find that almost touching his right shoulder if he faces north is a tremendous layer of the same rock marked in the same way.

Even if we did not quite give credit to the fact that only by being deposited under water could such rock as is "in situ" in the Niagara Peninsula be formed, such ripples undeniably prove this origin. Has the reader never gone wading near the shore in Lake Ontario or Erie when the water is clear and still? And has he never felt the hard ridges which even the sand not yet turned to rock can form, ridges so hard that they are painfully tiresome to tender feet? Supposing these same ripples were left behind as some gentle and fairly long-time ebbing of the waters occurred. The silica particles of the sand already fitting together with their joints and facets in geometrical fashion would be still further bonded by the small quantity of limestone which is always deposited, or by the small amounts of iron oxide which here gives this sandstone its characteristic red, rust and yellow colour. When the seas came again, slowly or quickly, these ripples would already be rock. Another layer of sand, mud or lime deposited by the new sea would protect the lower and older one as it in turn hardened to rock, aided by the immense pressure of water. Thus the ripple-marked stone would be preserved until some minor change in topography, such as cutting back of a river-bed by a falls, split the bonded layers apart.

The other phenomenon along this pathway which gives food for thought is a glacial mill or pothole – the largest in the Glen. This occurs on the same part of Foster's Flats, but is nearer Cripps Eddy. Un-

fortunately this one is split. One interested in the geology illustrated here will ignore the initials and love-symbols scratched or pencilled on its smoother inner sides. Just here it occurred to me to wonder if mortals feel that they are storing up some small measure of immortality for themselves when they do such carving. If this is so, some few people whose names appear nearly everywhere on prominent rocks in the Glen have already assured themselves more than their fair share of the godlike characteristic.

Walking on the pathway under a ledge of Medina (Whirlpool) Sandstone below Foster's Flats in the Glen. Areas of the ledge collapsed on this pathway during the 1950's effectively cutting off any access along the river path, except for a short way at the downriver end, where there is still access to the spring.

An example of sandwaves in the Medina sandstone found at the edge of the Whirlpool on the U.S. side. This sandstone, also called Whirlpool Sandstone because it was first visible out of the water at the Whirlpool, is the Foster's Flats Terrace layer.

Looking through a giant pothole.

The lower river path at Foster's Flats, circa 1906, near the spring. This picture shows the rustic benches, long since destroyed by vandals, which were placed throughout the Glen. The water level in the river covers the huge blocks of sandstone which are visible today.

The river path in the 1930's. The large piece of rock broken off from the sandstone ledge is a forecast of what was to happen over twenty years later, when the whole ledge along the path dropped onto the path, cutting off access. The rocks to the left, over which the river is flowing are now well out of the water and often used by fishermen, some of whom have been marooned temporarily when the water behind them rose suddenly, leaving them with a stretch of water too swift to cross.

George Bailey

The river path leading to the spring which is just to the left outside the photo. The paths at this level are red in colour, from the red Queenston Shale which is exposed here.

George Bailey

The spring which has been flowing continually since the Glen paths were laid out. At one time there was a tin cup attached to a chain, where hikers could refresh themselves. Later, when people became more concerned with sanitary measures, the cup was removed and you had to get your drink of cool, refreshing water with your cupped hands. This spring water is no longer potable, due to the development of the land areas adjacent to the Glen above the Gorge.

Potholes

It seems a good idea to investigate a well-known phenomenon in the Glen, with the purpose of determining whether this was due to glacial action. The only hard part about that assignment was the physical activity of going up and down between the various sections of rock in the high Lockport Limestone layer and the lower Clinton Limestone layer comparing them with the chemical nature of the rock in which the potholes occur. To do this for the one massive block pictured here was not too difficult but in order to be scientifically accurate and to be able to say that potholes at the Niagara Glen do not occur in the Lockport Limestones, it was necessary to explore the beautiful park examining all such strange formations, whether whole or split, to see if just one pothole was not in this upper layer of rock over which the glacier passed.

Thus, in such work that attemps to be anything more than guessing, very much labour has to be done before anyone can make even a completely negative statement. The negative statement which resulted from so much climbing: there is no visible sign of glacially made potholes at Niagara Glen. Since most of the Niagara District is covered with glacial silt it is impossible to say that there are no glacially made holes in the entire district.

It must be explained at this point that such holes can be formed by two agents: larger crevices in a glacier, or swift currents of water not far from the foot of a falls. If water from the top surfaces of a glacier pours perpendicularly, or almost so, down one of the huge cracks or crevices usually found in such mighty masses of ice when they go down a steep slope slowly, or when they are pushed up over broken country by the pressure behind, and if that water descends upon gravel, sand or large boulders lying in a depression on the rock surface under the ice, then the whirling matter grinds a pothole. I do not expect to find any glacially eroded giant's kettles, as they are called in Europe, in any place where the slope of the land is gentle as it is in this Niagara District. These are commonly formed too by the swift streams issuing from beneath the front of the ice-mass. Such places are Diana's Baths, near North Conway, New Hampshire, in the heart of the winter skiing paradise; Lost River section of the Glen Ellis River not far from Conway – one pothole here has a ladder 4.5 metres (15 feet) long placed down in it for the sightseers. This last named is not a basin-shape as many potholes are, but is pipe-shaped with a corkscrew twist to it. The most famous giant's kettles are at Lucerne, Switzerland, in the Gletscher (Glacier) Garden. The largest there is 7.9 metres (26

What could cause a pothole? The answer is – a pot boiler. The round object to the left of the softball in the picture is a pot boiler. A brown limestone boulder, it was found by the author in a conical twisted hole in a large boulder at the edge of the Horseshoe Falls. To make a pothole, take a cascade of water falling from a great height, a small depression in the bed of the river, add a more or less round boulder, some gravel and sharp sand – then stand back! The boulder swirling with the sand as the abrasive will soon cut a pot in the bedrock, even through a 3 metre (10 foot) thick rock layer.

A.H. Tiplin

feet) across and 9 metres (30 feet) deep. Most significant and interesting of all, the largest of the boulders which did the grinding are still there at the bottom of many of the holes.

All the potholes at the Niagara Glen are in the second and third layers of rock, counting from the top down. Nearly twenty of them are visible, whole or split, and mostly away from the beaten path. None is in the top layer of Lockport Limestone over which the glacier passed; since the gorge was cut after the glacier retreated, then none of the lower layers of rock was exposed at that time.

The mechanics of such formations created by swift currents or eddies at the foot of a falls are very interesting. Dr. Spencer has recorded an incident which is most instructive. It seems that while fishing in the rapids near the Glen, a fisherman lost a lead sinker. It was about 1.3 centimetres (half-inch) in diameter, and pear-shaped, being about 5 centimetres (2 inches) long. About a month later this was found somewhat lower down-stream curious-

ly embedded in a rock. It had ground out a hole about 2 centimetres (three-quarters of an inch) in width; sand was in the hole at the bottom and sides but only loosely; sand was also embedded in the lead of the sinker making it a rather effective sort of auger. The sinker had done a fair job of grinding with the sand because it was sitting up in a hole nearly as deep as its own height.

Thus as the reader gazes at the various interesting eddies all along the gorge, he may be fairly sure that more potholes and Diana's Baths are being formed in our river wherever the stream is swift.

Unfortunately this pothole, the largest in the Niagara Glen, is split. Also called a glacial mill, a pothole is formed when a rounded stone, usually granite, called a pot boiler, is held in a depression in the bed of the river. As the river current passes over it, the stone revolves. This constant turning, aided by grains of sand worn off the stone, becomes a grinding action which wears a circular hole in the softer, more pliant limestone or sandstone. After many hundreds of years of continual grinding a pothole is created.

A.H. Tiplin

Looking up at the sky through the 2.4 metre (8 foot) deep, conical shaped Devil's Oven Pothole along a path in the Glen.

When the hole made by a pot boiler does not pierce through the layer of rock, it is called a kettle. These twin kettles are to be found beside a stairway in the Niagara Glen.

Fossils in the Niagara Glen

One of the most remarkable features of the Glen is the undercut top layer of Lockport Limestone that makes up Wintergreen Terrace. This was no doubt first made into a shelf by the action of the first cataract 36.5 metres (120 feet) high which cut through the Glen. The chemical action of the acids in air and water, in the rootlets of live trees and plants, and in decaying vegetable and animal remains, surely added to the weakening of the 24 metres (60 feet) layer even where the rock was solid. But in my opinion there is another factor in the cutting back of the mighty side-wall of the gorge which I believe has been overlooked. The science books say that certain masses of uncertain form and of various temperatures which are called coral secretions are very hard. These masses are very conspicuous in the top layer of rock which forms the present floor of the Falls and of Wintergreen Terrace at the Glen. But strangely enough, in view of what the text books say of coral reefs in general, wherever there is the most undercutting of this layer there will be found the largest and the softest coral formations.

The officials of the Niagara Parks Commission tending the Glen are well aware of the danger attending a walk beneath these far overhanging masses of heavy limestone. They have accordingly barred certain paths. I have heard many people who frequent the Glen even oftener than I do, express a doubt that these layers were weak. Presumably the reasoning is that since they have been this way for so many years they must therefore be very strong. That is precisely the reason why they are weak now. It is well to remember that a breaking of the rock had to take place many times before the rocks could become shaped in this interesting and dangerous fashion; just because our lives are on a small scale in time, while the rocks are enduring on a larger time-plan than ours, we should not forget that more rock-falls are bound to take place. What a tragedy it would be if, without the slightest warning, and with the force of a mighty trip-hammer, one of these ledges were to blot out a party of carefree visitors. N.B. This danger no longer exists because the rock wall mentioned has long since been scaled.

Close-up view of the fossil bed found in the Wintergreen Cliff below Wintergreen Flats. The Niagara Glen is a Nature Preserve and it is unlawful to destroy the rock wall to collect fossil samples.

Niagara Parks Archives

On Saturday a week ago, I took a friend and three pupils from the physiography class at Stamford Collegiate on a fossil-hunting tour of this part of the Glen, Smeaton Ravine, and then over the Lewiston-Queenston Suspension Bridge to the railway which goes through a tunnel there and slowly mounts the gorge side to disappear inland just past Niagara University. N.B. The Niagara Glen is now a Nature Preserve and fossil hunting is no longer permitted. The railway referred to, the Rochester, Watertown and Onondaga Railroad, ceased operating in 1937 and the former roadbed mentioned was obliterated when the Robert Moses Generating Station complex was constructed.

This one coral reef in the Glen I want very much to have the reader see. I think it distinctly shows the coral mass to be softer than the rest of the rock. Equipped with a hammer and chisel, one of my students found that very small specimens of crushed coral, especially pieces of the jointed stems of the ancient sea-lily, called the crinoid, come out with only the pressure of the fingers. The hammer and chisel and goggles were of no use there because the whole mass is so sedimentary, incoherent and ground up, or so changed by crystallization that no separate structures were discernible.

On examination, I found there a fairly extensive crack in the limestone which supports the unweathered part of the coral. Coral, by the way, in the Gulf of Mexico and the Caribbean, does not form below the 100 fathoms mark. It has always been considered that these ancient corals were formed in shallow, warm seas. Those found in the Silurian limestones which characterize the Niagara District are the oldest known. There are many things about their formation which are not yet explained. It is generally thought that such masses as are shown here were caused by various corals, none of which were as colourful as those of our present warm seas, growing in colonies as they do today here and there in the world. The bottoms of the shallow seas nearby were continually being raised by sediments being deposited, but for a time the corals grew more rapidly. This was possibly because their deposits were augmented by the myriads of bodies of small free-swimming animals (which were not yet of the back-boned type) which came to feed on the coral polyps. The trilobite, an ancient ancestor of our present horseshoe crab, is often found in such reefs, unfortunately broken up and sadly treated by the grinding of the wave-borne sands and the weight of the deposits which were later made on top of him. We all looked for such in every accessible coral reef we found; tiny shells, stems of coral lilies which are too fragile to keep, and some round heads of the trilobite were ours in abundance. Later in the day we tried the lower coral reefs on the American side of the gorge nearly opposite the Queenston Power House. (Now the Sir Adam Beck Generating Station No. 1). Here it was the same story, traces of the trilobite but not one even half-complete specimen.

Our examination of the Rochester Shales which are known to be fairly rich in this rare trilobite was very cursory because about one hundred American geology students from colleges in New York State were then studying around the Falls and gorge for two days. One of their professors was later reported in the *Niagara Falls Gazette* to have found four trilobites. These students were astute enough to be digging in the best sections of shale. We were too polite to interfere. In any case our chance had been spoiled because trilobites are most surely and easily found after a long period of weathering has greatly separated the shale layers. Anyway, every knapsack in our party was crammed with specimens of various minerals and fossils and many a pocket was stretched.

Eurypterids – Eurypterida existed approximately 425 million years ago. Commonly called sea scorpions, distantly related to our modern horseshoe crab. Had flounder-like body with twelve movable segments on its back and a dagger-like tail. Moved with one to four pairs of walking legs depending on the species. This fine specimen of Eurypterid fossils, from the author's collection, was found in an unknown location in Bertie Limestone near Lake Erie.

Fossils Present in Niagara River Gorge Strata

Nautilus – Cephalopod

*Horn or Cup Coral
– Enterolasma Caliculum*

Lamp Shells – Phyla Brachiopoda

Sea Lilies – Crinoidea

Trilobites – Trilobita

Snails – Gastropoda

Trilobites – *Trilobita*

Bottom feeding crustaceans with a semi-hard shell back composed of articulated segments, and a soft underbelly. They swam or walked on the sea floor in search of food, and moulted, shedding their shell covering as our modern day crabs and lobsters. Existed about 425 million years ago and became extinct about 240 million years ago. They are found in Rochester, Grimsby and Clinton layers. The discovery of a complete fossil is rare and indicates a sudden burial.

Snails – *Gastropoda*

These spiral shells of snails are found in the Silurian rocks which make up the strata of our Niagara Gorge.

Sea Lilies – *Crinoidea*

Early in life they attached themselves to the sea bottom. When they matured, with long stalks, they broke away and became "feather" starfish. They still exist on the Atlantic Ocean floor, over 1.6 kilometres (one mile) down. Found in Rochester Shale, they date to 425 million years ago.

Horn or Cup Coral – *Enterolasma Caliculum*

They grew individually on the sea bottom in an upright position, cemented to shells or other hard debris. Found in Lockport and Clinton strata, they are 400 million to 425 million years old.

Lamp Shells – *Phyla Brachiopoda*

These Brachiopods are clam-like shells. Over eighty different species are to be found in the Clinton and Rochester strata.

Nautilus – Cephalopod

These ancestors of our nautilus, squid and related cuttlefish, range from 5 to 7.6 centimetres (two to three inches) in diameter. They were in existence when the Lower Silurian (Medina) and the Ordovician (Queenston Shale) strata were laid down over 425 million years ago.

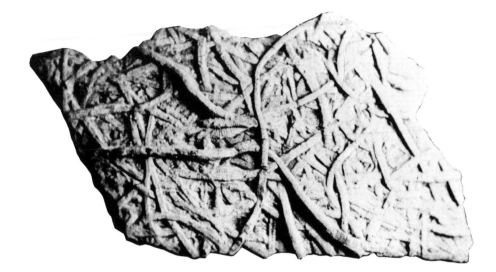

A.H. Tiplin

Fossil in Grimsby Sandstone of horizontal feeding burrows of a worm-like organism. The Upper Grimsby Sandstone layer from which this fossil came is classified as "massive to slightly stratified" (that is, it separates easily), by Ontario Hydro geologists who were conducting a geological study of the rock strata here prior to the construction of the twin tunnels in the 1950's. The ease with which these layers separate accounts for the clear, distinct fossil shown in the picture.

A.H. Tiplin

Albert Tiplin is shown in this photo, beside the highway on a vacation trip through Northern Ontario. He is holding his rock hammer, and a rock sample which he will use in his classroom teaching.

Former Outlets of the Upper Lakes

Before a certain enlarging of the Gorge at the Glen can be understood, we must realize the former size and use of the Niagara River. The volume of this river has been greatly magnified in the last 7,000 years. There is plenty of evidence to show that while it was cutting back from its birthplace at Lewiston-Queenston to the rear of the Glen near the Whirlpool our historic river was only a small but powerful exit for the drainage of a Lake Erie which was only one-fifth the size of the present Lake. All this evidence is proven by other traces of geological changes much farther north than our district.

The arrow on the map represents the retreat of the melting glacier as slowly, over a period of thousands of years, it moved back to its birthplace in the north. This direction is shown by glacier scratches on rocks in the quarries near here at Port Colborne, Queenston, Walker Brothers Quarries and also on Goat Island. One must think of our rock crust as a sponge rubber matting; when the great mass of ice was smothering the country, this matting was naturally pressed down. But when the ice retreated towards the north, this elastic matting just as naturally slowly resumed its former higher level. N.B. Ice a mile deep exerts a pressure of 7.2 kilopascals m^2 (150 tons a square foot). Glaciers ranged up to 4.8 kilometres (3 miles) thick, and this

depressed the earth underneath   61 metres or more (several hundred feet) below its present level. When the pressure of the glacier's weight was removed from the land it gradually rose; this is called glacial rebound. (Forrester 1976). This upward movement is not a thing of the past but is even now continuing as the glacial masses still in the north of Canada and Greenland slowly retreat.

When the glacier was just northward of the district "A" on the map, the lowest part of the land was naturally in front of the glacier and was still pressed down greatly by its weight. The melting ice produced floods which had to find an outlet to the sea-level. The easiest course was from Georgian Bay to Lake Nipissing and to the ocean via the Ottawa River. Along the shores of these bodies of water and on the banks of the Ottawa are marks and deposits of sand, clay and gravel which are now high above the present water level. These are high-water marks which definitely tell how much higher the land is now than it was then, or how much more water was flowing then than now. Geologists have decided that both these conditions existed.

But the glacier was slowly retreating for thousands of years and gradually the land along the Ottawa rose as its oppressor receded farther and farther northward. Soon this channel was no longer

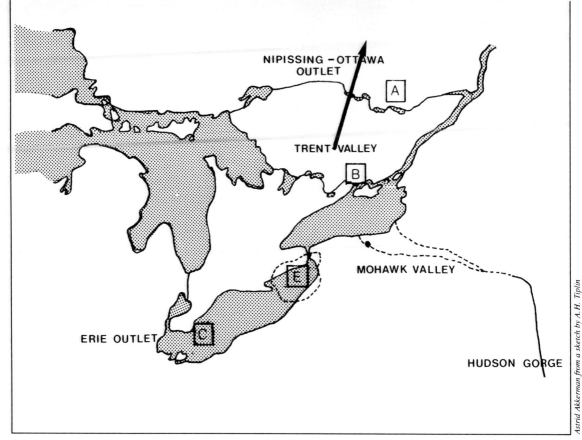

NIPISSING – OTTAWA OUTLET

A

TRENT VALLEY

B

MOHAWK VALLEY

E

ERIE OUTLET

C

HUDSON GORGE

This sketch shows the former outlets of the Great Lakes before the Falls cut back to the Glen. The arrow represents the slow retreat of the melting glacier, over a period of thousands of years. When the glacier was north of District "A" on the map, the easiest course for the melt waters was the Nipissing-Ottawa Outlet. When the surface of the land along this outlet rose after the weight of the glacier was removed from it, a new and lower passage for lake drainage opened up at "B", through Lake Simcoe and the Trent Valley System on to Lake Iroquois. The dotted area marked "E" shows the approximate size of the small Lake Erie whose waters formed Stage II, the Old Narrow or Erie Gorge. Modern Lake Erie is shown at "C".

such an easy one for the waters to take. The rim of the Lake Nipissing Basin was by this time a good deal too high to make a deep outlet for a mightly flow of water. Up to the present time in fact, it has risen some 76 metres (250 feet) above its old level. The Nipissing-Ottawa channel was for a long time the only escape of the lake waters to the ocean. This is shown by the strength and definite character of the old shore line along the outlet.

A new and lower passage had to be found. The

waters now opened a way "B", gradually through Lake Simcoe and the Trent Valley System to Lake Ontario. For some reason, the St. Lawrence passage was blocked by masses of glacial debris along its floor, or by some unusual temporary rising of the land across the Quebec region. The waters did not use this former channel for a long time although no doubt they were continually trying to force a way through. The great mass of the flood was diverted by a lower valley leading toward the headwaters of the Hudson River from the southern shore of Lake Ontario. On the map the dot on the side of this Mohawk Valley represents the city of Rochester. So for perhaps a thousand years at least the mighty Palisades of the Hudson Gorge saw the waters of the Great Lakes flowing southeastward towards Long Island, New York. But it seems that Long Island then did not exist except as part of the mainland. Nearly 161 kilometres (100 miles) out in the Atlantic beyond the present shore and many fathoms below the present ocean level the very deep submerged mouth of that ancient Hudson Gorge exists. In size and sculpture it may compare favourably with the present Grand Canyon in Colorado. The land then has since submerged along the coastal plain of the Atlantic.

The upper section of the Lower Great Gorge as seen from above Cripps Eddy, looking towards the Whirlpool, circa 1938.

Yet the bosom of the land was all this time swelling higher and higher as the ice in the north retreated; the glacier retired as slowly as it had come. Even this second outlet in the district marked "B" proved soon to be too shallow for the hurrying waters. During this Trent Valley Passage period glacial Lake Iroquois, crammed with all the Upper Lake waters, seems to have been much higher than its present level. It was as high as Roy Terrace at the Niagara Escarpment, and Eldridge Terrace on the American side of the River, only about 11 metres (35 feet) below the Lockport Limestone layer at Queenston Heights.

The Niagara River at this time was merely the local outlet for the small Lake Erie drainage. It was not connected with the flow of waters from the Upper or Great Lakes in any way. During the preceding stages of northeastern drainage of the lakes it had been painfully cutting back the hard layers of rock for more than 7,000 years. It had by this time, succeeded in making a comparatively small narrow gorge as far as the Niagara Glen and was eating out

the Whirlpool end of that idyllic spot. This much of the gorge is therefore called the Erie stage because it was formed only by the waters of Lake Erie, and of a very small Erie, at that. A great change was about to come; the pygmy was to grow to giant size almost overnight, geologically speaking.

The new and present outlet of the waters began about 7,000 years ago. The walled-up waters poured into a new valley, the only one now left open and the most southern one, the Detroit River to Lake Erie. The dotted area marked "E" on the map shows the approximate size and location of the small lake which had swelled forth waters to form the Erie gorge. Now the lake suddenly – that is in a few hundred years – grew to modern size, "C" on the sketch; the Niagara River had to bear the whole Lake Huron discharge. Accordingly it eroded a bigger channel from now on. In other words, the channel at the south end of the Glen suddenly was cut from a width of only 61 metres to 274 metres (200 to 900 feet). This began the last section of Stage III the Lower Great Gorge. N.B. Geologists today are reluctant to assign numerical designations such as 7,000 years, 8,000 years, to the stages of development for the Niagara River Gorge. Radioactive carbon dating has established that the Falls began about 12,000 years ago at Lewiston-Queenston. The intermediate stages such as the time taken to erode back to the Glen could now be in the order of 4,000 to 5,000 years.

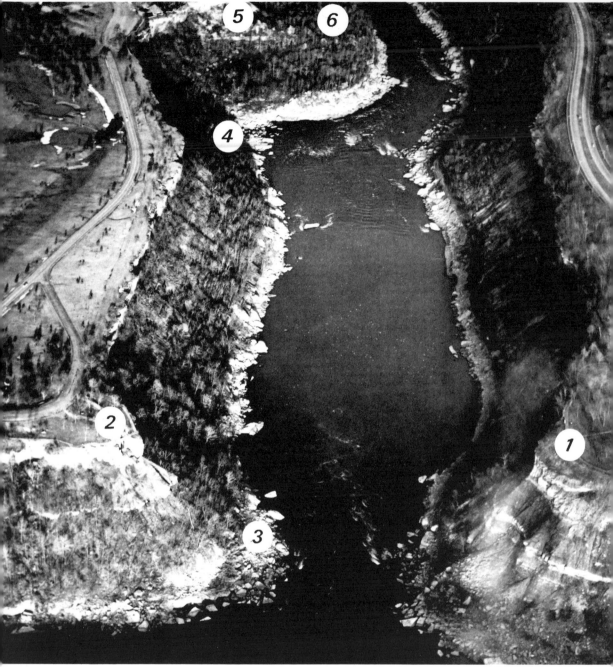

New York Power Authority

Stage III, the Lower Great Gorge from the Whirlpool exit to the Niagara Glen. No. 1, Whirlpool State Park and Whirlpool Point on the U.S. side; No. 2, Thompson Point; No. 3, exposed Whirlpool Sandstone ledge showing the narrow exit from the Whirlpool during winter water diversion; No. 4, Cripps Eddy at low water; No. 5, Wintergreen Flats, Niagara Glen; No. 6, Foster's Flats. Photo circa 1963.

The Whirlpool and The Whirlpool Rapids

When the Falls of Niagara reached present day Thompson Point on the Canadian side and Whirlpool Point on the American side, the river found its strenuous work of eroding the rock layers much easier. Suddenly at Thompson Point, it broke through the rock barrier which held back the glacial debris packed into what was the old gorge of an inter-glacial river, and began to flush out the debris, sand, gravel and boulders which filled this part of the gorge.

The full force of the river was directed at this glacial debris in the fashion of a placer-mining stream of water from a gigantic hose. Once the river found the buried gorge, in a comparatively short time – geologically speaking – it excavated enough of the debris to form the Whirlpool basin we see to-day. N.B. It is possible that it eroded back up its course, excavating the glacial debris in a buried channel over which it had been flowing on its way to the Falls, until it was about 152 metres (500 feet) south of the present Railway Arch Bridge. Here, it is possible that the river found the edge of Lockport Limestone which was the crest of the Falls before the glaciers advance diverted the river and filled in the gorge.

When you visit the Aero Car terminus at Sinclair Point, here within your view is what was once one of the most debated puzzles in the geological history of our Romantic River. The gorge to the left of the cables of the Aero Car is the deep debris-filled channel of a river which existed before the coming of the most recent, pushing, sliding plateau of ice, some 22,800 years ago. Called the Whirlpool-St. Davids Buried Gorge, or the buried St. Davids channel, it is packed with the scrapings and spoils of the glacier, compressed under its enormous weight.

Can you imagine yourself standing at this view-point – Sinclair Point – at the Aero Car terminal, with the ancient river flowing below you, from right to left – not making the sweeping curve you see in front of you? That much does not strain the fancy. But then picture yourself gazing upward at a towering blue-green and dirty brownish-white layer of advancing ice above your head grinding slowly but surely from the general direction of Kingston. With an accompaniment of thunderous avalanches of loose ice and snow falling from its frontal edge it remorselessly slides southwestward towards you, perhaps only 6 metres (a score of feet) a day. But a long day in mankind's experience is hardly as a split second to Nature.

The glacier you see is but a part of a larger mass of sinuous destruction which reached as far south as the Ohio River at its farthest travels. There is evidence that such awesome and mysterious ice-layers have at least four times oppressed the bosom of our planet on this continent and in Europe. Each period of terrible cold has been separated from the next by some 200,000 years.

The last ice age has hardly gone and we thin-skinned creatures shrink each time our winter breathes with the same frosty breath that nurtured and fostered these dreadful ice monsters of the past. When the next one threatens from the North, if it covers and then melts back from our present Niagara Gorge, will mankind find another buried gorge in its place?

The evidence of this inter-glacial river is still visible today when you stand at the bottom of Bridge Street in Niagara Falls, Ontario and look west, away from the gorge. There is a very definite slope upward, from where you are, to Clifton Avenue (now Zimmerman Avenue). There is a comparable slope on the American side, which is most noticeable when you turn left on Whirlpool Road after you have crossed the Whirlpool Rapids Bridge, to go towards the North End Business District in Niagara Falls, New York.

As you go north along River Road (Niagara Parkway) in Niagara Falls, Ontario, towards the Whirlpool, you will notice that the ground slopes upwards to your left, and the intersecting streets such as Buttrey, Ferguson and Elgin have steep slopes. This slope is the bank of the inter-glacial river, which flowed along the same course here, as our present river. Its terraced sides are uncovered today in the cascades above the American Falls and the Upper Rapids above the Horseshoe Falls. The Horseshoe Falls is turning, trying to climb out of this ancient inter-glacial river valley which was a tributary of a more ancient stream called the Erigan after the Indian name for water.

Thompson Point at the top left, where the Falls broke through into the soft glacial debris of the Whirlpool-St. Davids Buried Gorge. The outlet is shown at regular summer flow of 2832 m³/sec (100,000 cfs). The Whirlpool Sandstone ledge is visible at the shore of the river.

George A. Seibel

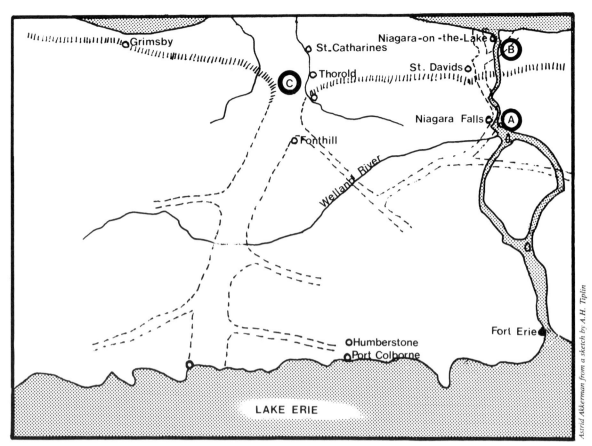

Astrid Akkerman from a sketch by A.H. Tiplin

This map shows the buried drainage pattern in the Niagara Peninsula as Dr. Spencer saw it as the result of his work in 1907. Present knowledge sees this drainage system in a different light as reported by Flint and Lolcama in Buried ancestral drainage between Lake Erie and Ontario. *"Over the past few decades, extensive data have become available and detailed bedrock surveys of areas within the Niagara Peninsula have been published. To date, however, no overall re-evaluation of the buried bedrock topography has been undertaken... Upstream from Niagara Falls to Lake Erie, the location of the St. Davids drainage system remains unknown. However, from information collected, we assume it is unlikely that the channel carried a river which flowed in an opposite direction to the present Niagara River, but rather that it was a tributary of the Erigan for a relatively short geological time, before another channel was opened to drain Lake Erie. The St. Davids channel may represent the only period, other than the present, when the Great Lakes emptied through the Niagara Peninsula."*

The accompanying map shows the Erigan channel and its tributaries. It was the inter-glacial channel that drained the area now occupied by Lake Erie, into ancestral Lake Ontario. On the shore of Lake Erie, near where the dotted lines show this ancient channel, is the community of Lowbanks. Here there is to be seen an embankment in the Erie shore some 3.2 kilometres (two miles) across. Closer examination shows that the limestone which should comprise part of this shore is entirely lacking. A well, bored here, indicates that there is gravel and sand drift to 42 metres (157 feet) below lake level. At Effingham in the Short Hills north of Fonthill, wells and borings have gone through the same material 30.5 metres (100 feet). Just north of Effingham the amazing depth further increases to 66 metres (216 feet); at the north of the Erigan channel where it cuts the Niagara Escarpment at Decew Falls, the depth is 82 metres (268 feet).

Here is to be observed a large embayment in the escarpment extending from just east of the town of Merritton to a conspicuous promontory at Jordan, 14.5 kilometres (9 miles) west. The two embayments, one on the Erie shore and the other on the Ontario shore, are joined by a depression on the

Milton J. Washburn

This photo, circa 1926, Stage IV of the Niagara Gorge, the Whirlpool and the Eddy basin of the Whirlpool Rapids, shows the river at maximum flow of over 5664 m³/ sec (200,000 cfs). No. 1, Whirlpool State Park in New York State and Whirlpool Point; No. 2, the double track right-of-way of the Niagara Great Gorge Railway; No. 3, Thompson Point, the Aero Car's northern terminus; No. 4, Sinclair Point, its southern terminus; No. 5, the double track right-of-way of the Niagara Falls Park and River Railway; No. 6, the railway car barns; No. 7, Eddy Basin.

surface of the countryside which reduces the altitude on the average by about 2.7 metres (9 feet), in spite of the great hills of drift nearby known as the Short Hills. Neither indentation is due to a bending in the bands of limestone, but has obviously been eaten out of the rock.

Those who were considering the various plans submitted for the location of the present Welland Canal, gave some thought to a plan submitted by a Mr. Wigley, who proposed this Erigan channel as the most economical and direct line for the canal. I do not know why his plan failed to meet approval. I believe that control of the water in a canal on this

route was in doubt because of its tendency to soak away in the sand and gravel. Such a location might therefore entail casing the whole channel in cement to conserve water – an impossible proposition in view of the great expense. It was found expensive and difficult to carry the Hydro Electric Power Commission canal waters over the gravels and drift of the head of the Whirlpool where the St. Davids Buried Gorge lies. (also called Whirlpool-St. Davids Buried Gorge). How much more so might it have proven for a large canal built over terrain not unlike that.

In inter-glacial times the Great Lakes did not exist. In their stead, or rather in their basins were three large rivers which led the waters in the same northeastward direction. These three rivers have been named the Erigan, Huronian and Laurentian. The line of the Erigan was from the dotted lines shown on the map along Lake Erie and on to Toledo, Ohio, just southwest of Detroit, Michigan. It was joined by many tributaries, one of which was a very small stream which poured over the escarpment by itself at Thorold, joining the Erigan stream somewhere in what is now the valley of Twelve Mile Creek, upon the banks of which the City of St. Catharines is situated. Another, the Falls-Chippawa Buried

Valley, whose discovery gives an explanation for the much debated Upper Rapids above the Horseshoe Falls, flowed in a direction opposite to the modern drainage. It swung around to meet this mighty Erigan River which in its turn was soon to join the more northern Laurentian canyon on its way to the St. Lawrence and the ocean. (Present knowledge disputes the hypothesis that the Falls-Chippawa River flowed in a direction opposite to the present Niagara River, but rather that it was a tributary of the Erigan and drained through the St. Davids Gorge to Lake Ontario).

The ancient Erigan channel reaches below the floor of Lake Erie. This modern lake is on the average 25.6 metres (84 feet) deep, but there is a deeper part 43.5 kilometres (17 miles) south of Lowbanks which is 62 metres (204 feet) in depth. This deep part is right in line with the Erigan canyon. The features of these ancient rivers are mostly obscured by post-glacial crustal warping and by the great mass of drift that smothers the former configuration of the Niagara District of inter-glacial days.

If a human inhabitant of this region who lived at the time (if such there were), were to look around his former fishing haunt, he would find things sadly changed – strange hills, great bodies of water too big even to see across, rivers flowing in another direction or no rivers at all where he knew there had been some. Truly such a devotee of the ancient art of Isaac Walton would shake his head, bewildered, and ask for a guide book. The most striking effect of glacial invasion is always modification of drainage.

The Whirlpool, August 8, 1916, on the first day of operation for the Aero Car. The double track roadbed of the Niagara Gorge Railway is visible on the U.S. side. Between the railway right-of-way and the river, the ledge of sandstone can be seen. As this is the first place along the river that this sandstone appears, it is called Whirlpool Sandstone.
Oscar Simon

The entrance to the Whirlpool at minimum water flow of 1416 m³/sec (50,000 cfs), November 1 to March 31 each year, when maximum amount of water is diverted for electric power generation. The effect of the underwater reef, holding back the water in the Eddy basin, can be seen in the smooth two-stage drop as the water enters the Whirlpool.

An air view circa 1980 of the entrance to the Whirlpool. The width of the Eddy basin in comparison to the much narrower Whirlpool Rapids, is clearly shown.

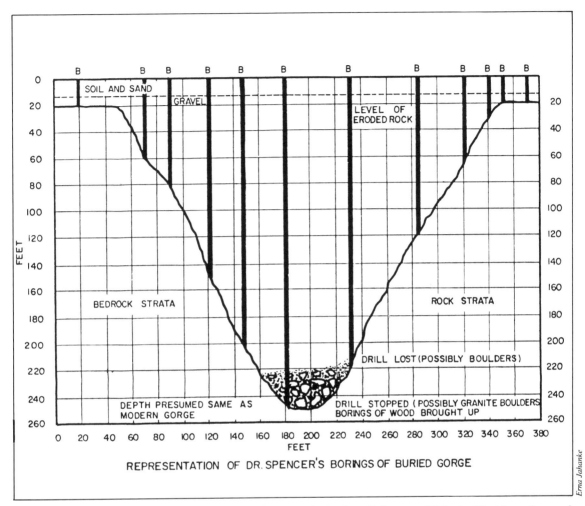

FEET

B   B B   B   B   B   B   B   B   B B   B

0
20   SOIL AND SAND
      GRAVEL
                                      LEVEL OF
                                      ERODED ROCK
40
60
80
100
120
140
160   BEDROCK STRATA   ROCK STRATA
180
200   DRILL LOST (POSSIBLY BOULDERS)
220
240   DEPTH PRESUMED SAME AS   DRILL STOPPED (POSSIBLY GRANITE BOULDERS
       MODERN GORGE   BORINGS OF WOOD BROUGHT UP
260

0   20   40   60   80   100 120 140 160 180 200 220 240 260 280 300 320 340 360 380
FEET

REPRESENTATION OF DR. SPENCER'S BORINGS OF BURIED GORGE

Erna Jahanke

This sketch shows the results of Dr. J.W.W. Spencer's borings made in 1906 to ascertain the existence of a buried gorge at the dead end of the Whirlpool. In 1969 geologists George D. Hobson and Jaan Terasmae drilled to bedrock to better define the buried channel and to bring up Pleistocene and fossil material for examination. Their results showed: clay, 3.6 metres (6 feet); silt, sandy, 8.5 metres (28 feet); clay, 10 metres (33 feet); silt, sandy, 14 metres (47 feet); sandy, gravelly till, 15.8 metres (52 feet); silt, clayey, 17.7 metres (58 feet); sand, 21.3 metres (70 feet); clay, 23.8 metres (78 feet); till with sand, gravel and cobbles, 28.62 metres (94 feet); gravel and boulders, 32.3 metres (106 feet); sand, some silt and clay, 42 metres (138 feet); silty sand, 44 metres (145 feet); clay with organic matter, 45.4 metres (149 feet); sand with twigs and wood, 46.6 metres (153 feet); sand, fine and medium, 54 metres (178 feet); sand, fine to medium, 55.7 metres (183 feet); gravel, cobbles, boulders with layers of glacial till, 84 metres (276 feet); bedrock, 86.8 metres (285 feet).

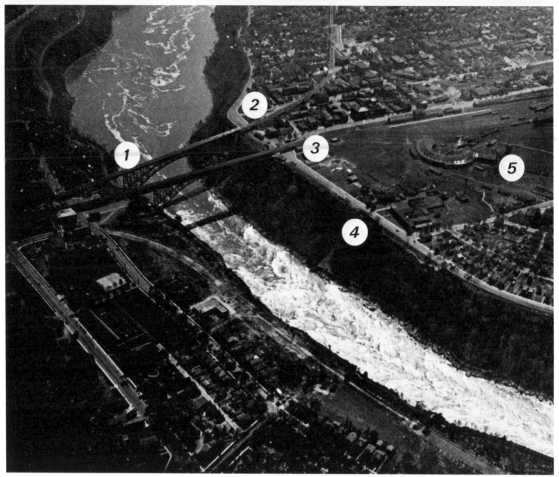

A.H. Tiplin

The south half of Stage IV Whirlpool Rapids Gorge ends at No. 1, at Swift Drift; No. 2, Railway Arch Bridge (built 1923); No. 3, Whirlpool Rapids Bridge also called Lower Steel Arch Bridge (1898); No. 4, elevator to the bottom of the gorge and the Great Gorge Boardwalk; No. 5, Canadian National Railway engine roundhouse. Photo circa 1935.

The Whirlpool Rapids

Viewing the Whirlpool Rapids from the boardwalk along the lower river spurs the imagination. The swellings and leapings of the torrent here which to the ancient Greeks with their neat turn for fancy, are so like myriads of horses leaping with arched necks and straining back muscles under the lashings of the river god, are caused by the mighty rock masses, torn from the gorge wall above and set in jumbled confusion in the river bed.

The depth of the river here is estimated to be 10.7 metres (35 feet) and the current runs at 35.4 kilometres (22 miles) per hour. No wonder the ice floes break up here. The speed of the current is caused by the narrowness of the gorge, the shallow bottom, but most of all by the rapid descent of the river here – 15.8 metres in less than 1.6 kilometres (52 feet in less than a mile). The canyon here is on the average 228.5 metres (750 feet) wide instead of 365.5 metres (1,200 feet) as elsewhere. N.B. Since 1962 when the Robert Moses Generating Station of the N.Y. State Power Project began operating, and the river's flow through the gorge was reduced almost 2128 m³/sec (75,000 cfs), the amount of water required to operate this plant, the original size of the river gorge has become visible. It is most noticeable in the winter period from November 1 to March 31 when the maximum amount of water is diverted for electric power generation. Then the level of the river is lowered, so that the layer of Whirlpool Sandstone that defines the old gorge is exposed, showing a much smaller gorge, perhaps as little as 38 metres (125 feet) in width in some places.

The Whirlpool Rapids from the air, circa 1980. Just above the second shadow on the water, that of the Railway Arch Bridge, is Swift Drift, the limit of navigation for all except dare-devils and stunters.

The boardwalk beside the Whirlpool Rapids, circa 1946, with the river in full flow before the major diversion of water for electric power generation, authorized in 1950, took place.

This view taken in the 1980's from the same perspective as the 1946 view, shows current summer water conditions with 2832 m³/sec (100,000 cfs) of water passing through the gorge. Sightseers are walking on the Whirlpool Sandstone ledge which in 1946 was the river bed. The large square boulder at the river's edge fell from the cliff above during the night of November 19, 1972.

The Whirlpool Rapids and gorge from the Whirlpool Rapids Bridge. This view taken on November 2, 1987 shows the narrow gorge which appears when winter diversion of water for electric power generation leaves only 1416 m³/sec (50,000 cfs) of water flowing through the gorge. The Whirlpool Sandstone ledge, still wet from having been just recently underwater, is visible at the right.

In this 1979 view of the Whirlpool Rapids, you can see how the river current which is directed toward the U.S. side, has cut away the rock fill and debris from the old railway right-of-way, and is eating away at the cliff. The large rock in the top left along the river bank, fell from the top in the 1960's.

George A. Seibel

Winston Bain

This photo taken on October 22, 1986, from the bank above the Whirlpool Rapids, shows the "Lelawala" in the most turbulent part of the rapids, where the velocity of the current is 29 kilometres (18 miles) per hour. The hair-raising trip through the rapids was made for the IMAX film, Niagara Miracles, Myths and Magic. It was a re-enactment of the trip made by the second "Maid of the Mist" on June 6, 1861.

This sketch, adapted from one made by H.G. Acres Ltd. for the American Falls International Board, shows a presumed cross section of the Whirlpool Rapids Gorge. The narrow gorge is shown under the mean water level of the rapids. The American bank is shown here as being a shorter distance from the river than the Canadian bank, accounted for by the erosive power of the shore current that drives into the U.S. side, eroding it faster than the Canadian side.

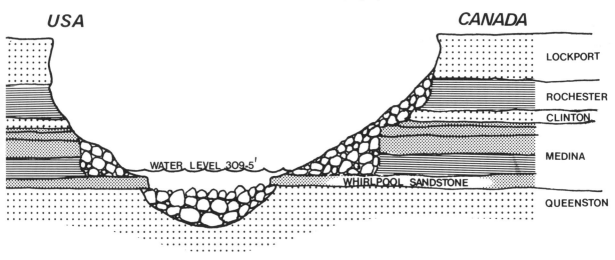

Gorge Wall Erosion at the Whirlpool Rapids

Most people, gazing across the gorge, are impressed by its great width. They cannot help but think of the might of the stream which could cut such a mighty chasm in solid rock, especially in the latter part of the canyon near the Falls. But the waters of the river did not cut the gorge as big as it is. The gorge widens by erosion and weathering, not by inches a year, but by sudden slides and falls of large pieces of rock, both of the more solid blocks and the lighter shale and slate.

The gorge wall on the American side at the Whirlpool Rapids seems to be particularly vulnerable to erosion. The huge fallen blocks of Lockport Limestone extend over the former road-bed of the Great Gorge Railway and the embankment, right down to the water's edge, completely obliterating the railway right-of-way in many places. One must be careful, in fact, while walking along this side of the gorge, right down to Devil's Hole. Every geology "bug" is warned of this by his university or association when he makes known his intention to visit this section of the gorge where the rock layers are most accessible and perhaps most productive of fossils.

In the 1920's when the Lewiston Branch line of the New York Central Railroad used to run along the upper cut near Niagara University, even then, when the cliffs were scaled each year so the rockfalls would not push a train off the track and over into the river, no visitor was allowed to walk along the tracks without a special permit. Such caution was exercised that several railway shantymen were stationed along the track at intervals, always on the watch for these sudden evidences of the ravages of time.

The forces of nature working here are slow as Time itself, silent as decay, and as powerful as eternity. Frost, especially in the autumn and spring days and nights when there is rather rapid and severe alternation between cold nights and warm sunny days, exerts, in the crevices on the surface of the rocks and deep inside, a prying force greater than any of our tension-testing machines used in the heavy industries. Experiments have proved that there is no force on earth which can resist the expansion which must take place when water changes to ice.

Even on warm sunny days, when the sun beams hot on the various rock layers with their varying content of minerals of different expansion coefficients arranged in crystals and particles of so many various textures, great forces are awakening which shortly demand scope and space. The sun expands these different minerals at unlike rates. Thus parts of a rock will tend to pull away from each other. Moreover, when the sun is gone and the rock cools, these heated materials must contract again and will do so at different rates, thus tending to split apart again. The variety of minerals in our top limestones along the gorge will no doubt surprise the reader. The most common are silica, alumina, iron compounds, sulphur, phosphorous. These may be present in amounts less than one percent, or some of them, especially the silica and alumina, may make up a large percentage.

Then too, there is the dissolving power of water, which is especially active in limestones and causes several caves along the gorge by enlarging natural crevices in the layers and making of them solution channels. Wherever there is enough water found to support plant life of any sort, clinging, prying moss and vines and grasses are able to take hold and spread, exerting a surprising force as their eager rootlets and climbing mechanisms reach out for life and room in further abundance. Also, in the process of living, these roots give off certain acids which render any top-soil water seeping through the interstices of the rock layers a more powerful dissolving agent. And in death and decay such organisms give off still more powerful rock-softening chemicals. Such silent forces are easily classified by most of my students as weathering.

In the usual run of things, these agents labour for years without any visible reward for their efforts. Then, like the avalanche of pain, suddenly and without warning climaxing the inroads of disease in the human tooth or appendix, comes the tottering and suddenly fluid rock pulled from its age-long perch by gravity.

Other forces are working now and have been since time began, to level the world with the aid of gravity. These other forces are more boisterous, and since they are easily seen, are more readily appreciated by the human mind. These are the waves of the shore, the currents of the rivers and lakes, the mad tumble of flood waters and the tamer rivulets of rain; they include the scrapings of ice in floe or glacier form, stinging grains of sand borne by the wind, the works of animals and of man, and lastly and perhaps more important than any, gravity – the universal leveller under whose laws all other agents of erosion seem to work, and into whose downward clutches they all deliver their burdens.

When the Niagara Gorge Railway roadbed was built in 1894 the workmen had to blast and cut into the gorge wall in places, to provide space for the right-of-way and rock ballast for the tracks. This process was to become the cause of the abandonment of the railway forty years later, when the weakened gorge bank collapsed at this point bringing an end to the operation of this railway. In the top centre, two of the viewing elevators can be seen.

This view of the Whirlpool Rapids from the early 1900's shows two definite currents in the gorge, one down the centre and the other directed at the bank on the U.S. side. No. 1, a Niagara Gorge Route car and trailer; No. 2, foliage growing on the talus slope. When the electric railway right-of-way was cut along the gorge, it was necessary to cut into the gorge bank. This disturbed the "angle of repose" (the angle where a slope will remain stable) and so it wasn't long before there were rock slides, which denuded the bank to the right, of foliage, hastening further erosion.

This 1907 view shows the stop-off point for the lower observation platform, where sightseers left the Niagara Gorge cars to view the Giant Wave. Of particular interest is the height of the water, right up to the base of the platform, No. 1. Although the railway had been in operation for 12 years, there is still some foliage on the steep bank, No. 2. The dark hole under No. 3 is the entrance to one of the viewing towers which were built along the rapids on the U.S. side prior to the building of the electric railway in 1895.

F.H. Leslie

A.H. Tiplin

(facing page top)

A Niagara Gorge Railway car on its route downriver, beside the Whirlpool Rapids. The Whirlpool Rapids Bridge is in the foreground and the Railway Cantilever Bridge, replaced by the Railway Arch Bridge in 1923, is in the background. Swift Drift, the point of no return for river navigation, is just under the Railway Cantilever Bridge.

(facing page bottom)

Shale covering the roadbed of the Great Gorge Railway, below the Whirlpool Rapids Bridge. This is the result of a collapse of the shale and slate layers of the gorge wall, sending tons of shale and friable slate on to the roadbed, and right to the water's edge. While this picture was being taken there was an occasional sprinkle of loose particles for seemingly no reason at all. There is a train crossing the Whirlpool Rapids Bridge, and it appears that the rumble of the bridge is communicated to the rock layers, and that the sprinkle of rock turned quite often to a rather heavy shower whenever a train went over the bridge. Photo circa 1937.

A.H. Tiplin

At about the same location shown in the previous picture, the gorge wall collapsed on September 17, 1935, piling 4920 tonnes (5000 tons) of rock on the Niagara Gorge Railway tracks. This brought the operation of this electric railway to an end.

A.H. Tiplin

The rock debris at the spot where the rock fall ended the Niagara Gorge Railway operations has increased in quantity in the 52 years that have passed.

This picture shows the damage done to the Gorge Trip boardwalk during remedial work on the gorge wall during the winter of 1982-83. Precariously perched overhanging rocks were blasted off and they destroyed the boardwalk when they fell. The falling rock from the three carefully controlled blasts swept the talus slope below clear of all vegetation and flattened many mature trees. The cliff was made secure by the installation of resin grouted rock bolts tensioned to withstand up to 9.8 tonnes (10 tons) each. This remedial work was necessary to forestall unpredictable rock falls such as occurred during the night of November 19, 1972 when 49,200 tonnes (50,000 tons) of rock fell, and during the night hours of April 29, 1977 when 19,680 tonnes (20,000 tons) fell. A system of rock-trap fences placed along the talus slope protects against smaller rocks which might become dislodged and fall from the gorge wall above.

This 1987 view shows that foliage has re-established itself on the talus slope since the 1982-83 remedial work done on the gorge wall. The rock-trap fences are barely discernible because of the foliage.

Rock Strata in the
Gorge at the Whirlpool

The Whirlpool and the Whirlpool Rapids Gorge are suitable places to pause in the story of *Our Romantic Niagara* for a discussion of the rock strata and side wall erosion of the gorge. At Sinclair Point where the Aero car begins its crossing, the banks are nearly 91 metres (300 feet) above the surface of the Whirlpool. At no other place along the Gorge do the characteristics of the rocks under the Niagara Escarpment appear so clearly. Perhaps it would show foresight to name them in order, top to bottom, once again now that their arrangement is clear. Anyone attempting to become familiar with this gorge could not do better than to memorize the names and relationships of these rocks. We have occasion to refer to them much more frequently than to any other feature of this great book of nature which lies here open for our inspection.

Beginning at the very top at Whirlpool Point on the American side, the layers of soil and rock run thus:

1 – Glacial Clays about 12 metres (40 feet)
2 – Lockport Limestone, 18 metres (60 feet)
3 – Rochester Shale and underlying shales, 18 metres (60 feet)
4 – Red Medina Shale and Sandstone
5 – Whirlpool Sandstone and Shale at water line

The surface clays at the top of Whirlpool Point are glacial in origin and very deep. On top are shell deposits from ancient fresh water seas which covered this whole district as far as Queenston in the form of a long and much broader arm of Lake Erie. These shells are of the same species now to be found in the river deposits, so the date of this deposit could not have been so very many thousands of years ago. They were no doubt accumulated in the smoother backwaters of the much broader river which covered these high and dry terraces.

All the rock under the surface layer tilts rather severely backwards and downwards from Lewiston-Queenston to Lake Erie. This very tilting caused the various top and bottom layers to appear and disappear in that same distance and they do so logically and regularly. For instance, the Lockport and Clinton layers do not appear past the cable towers of the former Lewiston-Queenston Suspension Bridge as one looks toward the north. There the Whirlpool Sandstone is exposed and makes a startlingly white capping for the red Queenston Shale. But just back of the cable towers the Clinton layer appears, thinly at first and then in its natural thickness. At Queenston Heights the Lockport Limestone layer is quite thin.

At Whirlpool Point these two late comers, the Lockport and Clinton Limestones are in their full thickness and strength. However, the Medina layer – Whirlpool Sandstone – which was so prominent at the cable towers and was 40.5 metres (133 feet) above the surface of Lake Ontario there, is here just above the waterline. In fact at the Whirlpool outlet this Grey Whirlpool Sandstone is just underwater and forms a sort of shelf which partially dams the swell of the Whirlpool flood. Furthermore, at the Horseshoe Falls itself this layer is part of the floor of the river and lies 27 metres (90 feet) beneath the surface of the Lake Ontario level.

Above the Falls another layer of rock of a different kind appears in the form of cascades and their ridges. One glance and it is clear that here are rocks which have suffered and which strangely bear the marks of their ancient purgatory. These are much more rich in fossils, gnarled and twisted by some gigantic forces coming from Heaven knows where during the days before the misty curtain of the Ages rose to signal the beginnings of History. They are harder than any other rocks in the escarpment layers, will undoubtedly slow the erosion of the river at the future rim, and yet they bear upon their faces the scratchings and polishings of the glacier. This layer is true Lockport Limestone; at diverse spots in its knotty texture there are evidently soluble materials for their surfaces are eaten into small, deep holes.

Whirlpool Point as seen from the Aero Car, shows the rock strata looking like a gigantic layer cake. The layer of Lockport Limestone is clearly visible under the surface layer of glacial clays. Beneath this the soft layers of Rochester Shale rest on the Clinton Limestone layer. Foliage is gradually covering the Red Medina Shales under the Clinton layer. The former right-of-way of the Niagara Gorge Railway has been completely obliterated by rock debris and foliage.

George A. Seibel

There is a tendency in these three main Silurian rock layers – Lockport, Clinton and Medina – so clearly defined at Whirlpool Point, to form three cataracts wherever a stream of any considerable volume flows towards Lake Ontario at right angles to the escarpment. For instance at Decew Falls, a few kilometres (a few miles) to the west of the Niagara stream, there are two large falls and a step rapids making a steep descent of 68 metres (224 feet) in less than a kilometre (a mile) of canyon. These falls are caused by the same layers of rock as the Niagara cataract, and are of the same age.

No. 1, Thompson Point, the northern terminus of the Aero Car; No. 2, Clinton Limestone layer; No. 3, Whirlpool Sandstone layer at river's edge; No. 4, Niagara Glen; No. 5, Robert Moses Generating Station. Compare the debris slope here at Thompson Point with the precipitous slope at Whirlpool Point. Photo circa 1970.

A.H. Tiplin

The conditions are repeated at Swayze Falls on a western branch of Twelve Mile Creek, 1.2 kilometres (three-quarters of a mile) north of Effingham, and at Letchworth Park on the Genesee River where there are three large and distinct cataracts over the same rock layers, Lockport, Clinton and Medina.

There remains only one feature at Whirlpool Point to be remarked on. The sloping sides of debris on the Rochester Shale layer are called talus. The talus would here fall in a longer slope starting from the bottom and reaching in one continuous sweep to near the top, if it were not for the shelf-like effects of the jutting layers. These support the talus in two main slopes. Such jutting layers doubtless make the work of the river easier because they hold back more or less permanently much eroded material which would otherwise tend to clog and fill the river in less turbulent spots, especially at the Whirlpool Rapids and below the site of the former Lewiston-Queenston Suspension Bridge.

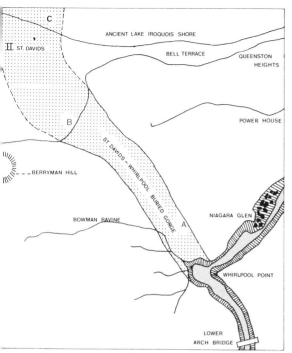

Astrid Akkerman from a sketch by A.H. Tiplin

The limits of the Whirlpool-St. Davids Buried Gorge are shown on this sketch. At "A" the water from Ontario Hydro's twin tunnels and canal had to be carried across the glacial debris of the buried gorge on concrete flumes. At "B" the escarpment rock is missing and is replaced by the many gullied hills of glacial drift. At "C" drillings revealed that the buried valley exists under the Lake Iroquois Beach Ridge.

The Whirlpool and the Electric Railway, a water colour by William Armstrong, circa 1900. The steel railway trestle in the background, centre left, crosses the Bowman Creek Ravine at the end of the Whirlpool-St. Davids Buried Gorge. At Thompson Point, on the right, the rock face of John Thompson's quarry is visible. Today, rock is exposed at the sides of the entrance to the Whirlpool; low water is caused by the diversion of water, upriver, for electric power generation. In the painting, the Niagara River was in full flow.
Amon Carter Museum, Fort Worth, Texas

Whirlpool-St. Davids Buried Gorge

George A. Seibel

In 1841 Sir Charles Lyell, an eminent British geologist, visited the Falls and discovered "an old ravine terminating at St. Davids" and deduced that this was the course of an inter-glacial river. In the intervening years many other prominent geologists visited Niagara Falls, but it was Dr. J.W.W. Spencer, a geologist with the Canadian Government Department of Mines, Geology & Survey Branch, who carried out borings and other observations which proved conclusively that this buried gorge existed.

After other visits here in 1895 and 1898, Spencer returned in 1906 and made "borings to ascertain the character of the buried channel beds over which the river afterwards flowed." He was the first to really interpret what must have happened to cause the great eddy – the Whirlpool. He concluded that the buried channel extended from the Whirlpool to St. Davids and beyond into the Iroquois plain – the former bed of Lake Iroquois, now the fruitlands below the escarpment.

The Hydro Electric Power Commission of Ontario (the forerunner of Ontario Hydro) conducted extensive surveys and borings along the buried channel site, in preparation for the twin tunnel project for the Sir Adam Beck Generating Station No. 2 project, which began in 1950. They found the channel from the Whirlpool extended 1219

metres (4000 feet) to St. Davids and that it was 305 metres (1000 feet) wide at the Whirlpool and widened to 701 metres (2300 feet) and then 823 metres (2700 feet) at St. Davids.

They reported that "the depth of the gorge has not been definitely determined... the deepest borings down to elevation 300 did not encounter solid rock... it is felt that the rock bottom of the gorge is well below this elevation." Elevation 300 is 91 metres (300 feet). As a result of their observations, the twin tunnels that carry water to the Sir Adam Beck Generating Stations were brought up to the surface at the edge of the buried gorge, and the water carried across the glacial debris of the buried gorge on a concrete flume, and then it enters the canal cut through the rock layer on its way to the forebay of the power plants at Queenston.

In the winter of 1965-66 geologists George D. Hobson and Jaan Terasmae carried out geophysical explorations, using a portable hammer seismograph and drilling equipment and confirmed the existence of the buried gorge beyond St. Davids. Their findings outlined a broad buried channel which extended to Lake Ontario, and dropped 22 metres in about 10.5 kilometres (73 feet in six and a half miles) on its way through the lower plain below the escarpment on the way to Lake Ontario.

While early geologists could only speculate on the time when the gorge was filled with glacial debris, the discovery of Carbon[14], a radioactive form of carbon, as a dating technique for recent geological events, made it possible for geologists from that time on to establish when a piece of fossil wood, pollen, or other organic matter found in a drilling bore sample, had been deposited. Using this technique, Hobson and Terasmae were able to establish that the gorge was filled with glacial debris about 22,800 ± 450 years ago and that the gorge was cut during the last inter-glacial interval or earlier.

From their boring in the area of the St. Davids sandpit they retrieved pollen and plant macrofossils in the silt, clay and mud at a depth of 32 to 33 metres (106 to 108 feet) from the surface. Pieces of fossil wood were picked up from the 46 metres (150 foot) level and Carbon[14] dated at 22,800 ± 450 years B.P. (B.P. = Before Present – i.e. before the date of the testing, 1966). Moss, leaves, fragments of bark, leaf cuticle, conifer needles, and twigs indicated the presence of local vegetation. Pollen from spruce, pine, fir and birch trees was recovered, bringing the geologists to the conclusion that the area was forested. Other pollen types investigated indicated that the climate then was much colder than it is presently in Southern Ontario.

Their findings in determining the route of the buried channel through the fruitland below the escarpment confirmed what the farmers who had land on top of the channel already knew. The soil to the east and west of the channel is reddish due to the underlying red Queenston Shale and contains a large number of pebbles, while over the channel the soil loses its red colour, the pebbles and stones are brown and in general it is better soil for agriculture.

Farmers living over the channel have also benefitted by having good wells, with an inexhaustible supply of water. In digging for their wells, they found that the depth of the gravel under their topsoil is rarely less than 31 metres (100 feet) and sometimes as much as 39.6 metres (130 feet), all the way back to St. Davids. The glacial till makes a good aquifer and the Regional Municipality of Niagara has a well, pump house, and reservoirs half way down St. Davids hill, at the head of Four Mile Creek. This pumping station formerly supplied the lower fruitlands and Niagara-on-the-Lake, but it is now kept as standby for emergency use.

The St. Davids channel in the fruitlands varies in

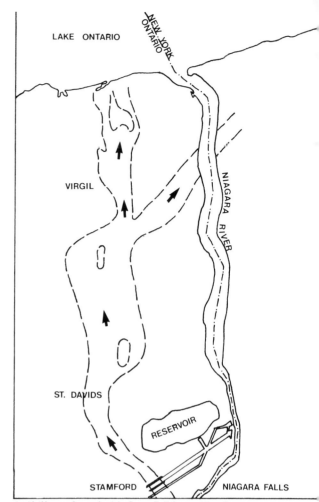

Astrid Akkerman from a sketch by George D. Hobson and Jaan Terasmae

width between 0.8 and 2.4 kilometres (one-half mile and one and a half miles). As well, there are several islands in the channel, similar to Goat Island and Navy Island in the present Niagara River. It was a meandering river. The borings reached more than 46 metres (150 feet) at their deepest, and found that the channel was cut 24 metres (80 feet) into the bedrock of Queenston Shale.

The channel enters Lake Ontario about 2.4 kilometres (one and a half miles) west of the present outlet of the Niagara River. A branch channel splits off around Virgil and crosses the Niagara River just north of McFarland House on the Niagara Parkway. Its location is marked by the deep gully which cuts the river bank there. There is evidence that it appears again at the Youngstown Yacht Club and goes on through the town of Youngstown, New York, towards Lake Ontario.

This sketch of the Whirlpool-St. Davids Gorge area is from the George D. Hobson and Jaan Terasmae study *Pleistocene Geology of the Buried St. Davids Gorge, Niagara Falls, Ontario; Geophysical and Palynological Studies*, published 1969 by the Geological Survey of Canada. It shows the location of the buried St. Davids River channel as it wends its way through the lower fruitland plain to Lake Ontario. The branch leading to the right is intersected by the present Niagara River just north of McFarland House on the lower Niagara Parkway.

Close-up view of a piece of fossil wood found in an excavation done for the New York State Power Project at Lewiston on November 26, 1958. Carbon^{14} dating of other pieces of fossil wood found near here at the former Lake Iroquois beach, has dated them as 12,000 ± 450 years old B.P.

New York Power Authority

The dead end of the Whirlpool, with Thompson Point at the right. The eroded glacial debris cliff of the end of the Whirlpool-St. Davids Buried Gorge is at the left. This view from 1981 was taken during high water conditions as the Whirlpool Sandstone ledge on the shore below Thompson Point is underwater.

Winston Bain

The steel trestle that carried the tracks of the Niagara Falls Park and River Railway across Bowman Ravine, from 1892 until 1903. Then the trestle was buried when the Canadian Niagara Power Company used the ravine as a dumping area for the rock debris taken from the wheelpit excavation made for the powerhouse under construction in Queen Victoria Park, just south of the Horseshoe Falls. The cut stone abutments are still visible today, marking the ends of this buried trestle.

The second hole of the Niagara Parks Whirlpool Golf Course lies on top of the buried gorge. The south wall of the buried gorge is to the left of the path leading up the embankment.

Construction of the twin tunnel outlets at the southern edge of the Whirlpool-St. Davids Buried Gorge, 1953. The tunnels were dug through rock and run as deep as 100 metres (330 feet) below the City of Niagara Falls, Ontario, and had to be brought up to the surface at this point because they could not be bored through the glacial debris of the buried gorge.

The concrete flume built across the glacial debris-filled buried gorge. Without this concrete sluice much of the water would seep away and be lost in the glacial debris. The tunnel outlets are at the bottom, out of the picture.

The buried gorge of the inter-glacial St. Davids River ends at the Niagara River just north of McFarland house, where a small stream has cut a deep gully through the glacial debris. On December 19, 1813, a British force under Colonel John Murray led detachments of the 41st and 100th Regiments of the Royal Scots, Royal Artillery and Canadian Militia on a night attack against Fort Niagara. They embarked in batteaux at the foot of this ravine, the only docking area available along the lower river, the river bank elsewhere in this area being steep and rocky.

Along the river bank north of McFarland House on the Niagara Parkway masses of hardened gravel layers make up the side of the present Niagara River, filling the channel of the inter-glacial St. Davids River. This buried channel was bisected by the waters of our modern Niagara River, and it begins again on the eastern bank at the Youngstown, N.Y., Yacht Club.

Glacial Debris in the Buried Channel

While clambering up the outwash gully in the Whirlpool glacial drift, I examined more closely something I had noted long before in the Spring when the slope was too slippery. A peculiar layer of bluish-grey clay of extremely fine texture had been so soaked by the rains that it had run down as a plaster over the yellow and red layers of washed sand. A further inspection showed that the large bed many metres (feet) thick was composed of many layers, some of them not more than 0.6 centimetres (one-quarter inch) thick. This phenomenon was especially noticeable wherever a little stream tumbled down over this sticky clay so as to wash away the outer weathered layer.

I was very surprised to find this laminated (layered) structure. I immediately knew that I would be obliged to alter my conception of the manner in which the glacier had filled up this deep ancient canyon, the Whirlpool-St. Davids Buried Gorge. I confess my impression of this was formerly that of a mighty blue-green and grey mass of ice pushing its muddy snout deep into the surface soil of the Niagara Glen area, slowly moving forward toward the only gorge in the district and dumping its scrapings into it as if to make a bridge for its further advance. I now wonder why I took so long to realize how too simple and childish this conception was. Glaciers do such things of course – but such tricks are characteristic of more quickly moving mountain or valley glaciers which have a definite slope to give them a momentum not obtained by continental glaciers. Now these tiny layers reminded me forcibly that our glacier was continental and probably always throughout its life advanced and retreated too slowly to do any work such as dumping earth into gorges.

More reasonably such work was done by the water which always pours from the top of such a continental mass whenever the sun strikes it and the season is not severe winter. Down through the countless crevices in the surface of the ice-layer the water tunnels until the ground level is reached. Then the water forms sub-glacial rivers flowing out to the foot of the ice-mass.

Where such a river empties its load of sand and gravel, a kame is formed such as Goat Island is. But such a steady melting may take place during a mild spell of climate lasting for hundreds of years that large glacial lakes are formed. These of course have the usual sort of currents and eddies which are prone to deposit gravel, sand and very small particles like a rock flour which form the compact clay mentioned above. Such a lake is quite similar to Lake Ontario except that one shore at least is resting against the ice-front, and obtains most of its substance from melting ice. The most intense melting is likely to occur in the summer season when the sun is more directly overhead; therefore the annual deposits of such a lake would consist of a summer-flood layer and another layer deposited during the rest of the year which we may conveniently call the winter one.

It is quite to be expected then that by careful counting of those annual layers, the age of a deposit of silt clay may be accurately told. The best place in the Niagara District, indeed in all the world with the possible exception of certain Alpine valleys in Europe, is Scarborough Heights, just a little east of Toronto. Here the inter-glacial clay which comprises most of the rock-like cliffs was formed in a northern bay of an inter-glacial lake which reached at least 16 kilometres (10 miles) inland from the present shore. These famous cliffs are delta deposits laid down by a great river which came down from Georgian Bay region, draining not the present great upper lakes which were not yet formed, but draining their basins into this much larger Lake Ontario. These astonishing formations, as slippery as greased glass in wet weather, as powdery on top as ground pumice-stone when dry, show almost countless layers or laminae throughout most of their greatest height of 62 metres (203 feet).

As at the Whirlpool, these laminae vary from 2.5 to 5.0 or 7.5 centimetres (an inch to two or three inches) in thickness. Where undisturbed by some too boisterous current which may have deposited sand in place of clay, these layers consist of a darker layer of fine grey or yellowish clay, and a paler part of a silty quality. Often the silty part contains matter similar to peat with an occasional twig or small bit of wood. From the peaty matter, moss, leaves and pieces of bark, seeds and parts of beetles have been obtained by the scientists who washed away clay, dried the peat, and examined it with a lens. Dr.

A unique sedimentary deposit of layers of sand and small pebbles, deposited by a glacial stream. This isolated deposit, with its horizontal layers of sand, is in the St. Davids sand-pit.

Scudder, now deceased, when he was working with Harvard University, found 72 species of beetles in these peaty layers in the talus slopes at the end of the Whirlpool. It is most probable that the silt-peat layers are, then, the summer deposits. In the Don Valley Brickyards at the east end of Toronto these laminae have been counted through a depth of 6 metres (20 feet) of clay by means of paper strips upon which the edges of the markings are carefully traced. Believe it or not, in these, the first series of beds recognized as inter-glacial in America, there were 672 laminae in 49 centimetres (20 inches), probably representing as many years of deposit. But how many years would be necessary to deposit the many thick beds of laminated clays visible at Scarborough? Surely several thousands of years. And this was during the time when the glacier was in only one of its phases, remaining then more or less always north of Toronto. How long did the glacier take throughout all its phases? How long a period of time did the four known and separate glacial advances take during the Glacial Age period? How long indeed was the central part of America and of Europe in the grip of the arctic cold of the

Glacial Ages? Was the fourth glacial advance merely the fourth in a series of five or more? These – perhaps the most leading and vital questions in geology – are mysteries as thickly veiled as the secret of how a blade of grass grows.

This chapter would hardly be complete without a word regarding the climatic changes which are of course inevitable upon the approach or retreat of a continental glacier. These changes are well shown in the Toronto inter-glacial clays which extend from the Don River valley to the Humber and on to Scarborough; the time element required for this period by nature is particularly clear.

The Whirlpool is not the only place on the Niagara Peninsula side of Lake Ontario which shows boulder clay of exactly the same sort. Extending between Garden City Beach, near Port Weller, and Port Dalhousie, are two remarkable layers of glacial till – one grey clay quite free of boulders; the other on top doubtless represents the last glacial advance. It varies from 0.3 to 1.2 metres (one foot to four feet) thick, red in colour with a thick massing of pebbles and boulders. On top of these two layers is a yellow and grey one which must represent the deposit of the later glacial Lake Iroquois. Strangely enough to the layman, it is the grey and bluish clay which, made into bricks and burnt in a kiln, forms red brick with which we are so familiar. The change in colour is made possible by the iron oxide content of about 7 percent. This boulder clay is made by the grinding action of the glacier on underlying shales. Paving-brick, pressed brick and terra-cotta sewer pipe made in Canada are from shales of the Palaeozoic era, or from boulder till and inter-glacial clays formed from these shales.

During the retreat of the first ice-sheet the climate of course changed slowly from arctic conditions like Antarctica's, to subarctic like Labrador's, and finally to temperate perhaps as warm as this district on the average. These earlier stages have left no indications in the lowest beds of the Don valley, but they must have taken thousands of years to accomplish. Then followed a time of warm climate with a river in the Don valley flowing into a lake lower than the present on whose shore there was a rich forest which like most of our trees here, lost its leaves in the autumn. This warm period lasted long enough for the formation of a delta of sand and clay 13.9 metres (45 feet) thick over an area of several square miles. The Don beds show traces of many generations of forest trees. Then came a rise in the waters of the lake, due to a warping of its outlet probably, so that the level was at least 46 metres (150 feet) above the present lake level, when delta beds were laid down covering more than 490 m² (100 square miles). During this time the 672 laminae in less than 6 metres (20 feet) of clay were laid down. The whole deposit was doubtless in the making for several thousand years. The climate had become colder, for the plants and insects changed, and no doubt was very similar to that of the northern Ontario region of today.

Next, the great lake was drained to a level 5 metres (16 feet) below present Lake Ontario. Three river valleys were carved in the great delta which had been formed before. One wide valley with gently sloping sides indicating maturity and old age was at the present site of Toronto, another narrower one at the Scarborough Bluffs, over 1.6 kilometres (one mile) wide at the top, and a wider one further east. To cut these rivers required certainly another several thousand years. Finally, arctic conditions came on again, the ice advanced from the northeast, and another sheet of boulder clay was deposited over the region. We are living during a period of retreat following this advance. The arctic conditions at the north of our globe are very slowly ameliorating but with a slowness imperceptible to any but the most careful scientific measurements. Two things are possible – either the retreat will continue so that the whole world becomes milder, while the Arctic is tropical again as it once was. Perhaps coal may one day form there as it did in Antarctica from the tropical swamps, according to the recent observations of Admiral Byrd. The other possibility is that the ice will not retreat much further but will someday come down upon this region yet again in the fifth glacial advance.

Hard packed sand and gravel found amongst the pure sand at the St. Davids sand-pit, where the Whirlpool-St. Davids Buried Gorge cuts through the escarpment.

George A. Seibel

Do you ever wonder where the large granite boulders you see throughout our city came from? The boulder pictured here is on the lawn of St. John's Anglican Church on Portage Road at the intersection of St. Paul Avenue. Granite is not native to this area but forms part of the Canadian Shield which extends from about 161 kilometres (100 miles) north of Kingston to Northern Quebec and Labrador. This boulder was wrenched from its granite bed by the glacier and carried here along with other debris in the glacier's ice. When the glacier retreated boulders such as this were left in an erratic pattern wherever they lay when the ice melted. For this reason they are called glacial erratics. A farmer in southwestern Ontario uses a different term – "leverite" – when he encounters such a large boulder in his field. Translated leverite means "leave 'er right there"!

George A. Seibel

This massive block of limestone is a glacial erratic, torn from its bed along the Niagara Escarpment by the glacier, and left in the St. Davids sand-pit. Its size reminds one of Stonehenge pillars and Easter Island statues. Just beyond the 12 metre (40 foot) embankment in the background is Mountain Road.

George Bailey

Quicksand in the Whirlpool-St. Davids Buried Gorge

In our search for a piece of fossil wood, one of my students and myself climbed down the west side of the buried gorge at the end of the Whirlpool early in the spring. We made our way along the ice piled on the shore which still made the air surprisingly chilly. We then came to an abrupt halt, unable to proceed further without careful change in plan. Flowing out upon these miniature icebergs was a four foot thick river of red mud and sand. It seemed somewhat dry on top, but remembering Dr. Spencer's borings in the drift at the top of the earth wall here, I used due caution. It was quicksand – of the quicker sort.

To the left, the winter thaws here have eaten into the soft drift which the glacier packed there so long ago – layer upon layer of various gravels, sands, boulder-clays, and even bits of ancient wood, which we hoped to find. The great 91 metre (300 foot) cliff of debris was cut so deep with a gully that all was revealed except the lower gravels. To overcome the barrier of quicksand which was too dangerous to take a chance with, we found it necessary to ascend the drift cliff about 15 metres (50 feet), climb a partially uprooted tree which sloped far out over the stream of peculiar sand; shinnying down a limb, we cat-walked a slippery log and finally reached the other side of the 15 metre (50 foot) river of mud. To make sure it was quicksand, I took a little for microscopic analysis. The grains proved to be strangely rounded in the manner which gives this soil its dangerous quality.

Quicksand is like a mass of very tiny steel balls. Can one imagine stepping into a pit full of ball-bearings and not sinking deeper with every vibration of the body as the balls just under the feet refused to pack into a firm support but continually slipped one against the others so that more room was always found somehow for the feet to sink?

Ordinary sand is formed of tiny crystals which are angular enough to pack once the pressure upon them is great enough, even though they are wet. When the grains are rounded however, moisture adds still further to the already great tendency of the ball-like forms to slip, especially under concentrated pressure. Hence it is better to spread out as much of the body surface as possible on top of the quicksand trap. As much as possible, that is, without running too much risk of immediate smothering before expected help arrives. If nearby twigs and even small branches are placed under as much of the body as possible, they will prevent the weight from being concentrated in any one place – and it must always be borne in mind that it is concentrated weight which causes the remorseless, steady sinking which needs only to last a little while to complete its work. However, in any quicksand worthy of its name, any weight is doomed to sink in time because most traps of this sort are kept well lubricated by an underground spring which may be far beneath the surface. Wanderers on the Whirlpool shores need have little fear, in as much as the sands are rarely exposed and are wet only in spring.

Pure sand of the Barre Moraine at St. Davids (Ravine Hill) sand-pit.

George Bailey

Harry Mottershead

The Modern Great Gorge, February 1988, looking downriver from the centre of the Rainbow Bridge. No. 1, River Road, is at the left, curving slightly as it climbs the rise to Hubbard Point, No. 2; No. 3, the Railway Arch Bridge where Swift Drift is located;

No. 4, the remains of the Schoellkopf Power Plant are visible in the lower gorge. Pressure ridges are visible in the centre of the ice jam which fills the river almost to the bridges.

Making Of Our
Modern Great Gorge

Until the falls of our now famous river had cut back as far as Swift Drift Point, just south of the present Railway Arch Bridge, it had the necessary great volume of water to make erosion easy, a volume of water newly acquired when it was at the Niagara Glen. It was then that the waters of the upper lakes first flowed into Lake Erie, and, swelling that then small lake, caused the roar of the falls to become more deafening.

When it reached the point just slightly southward from the Railway Arch Bridge, the falls found the going much harder. It encountered the highest limestone ridge in the Niagara District. This ridge ran across the river's path, and extended 1.4 kilometres (nine-tenths of a mile) from Swift Drift Point to Hubbard Point, its southern edge, just north of present day Eastwood Crescent.

At this stage of the gorge, the waters of the upper lakes were for a long time considering joining their forces permanently with the "Father of the Waters", the Mississippi River. Residents who live along River Road in Niagara Falls, from Hiram Street to Eastwood Crescent, must pull their cars up narrow, steeply graded driveways.in order to park them off the road. They live in an area that was submerged under the waters of the river. N.B. It is interesting to note that the level of the River then, at Hubbard Point, was about the same as the level of the river today at the northern tip of Navy Island.

The accompanying picture was taken looking almost due north while I stood on a point of land jutting out over the gorge, just south of Hubbard Point, the highest point on Hubbard Ridge. It is almost 15 metres (50 feet) above the level of the present Horseshoe Falls, the Falls being about 2.4 kilometres (a mile and a half) back of the camera. The barometer used was not accurate enough to record this change in altitude, and I did not then have available a topographical map of this area. However much that estimated figure may err, the camera was level when the picture was taken. It clearly shows the Lockport Limestone layer at Hubbard Point to be at a much higher level than the position of the camera.

This high rock ridge is elevated abnormally because of some local folding of the Earth's crust in ages past, no doubt at the same time that the Niagara Escarpment was formed. One expects that the river would have had great difficulty cutting a gorge through this hard barrier. Any stream will cut deeply and more quickly if the falls in its system is a high one, or if the falls is low but has a great volume of water.

George Bailey

Hubbard Point, the remains of Hubbard Ridge, is shown here. When the cataract was here, it was almost 15 metres (50 feet) higher than the present Horseshoe Falls. The river behind it was level with the present upper cascade at Dufferin Islands and all of present Queen Victoria Park was submerged. Goat Island was covered with about 9 metres (30 feet) of water.

Hubbard Point as seen from the U.S. side. The dark spot in the gorge wall, to the right of the Point is the opening of Indian Cave (Redskin Cave). Bender's Cave and Sunny's Cave are out of sight, to the left of Indian Cave.

Schoellkopf Geology Museum

Since the waters had to fall over this great height, the gorge was now cut more deeply. But obviously, if there were a large wall of rock layers like this one across the river's course, the volume of water going over the falls must have been decreased until the river had cut the ridge lower. Lake Erie at this time seems, according to some authorities, to have been much higher in its water level than it is today, so that the spot where the camera was placed for this picture would not be much above the level of ancient Lake Tonawanda (which was an extension of ancient Lake Erie). Goat Island would then have been covered by at least 9 metres (30 feet) of water and the area we now know as Queen Victoria Park would have been submerged, with the water level reaching the top of the embankment that presently borders the Park.

When we were very young, I remember that my chums and I used to find special fun at any picnic held in Queen Victoria Park because of the steep wooded hill at the back. There used to hang long vines from the network of branches at the top of the trees which interlocked closely. We used to cling to one of these vines, stand at the top of the "mountain" or as near to it as intervening trees would allow us to get, and then swing scores of feet down and out to the bottom, where we let go and dropped with more or less of a bang. Recently (1938) I tried to find these same monkey-swings, as we used to call them,

Stage V of the gorge, the Modern Great Gorge, as seen from the U.S. side. The Minolta, Maple Leaf and Skylon observation towers dominate the skyline on the Canadian side. The American and Horseshoe Falls are beyond the Rainbow Bridge.

for I am still most interested in gymnastics, but I found none. I believe the excellent gardeners of the Parks Commission realized long ago the danger of that sort of adventure.

But the "mountain", as we used to speak of it, is still there; I know that it was our small size that made it appear so big. It is on the average only 31 to 39.5 metres (100 feet to 130 feet) higher than the adjoining flat land of the park. I have since learned, too, that it is not a "mountain" but the ridge or bank which used to hem in the curving waters of the mighty river and bar them from going westward where they might easily have found another exit rather than the one at Queenston.

This very ridge which appears behind the spring-fed island pond shown in the picture, was, before it was cut out by the river, merely a fairly level or undulating plateau of glacial debris extending to the American side. This plateau formed a mantle, and still does, over the ancient Falls-Chippawa Buried Valley underneath. The plateau is situated quite near the centre of this very old, inter-glacial, shallow, broad stream and is parallel with it. The east side

The ridge of glacial debris which borders the flat land of Queen Victoria Park is visible between the trees in the background. When Queen Victoria Park was opened in 1888 there were a number of springs flowing out of the base of this embankment and six spring-fed drinking fountains were placed throughout the Park. The small island in the centre of the picture is surrounded by a spring-fed pond, the site in 1888 of a drinking-trough for horses.

George Bailey

of this ancient river may be seen plainly in the cascades over which the Horseshoe Falls is now trying so hard to cut a path, and in the cascades above the American Falls. The west side does not appear, being covered by the shallow overburden of soil of Queen Victoria Park Terrace. Traces of it were found during excavations for the foundations of the Administration Building (now the N.P.C. Police Headquarters).

Excavations for one of the conduits of the Ontario Power Generating Station have revealed that the rocks underlying this Park, as indeed all of the

underlying rocks of this district, have been scratched and polished by the glacier. In other words, as one walks through the gardens of the Park, here at least, and doubtless all along the gorge at its edge, he is supported by a layer of glacial drift which overlies the polished rock beneath. The rock beneath, in its turn, forms the sloping sides of the ancient Falls-Chippawa River whose shape is now affecting the form of the Falls itself and the river above it, at the cascades. This is the plainest illustration for which one could wish of the storied character of our district. These "pages of days that were" lie open for geologists the world over to read, and, from the lessons learned in them, to interpret the nature of the earth in pre-historic times in other parts of the world.

N.B. The Falls-Chippawa Buried Valley was Albert Tiplin's name for what is now called the St. Davids Buried Valley.

This picture taken in 1903 at the north end of Dufferin Islands, during the construction of the second Ontario Power Company conduit, shows the undulating surface of the limestone which lies beneath the glacial debris. These round ridges of limestone are an extension of the Buried Falls-Chippawa Valley, and make up the lower cascades in the river above the Horseshoe Falls. The glacial drift bank is to the left. The layers of rock, sand and gravel which were eroded from this bank when the river overflowed and were deposited in layers over the limestone, are visible at the edges of the excavation in the centre of the picture.

Ontario Hydro Archives

The Hubbard Point Caves

George A. Seibel

There are three caves in the gorge wall north of Hubbard Point. They are Bender's Cave, also known as Devil's Cave and Sorcerer's Cave; Sunny's; and, Indian Cave, also known as Redskin Cave. They are found along the same rock layer in the Lockport Limestone, about 6 metres (20 feet) down below the upper gorge bank, and some 12 metres (40 feet) up from the top of the talus slope.

Their origin can be traced to the time when the falls was at Hubbard Point, and the water behind the ridge found weak spots in the rock strata and gradually forced its way through the fractures and out small openings beyond the ridge, downriver from the falls. Constant pressure from the weight of the water behind the ridge, which was six or more metres (20 or more feet) deep where the water seepage began, caused an enlargement of the outlets. Water continued to cascade out of the openings, which became larger as time went on.

When the falls broke through Hubbard Ridge, the river behind the barrier lowered, until it cut off the source of water for the subterranean streams and their side falls. The caves that remain today are the result of the constant erosive action of the water.

Spelunker Scott A. Ensminger with H.E. Krog, B. Carr and B.R. Horncastle, have explored all three caves and made measurements. The sketches Mr. Ensminger made, showing the dimensions of the caves, and the descriptions of each cave, are reprinted here with Mr. Ensminger's permission.

Bender's Cave, the most accessible of the three caves, is just north of the outcropping of rock known as Hubbard Point. It is a shelter cave, measuring 9 metres (30 feet) deep, 7 to 9 metres (24 to 30 feet) wide and averaging 2 metres (7 feet) in height. The entrance is 5.5 metres (18 feet) wide and 2.4 metres (8 feet) high in the centre. Small stalactites, in colours of black and white, can be found there.

The first record of the cave is found in Elizabeth Simcoe's Diary, in August, 1795. She wrote that she visited a cave at Painter's Point, and then she had tea at the Painter home. Painter is the name she mistakenly gave the Bender's, who were Crown Grant settlers on the land along the gorge, from present day Otter Street, south to Robinson Street, just south of the present Niagara Parks Police Headquarters in Queen Victoria Park.

The cave was mentioned in J.W. Ingraham's *Manual for the Use of Visitors to the Falls of Niagara,* published in 1834. Ingraham described the cave as being "20 feet (6 metres) in width and in some places high enough for a man to stand upright.

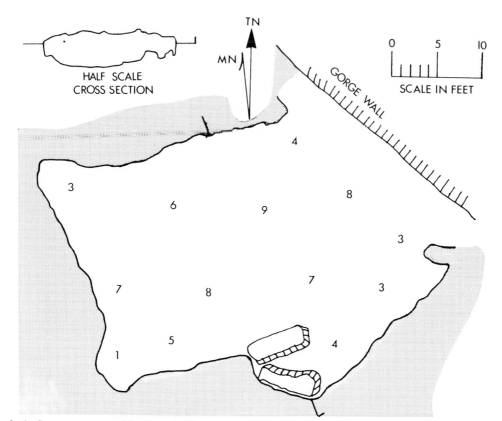

HALF SCALE
CROSS SECTION

TN

MN

GORGE WALL

0   5   10
SCALE IN FEET

Astrid Akkerman from a sketch by Scott Ensminger

Bender's Cave was surveyed by Scott A. Ensminger and H.E. Krog in January 1978. The numerals on this and the following sketches represent the height inside the caves, in feet. The approaches to these caves are dangerous and caution is advised to those who would attempt to explore them without rock climbing equipment.

It was made by the decomposition of limestone." In July, 1848, the Ordnance Board, which had jurisdiction over the Crown Reserve along the gorge, granted a Mr. Price permission to clean out Bender's Cave and construct an approach to it. For the rest of that year he was allowed to conduct visitors to the cave, and charge 25 cents for the privilege. At the end of the season, the concession was to be put out for public tender, for a period of seven years. The cave appeared in guide books until 1862, when it lost favour as a tourist attraction because of the competition of other attractions.

Bender's Cave is well known to many residents of Niagara Falls who grew up at a time when the river bank along here, and the river below, were their recreation areas. Tradition has it that Bender's Cave was a smugglers' cave. But this fanciful supposition which had smugglers carrying contrabrand goods into the cave and through a tunnel at its back up to the centre of present day Epworth Circle, where the Niagara Falls Collegiate now stands, was

impossible. First, no smuggler in his right mind would haul goods from the River, up the talus slope then straight up the gorge wall to the opening of the cave, some 12 metres (40 feet) from the top of the talus slope. There were easier ways to get merchandise into Canada from the United States. Besides, there is no tunnel at the back of the cave, just a very small throat, choked with rocks.

The origin of the name "Hubbard" for this geologically important point, originally called Bender's Point, is explained on page 114. In the 1880's, the Wesleyan Methodists had a summer camp meeting each year at what is now Epworth Circle. During that time, the Point was fenced off and a wooden stairway was built down the gorge wall, leading to a path which wound down the talus slope to the river's edge. It was an evening's entertainment for some to descend the ladder, and go to the river, where the more venturesome would take a dip in the water.

In the 1970's, as a safety precaution, the Niagara Parks Commission closed the opening in the stone wall along the gorge, which gave access to the Point. This was premature as only the tip of Hubbard Point is undercut by erosion. The railing could have been set back 3 or 3.6 metres (10 or 12 feet) and the rest of the Point left accessible to those who use the Niagara River Recreational Trail and who wish to walk out on the Point to enjoy the view.

Readers are cautioned against planning any exploration of these caves at Hubbard Point, as the approach is dangerous and rock climbing equipment should be used.

George A. Seibel

This is the opening to Bender's Cave. This photo was taken in 1973, from the edge of the narrow ledge outside the cave. Beyond this ledge there is only space and a sheer drop of 12 metres (40 feet) to the talus slope, and then another 58 metres (190 feet) sloping down to the Niagara River.

Inside Bender's Cave, 1973, the small stalactites visible were formed by water dripping from the ceiling above, leaving particles of limestone which had been in solution in the water. The stalactites are very small; any larger specimens would have been broken off years before by earlier visitors to the cave.

Sunny's Cave, 1972, with a flow of clay which has evidently been carried down from the overburden by water seeping through the limestone.

George A. Seibel

George A. Seibel

"Old Mother Hubbard"
Gets the Point

In 1852, the St. Catharines, Thorold and Suspension Bridge Toll Road Company was granted permission to establish a toll-road along the top of the gorge bank, on the Chain Reserve, from the Railway Suspension Bridge (present day site of the Whirlpool Rapids Bridge), to Table Rock. The rise of land at Bender's Point was chosen as the site for a toll-gate. There, travellers had to stop and pay a toll before they could proceed.

The Toll Road Company removed earth from the glacial debris bank opposite the Point, constructed a toll-house, and installed the toll-gate. At some time after 1861, Mrs. Sarah Hubbert, a widow with small children, became the toll-gate keeper and lived in the toll-house. To add to her income, Mrs. Hubbert made her parlour into a saloon; according to Lovell's Province of Ontario Directory *of 1871, she is listed as the proprietress of Bender's Cave Saloon.*

The Queen Victoria Niagara Falls Park Commissioners took over the toll-road, and abolished tolls on it, in June, 1887. Mrs. Hubbert continued to live in the former toll-house until her death.

Mrs. Hubbert died at age 74, in 1890. The notation in the records of Drummond Hill Cemetery, where she is buried, reads: "Dec. 11, 1890. Old Mrs. Hubbard or Linkey, (who) lived down along the river bank between the Bridges so longe, died at the Old Toll gait stand, Clifton." The Welland Tribune *reported: "Hubbard, Mrs., better known*

as Mother, died at her home on the riverbank in the small hours of Tuesday morning (Niagara Falls Town)."

Over her long tenure, almost thirty years, at the toll-house, her name had changed from Hubbert to Hubbard, in the public's mind. Local use of the name Hubbard persisted. When the Niagara Falls Park and River Railway tracks were laid along the gorge in 1892, a regular electric car service began. The cars had difficulty climbing the hill leading to Bender's Point, and local passengers referred to it as Mother Hubbard's Hill. That name for the hill was used even after the electric railway ceased operation in 1932. At sometime in that era, Bender's Point became Hubbard Point, the name we use today.

Romantics among us may credit patrons of the saloon with creating the folklore which surrounds Bender's Cave, which was just across the road in the gorge wall. Fueled by the liquid refreshments which Mrs. Hubbard sold, stories of smugglers and other surreptitious activity, and exaggerated accounts of the size of the cave, would flourish. The indentation in the bank where the toll-house stood, is still visible on River Road; the toll-house and the toll-gate are long gone; Mrs. Hubbert (Hubbard) has been dead for almost one hundred years but she is commemorated in Hubbard Point.

Sunny's Cave is 4.5 metres (15 feet) north of Bender's Cave. It was surveyed in June 1978 by Scott A. Ensminger and H.E. Krog. The entrance is 3 metres (10 feet) wide and 2.4 metres (8 feet) high. A passage to the west tapers to 0.9 metres (3 feet) wide and 15 centimetres (6 inches) high in 7.6 metres (25 feet). On October 16, 1982, a trench 1.2 metres (4 feet) long, 0.61 metres (2 feet) wide and 18 centimetres (7 inches) deep, was dug at the back of the cavern. The top layer

of gray flowstone is only 0.08 centimetres (1/32 of an inch) thick. Under the flowstone, a 15 centimetre (6 inch) layer of red clay was found. Below the clay, a layer of brownish sand was encountered. The sand is apparently the result of Lockport Limestone rocks that have decayed. Beyond the trench, the passage is 15 centimetres (6 inches) high. The passage widens, continues for roughly 7.6 metres (25 feet) and then turns to the right. Two dead bats were found in the cave.

Astrid Akkerman from a sketch by Scott Ensminger

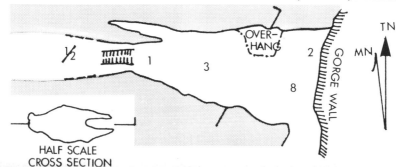

HALF SCALE
CROSS SECTION

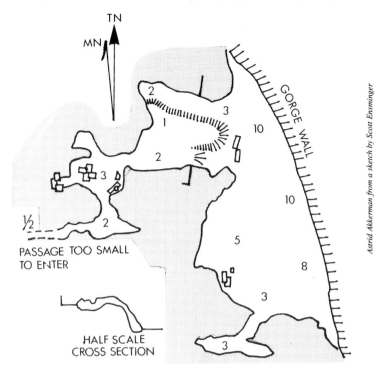

TN

MN

2
1
3
10
2
3
10
2
5
8
½
3
3

PASSAGE TOO SMALL
TO ENTER

HALF SCALE
CROSS SECTION

GORGE WALL

Astrid Akkerman from a sketch by Scott Ensminger

Indian Cave or Redskin Cave is located 18 metres (60 feet) north of Sunny's Cave. It was explored and its measurements were recorded by Scott A. Ensminger and B.R. Horncastle, in 1978. It is a much larger and more interesting cave than Bender's Cave, but it is in-accessible, except by the use of rock climbing equip-ment. The entrance is 15 metres (50 feet) wide, 2.4 to 3 metres (8 to 10 feet) high, and 2.1 to 6 metres (7 to 20 feet) deep. Near the north side of the entrance, at the top of the slope, there is a 7.8 metres (26 feet) long crawlway to the west. This leads into a small room, 3 metres (10 feet) in diameter and 0.9 metres (3 feet) high. Two more crawlways lead from this room. One to the west is blocked by breakdowns in 1.5 metres (5 feet). The other, to the south, connects with a small room. A crawlway from this room, to the west, is blocked by dirt in a few feet. The cave con-tains small stalactites, romstone dams that are 5 cen-timetres (2 inches) high, and flowstone. Near the south side of the entrance is another short crawlway which leads to a small room.

This photo is taken from the American side of the River. Hubbard Point is the rock projection on the left of the picture. Bender's Cave and Sunny's Cave are in the shaded area to the right of Hubbard Point. The entrance to Indian Cave shows as a smaller black area in the gorge wall at centre right.

George Bailey

This photo of Indian Cave was taken by Paul Hibbard of the Niagara Falls, Ontario, Fire Department as he was in a sling suspended from an extension ladder of a Fire Department ladder-truck. Paul Hibbard was twisting back and forth in the sling while he was taking this and other pictures of the cave, during a training exercise.

Indian Cave, 1986, taken from a point of land downriver from the cave.

Recession of the Falls

Falls of the sort we have now in our district depend on geological conditions of a peculiar sort – that is, hard resistant layers must uniformly be underlain with soft, easily-eroded strata. This arrangement of hard Lockport Limestone and soft layers of shale keeps the falls from degenerating into rapids, or from becoming cliffs whose recession is extremely slow. Over such a rock formation the falls must remain vertical, tumbling over the overhanging ledge.

It might be well to explain once again why such a layer as the Whirlpool Sandstone is not to be seen at the Falls. At the Lewiston-Queenston Suspension Bridge this white layer is nearly 30 metres (100 feet) above the water; at the Whirlpool it dips beneath the water and does not reappear.

This, the reader will remember, is partly because of the south-westward dip of the strata in the district at an average rate of 6 metres in a kilometre (20 feet in a mile). In the course of a gorge as long as the Niagara gorge, this means a change in altitude of about 43 metres (140 feet) at least. For example, the rock escarpment shown in the sketch, mostly all limestone and soft shale at the Falls, is thin limestone, and very deep soft shale, at Queenston. Thus, as the hard top layer becomes thicker run-

ning upriver, the rate of recession of the Falls tends to become slower. At Queenston, it is 6 metres (20 feet) thick; at the Falls, 24.4 metres (80 feet). One mile above the Falls, it is 40 to 46 metres (130 to 150 feet) thick, as shown by drillings.

Even with this increased thickness, the curve of the Horseshoe wears back about 2.4 metres (8 feet) per year, according to the Geological Survey of Canada in 1911. The mean rate, however, is about 1.1 to 1.5 metres (3.5 to 5 feet). Since 1842, and possibly since 1700, the rate was apparently much slower, according to the experts. The deepest flow at the crest of the Horseshoe (1938) is probably from 6 to 7.6 metres (20 to 25 feet).

N.B. Since 1962 when the maximum amount of water was diverted for electric power generation at the Robert Moses Generating Station, the layer of Whirlpool Sandstone mentioned above, is exposed each year during the winter water diversion. Then it is visible and extends as far as the Whirlpool Rapids Bridge, before it disappears underwater.

N.B. The rate of future erosion of the Horseshoe Falls has been estimated by Environment Canada, as 30 centimetres (one foot) in ten years, but no one can be certain that this is what it will be. Several factors must be considered. First, no one knows when the next significant fall of rock from the crest of the Horseshoe Falls will occur. It may be in 50 years, or 100 years. Such a rock fall would suddenly and dramatically increase the rate of erosion, and only then would it be possible to work out an average rate of erosion for the intervening years.

Another possibility is that rocks falling from the brink might pile up on the ledge of Clinton Limestone at the base of the Falls, because the plunge pool is not being carved out deeply enough. The current fall and volume of water may not be sufficient to carve out a deep plunge pool, which would allow the Clinton Limestone ledge at the base of the Falls to break off when a large block of Lockport

Limestone drops on to it from the crest. If this happens the Horseshoe Falls would become a cataract similar to the American Falls, with huge blocks of limestone piled up as talus at its base.

It is not out of the realm of possibility that at some future date, it might be considered expedient to dry off the Horseshoe Falls and shore up with cement the underlying shale layers, to retard future erosion. This would stabilize the Horseshoe Falls in its present position. When the water was put back over the Falls, the curtain of water would hide any remedial work, and there would be no noticeable change in the spectacle of the Falls as we know it today.

This sketch of the Falls of Niagara appeared in one of the many editions of Isaac Weld's Travels through the states of North America and the provinces of upper and lower Canada, during 1795, 1796, 1797. Weld, who was a landscape painter, has depicted the beginning of the formation of the horseshoe shape in a previously straight crest line of the Great Falls. The American, or Schlosser Falls as it was called then

(named after Captain John Schlosser of the Royal American Regiment, who built and commanded the fort known as Fort Schlosser, on the upper river above the American Falls), is depicted as having a straight crestline. Weld calculated that the Great or Horseshoe Falls was 549 metres (600 yards) wide and 43 metres (142 feet) deep.

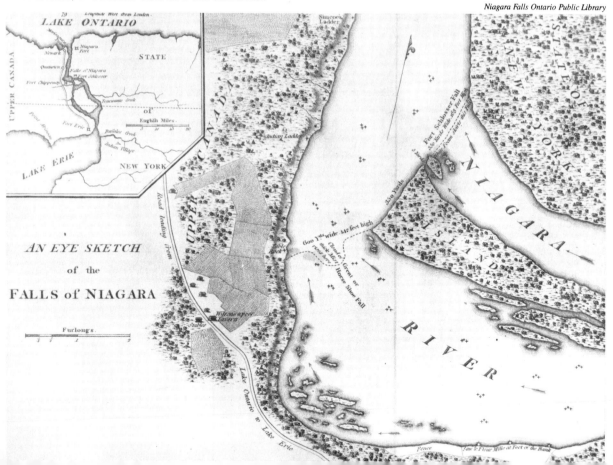

About 600 to 800 years ago the American and Horseshoe Falls were still one cataract. After the two separated, the crest of the American Falls remained in a more or less straight line until some time after 1775. This daguerreotype by Platt D. Babbitt, taken in the 1860's, shows that a large section has fallen from the lip of the American Falls, giving it a moderately curved crestline. Terrapin Tower, razed in 1873, is in the distance on Terrapin Point.

The depth of the river just north of the Horseshoe seems to be close to 56.6 metres (185 feet) but great blocks of talus fill part of this depth to about 22 metres (72 feet) from the surface. The tremendous force of the falling water – one good pail full weighs about 27.2 kilograms (60 pounds) – is met by the buoyant force of this depth of water to produce a swirling action and a powerful erosive force which works backwards underwater, against the soft shale. Combined with this is the prying action of the frost from the intense spray, as well as the dissolving action of the spray itself which is considerable. When one block of limestone is pried off its undermined perch, it is caused to swirl round and round, grinding the shales below the base of the Falls. Thus the fall of one block means a lengthening of the gorge, it is true, and the fallen block is also a powerful tool for bringing down its former neighbour on the brink above.

120

Captain Basil Hall, a British Naval Officer made the first actual sketch of the Horseshoe Falls, in 1827. With the aid of a Camera Lucida he was able to depict correctly its contours. Basil Hall's Camera Lucida was not a true camera. It consisted of a four-sided reflecting prism, with one angle of 90° and the opposite angle of 135°. The prism was positioned above a horizontal sheet of paper, set on a table in a darkened tent. The prism was directed towards the Horseshoe Falls, and Hall, by looking over the edge of the prism, was able to trace the reflected image of the Falls, and so produce an accurate sketch.

During the 1880's and early 1890's, great pieces of limestone fell from the crest of the Horseshoe Falls. This picture taken by John Zybach from the observation portico of old Table Rock House, shows the large notch in the Horseshoe, the result of the 1880's fall. In early January of 1891, on two successive nights, at 9 p.m. and 10 p.m., large masses of rock broke away from the crest. The Buffalo Times reported "...the noise made by the tumbling rock alarmed the residents. The massive stone building known as Table Rock House was jarred to such a degree that the doors were thrown open.'' They went on to report that ''the effect of these displacements of rock on the contour of the Falls is quite marked – the change being from that of an angle at the vortex to the original horseshoe shape.''

As the Horseshoe Falls eroded, more water flowed over the crest at the centre, and the river bed dried off on the Canadian shore at Table Rock. The fractured top layers of limestone are evident in this 1905 view. The continual breaking away of pieces like these contributes to the erosion of the Falls. It is no longer possible to sit on the brink of the Horseshoe Falls. This dried-off area has been filled in and forms part of the present Table Rock viewing area.

In this view of the Horseshoe Falls circa 1900, water was not being diverted for electric power generation, and the full volume of the river's flow, about 5664 m³/sec (200,000 cfs) dropped over the brink. This photo must have been taken on one of those rare occasions when a south-west wind blows the spray downriver and away from the Horseshoe Falls making possible a clear view of the crest. The volume of the river's flow indicated includes 10% which goes over the American Falls, the remaining 90% goes over the Horseshoe Falls.

This photo, taken in August, 1961, shows the present crestline of the American Falls. In the late winter of 1931, more than 74,784 tonnes (76,000 tons) of rock fell from the crest, giving a modified "W" shape to the crestline.

These massive talus blocks were exposed in 1969 when the American Falls was dewatered for a geological survey. These blocks are from the major rockfalls of the early 1800's and 1931.

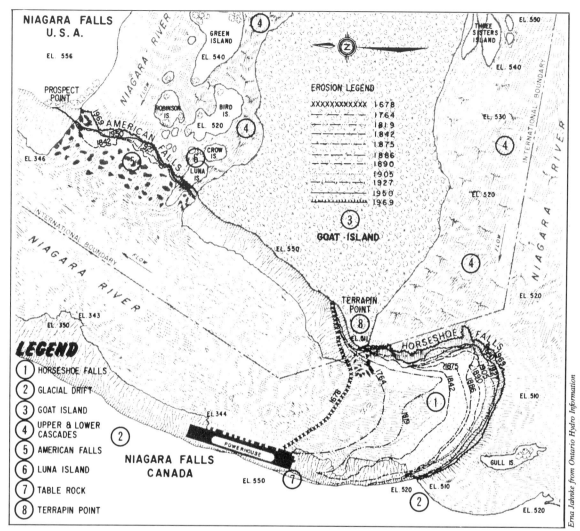

NIAGARA FALLS
U.S.A.

EL. 556

PROSPECT
POINT

EL. 346

NIAGARA RIVER

GREEN
ISLAND

EL. 540

ROBINSON
IS.

BIRD
IS.

EL. 520

CROW
IS.

LUNA
IS.

AMERICAN FALLS

THREE
SISTERS
ISLAND

EL. 550

EL. 540

EL. 530

EL. 520

EROSION LEGEND

XXXXXXXXXXXX 1678
—·—·—·— 1764
————— 1819
————— 1842
————— 1875
—·—·—·— 1886
—·—·—·— 1890
········· 1905
—·—·—·— 1927
————— 1950
xxxxxxxxxx 1969

GOAT ISLAND

EL. 550

INTERNATIONAL BOUNDARY

NIAGARA RIVER

FLOW

EL. 520

NIAGARA RIVER

INTERNATIONAL BOUNDARY

NIAGARA RIVER

FLOW

EL. 343

EL. 350

TERRAPIN
POINT

EL. 511

HORSESHOE FALLS

EL. 520

EL. 510

LEGEND

1 HORSESHOE FALLS
2 GLACIAL DRIFT
3 GOAT ISLAND
4 UPPER & LOWER CASCADES
5 AMERICAN FALLS
6 LUNA ISLAND
7 TABLE ROCK
8 TERRAPIN POINT

NIAGARA FALLS
CANADA

EL. 344

POWERHOUSE

EL. 550

GULL IS.

EL. 520

EL. 510

EL. 520

Erna Jahnke from Ontario Hydro Information

Prior to the additional diversion of water in 1956 and 1962 for electric power generation, the depth of the water in the centre of the Horseshoe Falls was about 3 metres (10 feet). Remedial work carried out before these diversions took place deepened the river channel on both flanks of the Horseshoe Falls. The water is regulated by the International Control Structure so that today the flow over the Horseshoe Falls is evened out, with an average depth of 0.6 metres (2 feet) of water more or less evenly spaced along the entire crest. This depth increases when the river's flow increases. That may happen for several reasons: sus-

tained rainfall; south-west gales on Lake Erie which force more water out of the lake and down the Niagara River; an authorized fluctuation in the amount of water taken out of the river above the Falls for electric power generation at different seasons. Note the location of the International Boundary as it passes close to Terrapin Point. The Horseshoe Falls is almost entirely within Canadian Territory. The statistical information on the river's flow used throughout this book was supplied by Ontario Hydro and Environment Canada, Water Planning and Management Board.

124

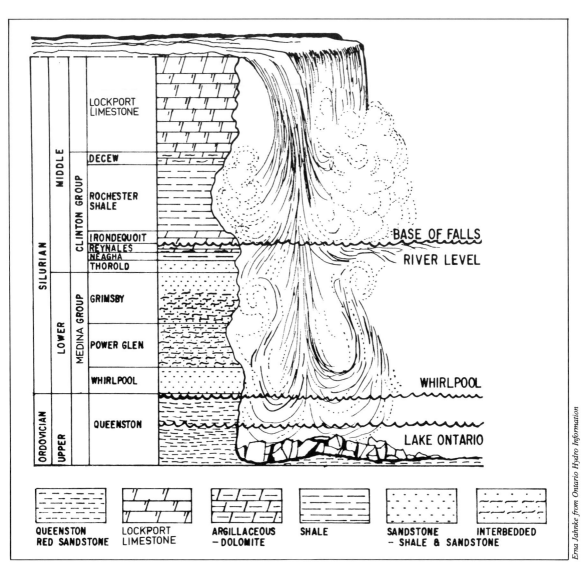

Erna Jahnke from Ontario Hydro Information

Throughout this book we have adhered to the same formula for naming the rock strata as used by the Schoellkopf Geology Museum at Niagara Falls, New York. In the most recent publications and reports on the geology of Niagara Falls, the top layer of limestone has been referred to as both Lockport and Niagara, and limestone has been further described as Dolomite, Dolostone, Dolmite and Dolmitic. In the in-

terest of clarity and simplicity, we refer to the top layer of limestone as Lockport Limestone. It is composed of four distinct types of limestone: Oak Orchard in New York (called Guelph in Ontario); Eramosa; Goat Island; Gasport. Anyone wishing to study the rock strata in more detail can consult the reference books listed in the bibliography.

This view of part of the gorge wall is taken from the road leading down to the Maid of the Mist landing. It shows the 24 metres (80 foot) layer of erosion-resistant Lockport Limestone laid down as sediment by the warm sea which covered the area during the Silurian Period of the Palaeozoic Era, about 400 million years ago. The softer less erosion-resistant layers of shale have been cemented over to retard erosion. This is the rock layer over which the Horseshoe Falls cascades.

George Bailey

The American Falls, 1987, from the deck of the "Maid of the Mist". The talus blocks, exposed during the 1969 dewatering project, are here partially covered by foaming water and shrouded in mist.

George Bailey

George A. Seibel

The Horseshoe Falls during a period of particularly high water, October 1987. A south-west wind forced additional water out of Lake Erie and into the Niagara River. The flow depicted was in excess of 4248 m³/sec (150,000 cfs), one third more than normal for that time of year.

The crest of the Horseshoe Falls, November 1, 1987, the day after an additional 1416 m³/sec (50,000 cfs) were diverted for electric power generation, leaving an equivalent amount to flow over the Falls. The glacial boulders which cause minor rapids when the river is higher, are exposed at this lower, winter water level.

George A. Seibel

Cross Channel Erosion

I suppose everyone has noticed, as one walks eastward away from the cataracts' roar, how the end of Goat Island and the Three Sisters Islands adjacent have been increasingly denuded of soil. Finally, one comes to a spot where he may climb down from a ledge of hard and slippery rock at the Three Sisters Islands, to a floor of fairly smooth dry limestone which is eaten into countless holes. Then, looking ahead towards Buffalo and the water to the east, our explorer may be startled momentarily to see the flood apparently coming down upon the very place where he is standing. Luckily, so it seems, these waters are diverted at the last moment, at the point called "Parting of the Waters", at the eastern end of Goat Island, to flow harmlessly by on either side towards their final stretch to ocean level. From the end of Goat Island one does not have this experience, for he may walk from the road which encircles the island proper, on slightly rising rocks, quite far toward the Parting of the Waters.

The first picture illustrates the view when one looks upriver towards Buffalo from the upper of the Three Sisters Islands. The water forms a green and white wall some 2.4 metres (8 feet) deep, curving over the rounded ledge of the Green Cascade. When there is a west wind one may walk on top of this ancient rock side of a stream which may be of inter-

glacial origin, or possibly of pre-glacial origin, that is, pre-dating all the glaciers in this region. There are traces in southern Ontario of at least two of these ice juggernauts. In most places, however, the debris or marks of the first glacier have been removed, or covered, by the last.

The rock ledge of the Green Cascade is the side of the ancient Falls-Chippawa Buried Valley (St. Davids Valley). Unfortunately this valley has not been traced for a very long distance and is not well studied. Its presence means, however, that the Horseshoe Falls is destined to climb over the lower ledges of this ancient valley until it comes to this higher ledge of the Green Cascade. Not far back of this ledge, up the river, the height of the water level in the river is about 15 metres (50 feet) above the height of the water level at the present rim of the cataract.

When the Horseshoe Falls has conquered this ledge it will be at least 61 metres (200 feet) high. But such a conquest will not be easy. The rock here is not quite the same Lockport Limestone formation which had to be cut through all along the gorge from Lewiston. The rocks above the Three Sisters Islands are of the same Lockport Limestone group, but are harder.

This photo of the Upper, or Green, Cascade was taken from the Three Sisters Islands in October, 1987. It is looking towards the U.S. shore of the Niagara River. The boulder in the left foreground is composed of the harder strata of Lockport Limestone, the same harder strata which make up the river bed under the

Upper Cascades. The pitted surface of rocks such as this, makes them very popular for use in rock gardens. Small deposits of gypsum or salt, laid down with these rocks, were dissolved when the limestone came into contact with water. As a result, holes remain where the deposits had been on the rock surfaces.

This photo of the Green Cascade was taken November 3, 1987, from the same location as the previous picture. The cascade is dry, being deprived of water because of the winter diversion of more water for electric power generation. Beginning November 1

each year less water is allowed to go over Niagara Falls. Instead it is diverted above the Falls, on both the American and Canadian sides of the River, into tunnels which carry it to power houses at Lewiston and Queenston.

To experience just how much harder, let the reader try, as I did, to collect specimens from the typical rocks of the Niagara Glen and from those above Goat Island. There, above Goat Island, I saw, but was unable to remove, a splendid fossil which was begging to be put in my box and taken in out of the weather where it had been fastened for so many millions of years, ever since the Silurian Period of the Palaeozoic Era. A conservative age for these extra hard limestone rocks is 300 million years. N.B. The Silurian Period ended about 400 million years ago.

In a previous chapter there are sketches of some of the simple life forms that existed in these rocks; for example, crinoidal or sea lilies. The rocks are grey to chocolate coloured and have many holes, none of which pierced their mass, because these holes were filled with a softer material, more readily dissolved away by water, or split by frost.

The newness of these rapids above the Horseshoe Falls is proved by the lack of evidence for any erosion in the stream bed or in the bank. From a viewpoint on the Canadian bank, just opposite the spot where the ancient rock ledge of the first cascade disappears under the terrace of glacial drift on Goat Island, it can be seen that the ledge is in a more or less straight line across the river. In other words there has been no cutting back, or hardly any that

can be noticed, since the limestone ridge came near the surface of the river. The river has, then, not been in this shape, or at this level, for very long.

Until the Falls had cut a gorge back to Hubbard Ridge, the bed of the river south of that place remained much higher and above the level of Goat Island. This fact of the submergence of the famous island we have referred to before.

When the falls reached Hubbard Ridge, the crest was 15 to 18 metres (50 to 60 feet) higher than it is now, after breaking through Hubbard Ridge.

After breaking through Hubbard Ridge, it began backing downhill, as it were, to the present height of 48 metres (158 feet) at the Horseshoe. This backing down caused the water-level of the river, and of the lake feeding the river, to lower, forcing the river to cut a channel out of its old bed of glacial debris and river sediment deposits, and causing Goat Island to appear above water. As the river lowered further, there was revealed in the form of cascades, the ridged side of the ancient Falls-Chippawa interglacial valley. The bed of the lowered river was now rock which had a westward slope. This slope turned the flow of the water towards the west bank, making it cut into the deep glacial debris filling of the ancient valley on the Canadian side. This in turn caused an eating away of the glacial debris, particularly in one spot – Dufferin Islands.

The roches moutonnées (sheep's rocks) of the Green Cascade above Three Sisters Islands are dried off and exposed in this view taken November 3, 1987, a time of low water because of diversion for electric power generation. A.H. Tiplin wrote about this spot in 1938: "The water forms a green and white wall some 2.4 metres (8 feet) high over the rounded ledge of the Green Cascade."

George A. Seibel

The second picture shows soils from glacial deposits on Goat Island which are not related to the bed rocks underneath. Most soil is formed by the decomposition of the rocks underneath; not this. The deposit here, not far from Terrapin Point at the edge of the American flank of the Horseshoe Falls, is known as a kame. This is a term used in glacial geology for a short ridge of gravel and sand deposited by a stream issuing from an ice-front. In other words, Goat Island is a mound of gravel formed by a stream of water from melting ice, carrying debris from the surface of the glacier to the ground at its base. Goat Island is part of the Niagara Falls Terminal Moraine which was deposited in Lake Lundy, the old and very large glacial lake. It is an isolated part of the larger mass which forms the high terrace back of Queen Victoria Park, and part of that drift bank which nearly engulfs the "old swimming hole" – Dufferin Islands.

Not all of the terrace shown in the second photo is glacial debris. There is a covering layer of soil deposited by fresh water. Near to us on the Canadian side, this layer is absent. On Goat Island and the adjoining American shore it is as much as 6 metres (20 feet) deep in spots.

This 1938 view was taken not far from Terrapin Point at the edge of the American side of the Horseshoe Falls. It shows the glacial soil deposit which makes up Goat Island, which is the isolated eastern tip of the Niagara Falls Moraine. Goat Island has a slight covering of fresh water sediment containing shells, deposited when it was under water.

Glacial Drift
Dufferin Islands

Are you an artist who paints with light, and do you stalk beauty with a little dark box in your hand? Or are you just an ordinary lover of the symmetry of nature so that you are content to sit and gaze?

In either case you will find what you are looking for all along our gorge and river. But be sure you do not miss Dufferin Islands. Here, in this embayment where the river once flowed deeper and swifter than it does now, are to be found a myriad of settings to delight the heart. And these are, more often than not, framed with all manner of trees, straight, spreading and drooping – drooping as though mourning the almost vanished waters which once cut through the several channels. For those who prefer to watch activity and fun in such an environment there are many swimmers with light hearts who are wont to visit the old swimming hole – "Duff", as the students call it.

In the photo can be seen the glacial drift. In the spot shown, it is 31 metres (100 feet) thick overlying the sloping rocks of the Falls-Chippawa Buried Valley. On it is situated Oak Hall, the former home of Sir Harry Oakes (now the Niagara Parks Administration Headquarters), with its unparalleled view of the rapids.

You can stand on the southern side of Dufferin Islands and, looking north-east, you are able to see that the drift forms a sharp semi-circle on the map at the point "A"; this sweep of the drift ends at "B" almost on a line with the first rapids and the rock terrace of the ancient Falls-Chippawa Buried Valley. The four main terraces cross the path of the river all quite parallel with each other.

There is one fact which is tell-tale regarding the age of Dufferin Islands. It may be observed that the exposed terraces in the river and the ridges formed by them at the water-edge, are still very much in line. The conclusion drawn, then is that since the terraces were not worn down very much by the river, the time of their first exposure, caused by the lowering of the water-level of the river after the falls broke through at Hubbard Ridge, was recent in geological time, about 4,000 years ago.

The depth of the river is much greater near the Canadian shore. Thus Canada has much the best deal in water-power here. This greater depth is due to the incline of the rock underlying all of this region. For instance, just above Goat Island, the rock bed is 166 metres (544.6 feet) above sea level; at the Canadian shore, near the end channel of Dufferin Islands, the height is 164.79 metres (540 feet); in the elbow of Dufferin Islands, near the drift bluff, the height is 163.83 metres (537 feet). This is a drop of 2.17 metres (7.6 feet).

The water flowing through Dufferin Islands channel, once turbulent and swift, is now placid. The broad channel is now dotted with man-made islands. Oak _Hall, the home of Sir Harry Oakes, is visible on the high bank in this 1938 photo. Oak Hall is now the Niagara Parks Administration Headquarters._

Naturally then, this slope slides the water to the Canadian side. On the map it will be noticed that this shelf tends to lead the waters right towards Dufferin Islands embayment and the terraces of Queen Victoria Park lower down the river. There is evidence to prove that the curve shown on the map between points "B" and "C" was formed when the water-level of the flood was higher and the Falls was near Hubbard Point.

Soon after this the river level fell, and some of the river flowed over part of what is now Queen Victoria Park. This was so in as late as 1678, when Father Hennepin saw the Falls for the first time. The engraving made in 1697 for Hennepin's book, shows that the Falls were in three parts, the present day Horseshoe and the American Falls, and also a side-fall sweeping to the north and west of old Table Rock. This side-fall location is pictured in a later chapter.

Dufferin Islands embayment seems to have been formed somewhat later than the arc of Queen Victoria Park. Before the Ontario Power Company development in front of the entrance to Dufferin Islands took advantage of the welling of the waters near this side of the drift bluff, there was much more water flowing through the islands' channels. Now the flow can be regulated more or less at will. When the river first formed the embayment, the channels were cut in the glacial deposits along the edge of the rock table beneath, causing the main centre islands to form more or less as they are now.

It is interesting to speculate on what would have happened if the drift bluff on the Canadian side had not been so high, or if the slope of the rock layers had at this point been slightly greater, as it is at other points along the gorge. Near Chippawa Creek, or the Welland River, there is a fairly low channel which is lower still, the greater the distance from

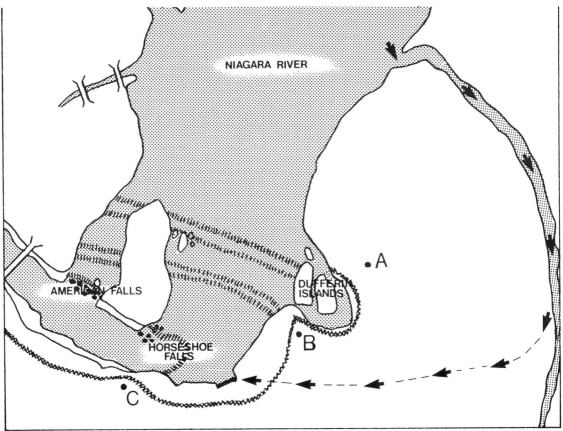

Astrid Akkerman from a sketch by A.H. Tiplin

Point "A" on the map marks the position of the first ridge of the ancient Falls-Chippawa Valley, which diverted the water of the Niagara River toward the bank, to form the Dufferin Islands embayment. The water of the embayment channel returns to the river along the edge of the lower cascade at "B". The curve on the map between points "B" and "C" was formed when the water level of the river was higher and the Falls was near Hubbard Point.

The banks along the inside of the Dufferin Islands embayment were constantly eroding. Soon after the Queen Victoria Niagara Falls Park Commissioners took over the Islands, Superintendent Wilson had a log crib work built against the drift bank all around the embayment. This was filled with rock, and topped with fine gravel. This became a walkway around the islands and was named "Lovers' Walk". By 1898, the ravages of the river, which ran as much as 0.9 metres (3 feet) deep, and at a speed of 16 kilometres (10 miles) per hour, in the islands channel, had damaged the cribwork. It was replaced in 1900.

Niagara Falls New York Public Library

the Niagara River, about 1.6 kilometres (one mile) to the west. The wonder is that the Niagara River did not flow this way along the course dotted on the map, eating deeper into the drift on top of the whole triangle here until it began to remove the drift from the ancient valley beneath. However, once it had done this, it seems likely that it would have turned and flowed north as it is doing now.

From these speculations, one can see that, had natural conditions varied to some degree, Queen Victoria Park and the terrace which forms it might never have existed. Further, if the river had taken the lower exit 1.6 kilometres to the west, the result would have been a lowering of Lake Erie and the Upper Niagara River as well as the height of the Falls, with the Falls then having a considerably decreased flow. On such slight considerations does gravity aid water, to shape the landmarks of a district.

This air view was taken November 1, 1961, when water flow over the Falls was only 1416 m³ (50,000 cfs), the least allowed by the 1950 international treaty. Many rocks and boulders are exposed. The picture shows the relationship between the cascades (the ridges of the ancient Falls-Chippawa River Valley) and Dufferin Islands, No. 1. The Canadian bank of the river has intake weirs to divert water into the various power plants; No. 2, Canadian Niagara Power Company gathering weir; No. 3, Toronto Power Generating Station gathering weir; No. 4, Ontario Power Generating Station intake structure, with the Screen House parallel to the river. The Gate House at the entrance to the three conduits which carry water to the Generating Station below the Falls, is at a right angle to the Screen House. The Screen House was razed in 1987 and there is now a fenced-in pedestrian walkway at this location; No. 5, the ice channel extending from the International Control Structure; No. 6, Goat Island, showing the roadway around what was formerly the tip of the island. The paved area to the right of the road is a helicopter pad, built on land reclaimed from the river; No. 7, the Green Cascade at the end of Three Sisters Islands; No. 8, Hubbard Point; No. 9, the water at the Canadian flank of the Horseshoe Falls flowing unnaturally smoothly, the flank having been deepened and the river bed cleared of glacial boulders; No. 10, Table Rock viewing area at the Horseshoe Falls; No. 11, Ontario Hydro Pump Storage Reservoir; No. 12, Oak Hall; No. 13, the stranded scow.

New York Power Authority

This is the bed of the south channel, dried off when the Ontario Power Company built a cofferdam in the river at the entrance to Dufferin Islands. The dam was necessary while the intake structures were being built for the Power Company. The Niagara Falls Park and River Railway bridge is in the background with the carriage and pedestrian bridge, Pollux, in front of it.

The Queen Victoria Park Commissioners Report for 1903 reported that the rock excavated from the Ontario Power Company forebay at the entrance to Dufferin Islands "was being used for the extensions of the islands". One condition of the agreement that the Park Commission had with the Power Company was that a series of cascades and artificial islands be constructed to compensate for the reduced water flow when the Power Company began diverting water for power generation. This 1904 photo shows the results of this work.

The Queen Victoria Niagara Falls Park Commissioners considered that the work done at Dufferin Islands by the Ontario Power Company in 1903, to "have a formal appearance, out of keeping with the natural surroundings". When the Power Company wanted to construct a third conduit, the Commissioners required as part of the new agreement, that the rock excavated be placed along the drift edges of the embayment, in an irregular shore line, with widened areas for planting. New islands were to be created, and several cascades shortened. This photo, circa 1920, shows this work in progress. When it was completed the Commissioners said: "the effect is agreeable".

Remedial work was undertaken at Dufferin Islands in 1986-87. Gabion baskets, made of galvanized fencing material, shown in the left foreground, were placed around the perimeter of the islands and filled with rock, to prevent erosion. Gabion baskets are already in place around the island in the centre of the picture. More than 6,000 tandem-truck loads of silt were removed from the river bed in the islands' channels. This silt which had accumulated over the past 60 or more years, supported the growth of Eurasian Milfoil, an aquatic plant which was depleting the water of oxygen, and choking the water courses. Oak Hall, the Niagara Parks Administration Headquarters is visible on the high bank.

The suspension bridge, Pollux, which formed the exit
from Dufferin Islands, at Dufferin Gate, circa 1880.
The speed of the incoming river current is apparent. A
similar bridge, Castor, formed the entrance to
Dufferin Islands. In Roman mythology, Castor and
Pollux were the twin sons of Leda and Jupiter.

Ontario Power Generating Station water intake
facilities at the entrance to Dufferin Islands are
shown in this October 1907 photo. On the right is the
Screen House, where ice, wood and other debris were
screened to prevent them entering the forebay, centre.
At the end of the forebay are three conduits, which
have their openings at the Gate House, in the left
background. The Screen House was razed in 1987,
and screens were installed at the entrance to the conduits. In place of the Screen House there is now a
covered pedestrian walkway over the forebay.

Ontario Hydro

This November 1987 photo shows water flowing again into the intake facilities of the Ontario Power Generating Station. The new fenced-in pedestrian walkway on the bridge across the forebay forms part of the Niagara River Recreation Trail. Those using the walkway will enjoy a view of the upper rapids which was obstructed by the former Screen House, which stood on this site from 1905 until 1987.

This air view was taken October, 1987, as remedial work was being completed on the Ontario Power Generating Intake facilities at the entrance to Dufferin Islands. While the 4.05 hectare (10 acre) forebay was dewatered, the former Screen House was razed and screen gates were installed at the Gate House – the white building on the left. The screens are designed to prevent ice and other debris from entering the conduits, which have their openings under the Gate House. The forebay ranges in depth from 4.3 metres (14 feet) at the entrance, to 10.6 metres (35 feet) in front of the Gate House screens.

Ontario Hydro

Future of the Falls

In the chapter on the Recession of the Falls we saw what the immediate future of the Falls is likely to be. Now let us inquire beyond the immediate future, and into the future story and nature of our cataract in the next several thousand years.

The caption under the map and the accompanying pictures make it clear what the future will hold for the Falls in the next few milleniums if the relative levels of the land surfaces round about us are left undisturbed. This is hardly to be expected.

Elsewhere in this book the canting and tilting of this section of the continent have been reviewed. Some scientists claim that this rising of the land in the north-east is still continuing at nearly the same rate as it did ten to twenty thousand years ago. If so, and so slow is the action that it is hardly noticeable in even a long lifetime, the influence on our Great Lakes system and, of course on our Niagara River, will be direct and tremendous.

If the land to the north-east is rising, either as a result of the great burden of the glacier having been recently lifted, or because of the earth's movements dependent on the mysterious convections in the rock plasma below the crust of the globe, then the St. Lawrence outlet will become too shallow for the overflowing lakes. Indeed, Lakes Erie and Ontario will be slowly turned to flow the other way, unless they can cut paths through the land as it rises. Lake Huron drainage would of course be reversed across the peninsula between it and Lake Michigan, so as to find eventually a way through the Chicago Valley to the Mississippi. It would then be hard to visualize Erie and Ontario any longer as inland seas. They would not be supplied with the upper lakes' waters, but would be merely local drainage reservoirs. Their outlets would be no doubt about as they were before the Pleistocene Age, about 50,500 years or more ago; that is, in the case of Lake Erie, south-westward to the tributaries of the Mississippi River Valley. The Niagara River could not exist, of course. It would get no sustenance from the upper lakes or Lake Erie, for their course would be the other way. Then naturally the famous cataracts would be dead.

Professor G.K. Gilbert and one or two other geologists have calculated the rate of this rise (which may or may not be continuing now) and have come to the following interesting conclusions: in about 600 years Lake Michigan would begin to find its way over the rock ledge at Chicago; in 2,000 years the outlets at Niagara and Chicago would be at equal volume; in 3,500 years Niagara would be entirely devoid of its waters and all the overflow would be through Chicago, with Lake Huron once again find-

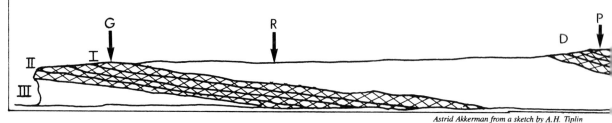

Astrid Akkerman from a sketch by A.H. Tiplin

ing its ancient outlet by way of Saginaw Bay, across the lower peninsula of Michigan, to Lake Michigan.

According to this calculation, Niagara Falls would have about half of its expected normal life span taken away. But if the natural course is followed over the various rock ledges as shown on the sketch, the life would probably be 8,000 years until it became a rapids divested of all its scenic beauty. However, it is by no means sure that such a tilting was ever slow and steady. According to the evidence of the ancient gravel beaches such as those Lake Iroquois deposited, (beaches which were later raised by the reflex action of the earth's crust), this tilting has been only at intervals, that is, spasmodic. It is a question not yet decided whether this last spasm is still going on; it is another and more obscure question whether this spasm, even if it is still effective, will last long enough to shorten the normal life span of the Falls.

In the 30.6 kilometres (19 miles) between the Lockport Limestone at Goat Island and the Onondaga Limestone at Buffalo, the types of bedrock will cause the cataract to change a great deal. In the sketch, S = Silurian Age sea-beds composed of: I, Salina Limestone; II, Lockport Limestone; III, Clinton and Medina shale and limestone formations; D, Devonian Age limestones which form the escarpment through Buffalo and which prevent Lake Erie from draining almost completely into the Niagara River; G, end of Goat Island. The Falls will be much higher after cutting through the terraces of the ancient buried Falls-Chippawa Valley; R, near here, at the southern end of Navy Island, the Falls will either become a terraced cataract, like Letchworth Lower Falls, or will become a rapids because of the soft Salina shales which form most of the bed of the upper Niagara River; P, Peace Bridge, where there now are rapids of a sort and the future site of another small cataract when the level of the Niagara River is gradually lowered by the falls cutting through the shales at "R".

The opposite shore in this photo is Navy Island. Beneath the silt of the river bed, near the tip of Navy Island (centre right), the Lockport Limestone layer ends and the softer, less erosion resistant Salina

Shales begin. When the Falls recede to this point, they will degenerate into rapids as they progress upriver, because the soft shales will be eroded quickly.

George Bailey

Niagara Falls Moraine

A terminal moraine is a great mound, or ridge, formed by material which was carried upon and within the glacial ice, as well as material which was pushed by the glacier.

The stippled parts of the map show where these have formed twice in our immediate Niagara vicinity. No. 1 is called the Niagara Falls Moraine. It extends faintly across Grand Island at about the half-way mark between the recently built Grand Island Bridges. It is deeper toward East Aurora, N.Y., just south-west of Buffalo, but fades out when it approaches the lateral moraines of the Finger Lakes District. To the west of Niagara, it gradually descends towards Hamilton, becoming a mere shadow of its highest point. The highest point is on Lundy's Lane Ridge, where Drummond Hill Presbyterian Church and Drummond Hill Cemetery are located. It is some 142 metres (465 feet) above the level of Lake Ontario.

No. 2 is the Barre Moraine, which is not as extensive nor as deep, as the more southern Niagara Falls Moraine. Its masses of assorted cross-bedded gravels and washed sands choke the head of the St. Davids Valley at the Indian Ossuary. Its finer sands and clays fill the ancient buried gorge called the Whirlpool-St. Davids Buried Gorge, represented on the map by the dotted line.

Each winding ridge of gravel, it will be observed, has its steep side to the north. Each has the washed sand deposit to the south on its sloping side (represented by dense black). From the material found on the surface of these ridges, or made to appear deep inside by digging in gravel and sand deposits, it can be determined that the continental glacier which changed the features of our country did not carry the principal part of its burden of gravel, boulders and sand upon its surface. On the contrary, it pushed it ahead, or carried it embedded in the more liquid ice at the bottom of its tremendously thick mass.

Consequently these moraines are made up of rounded pebbles and boulders (aside from sand and clay) which, because of their very shape show that there was great wear and pressure in the past. If the rocks on the surface were angular (and they are not), such lack of roundness would definitely indicate a lack of abrasion, because they would have been carried on top of the glacier. In this way our moraines were pushed up.

To the south of the Niagara Falls District there are other terminal moraines. To the north there are many others. Each one represents a pause in the more or less steady withdrawal of the invading ice barrier from its most southerly point of invasion.

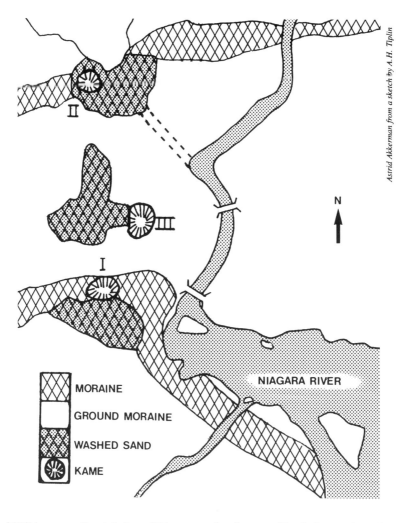

Astrid Akkerman from a sketch by A.H. Tiplin

MORAINE

GROUND MORAINE

WASHED SAND

KAME

NIAGARA RIVER

N

No. 1, Drummond Hill kame, on Lundy's Lane Ridge which is on the Niagara Falls Moraine, shown by the checkered lines; No. II, Barre Moraine (St. Davids or Ravine Hill sand-pit), Indian Ossuary and edge of the escarpment; No. III, Fairview Cemetery, a kame, at the western end of Bridge Street in Niagara Falls.

In our part of the continent, this invading ice-front went as far south as the State of Ohio.

Whenever the retreat of the ice barrier is gradual and steady, ground for kilometres (miles) in front of the ice-sheet will be level like a bedspread. Such a ground moraine covers most of the Niagara District between Falls View (the heights above the Horseshoe Falls) and Lake Erie, with the notable exception to the west, of Fonthill, or Short Hills region. These ground moraines were formed by

shoal water. Doubtless, when the water from the melting edge of the ice-front put down these ground moraines, the depth of the water would be partly determined by the height of the Lundy's Lane Ridge of the Niagara Falls Moraine and of the Barre Moraine. The Lundy's Lane Ridge is, at a spot about 1.6 kilometres (one mile) west of the Battle of Lundy's Lane Monument in Drummond Hill Cemetery, 27.4 metres (90 feet) deep to solid rock. The monument location is higher since it is on a kame.

On several occasions, to judge from the number of terminal moraines in this region once traversed by the glacier, the melting retreat of the glacier was not slow or steady. Why there should have come times when the rate of retreat northward was balanced by the rate of melting, we can no more determine than we can tell why there should have been continental glaciers at all, or why, once having come upon the world, they should have seen fit to retreat.

But at least the reader will easily surmise that these terminal moraines may be valuable some day to scientists who wish to study more intensively the problem of long-time climatic changes. Each ridge certainly indicates a fairly sudden warm period in the distant past. How long each warm change lasted can only be guessed at yet, since we are almost totally in the dark concerning the thickness of the ice barrier, and the amount of debris it carried in each cubic mile of ice.

Each pause caused by a warm period may have been thousands of years long. At least the top of the ice barrier must have been much higher than the top of any of its terminal moraines. This is chiefly why these great mounds or ridges are interesting to me. They definitely show the approximate height of the crunching monster.

It will be noted that in three places on the map there are kames. In the chapter dealing with Goat Island I explained briefly what a kame was. On the map there are three on the Canadian side near Niagara Falls – Berryman Hill (most northerly); Fairview Cemetery; and Lundy's lane kame at Drummond Hill Cemetery (most southerly). A kame is a short ridge or hillock of layered sand and gravel heaped up by streams under the glacier's surface, as they flowed from the margin of the ice.

The Drummond Hill Cemetery kame on Lundy's Lane Ridge was the scene of fierce fighting during the Battle of Lundy's Lane, July 25, 1814. British General Phineas Riall chose the top of the kame, the highest point of land in the district, as the strategic position for his artillery battery, in preparation for battle with the invading American forces. Throughout the battle, at one time or another, both sides had control of the hill. Almost 2,000 soldiers, British, Canadian and American, were killed, wounded or missing in this bloody action.

The monument commemorating the Battle of Lundy's Lane, July 25, 1814, stands in Drummond Hill Cemetery, on a kame on top of Lundy's Lane Ridge, which rests on the Niagara Falls Moraine. This is the highest point of land in the area, 142 metres (465 feet) above Lake Ontario. It is 27.4 metres (90 feet) through glacial debris of sand and gravel, down to bedrock, one mile west of the monument.

The Battle of Lundys Lane Monument, on Drummond Hill kame, is shown in this 1983 view. The Union Jack is flying here because it is the flag under which the British and Canadian forces fought in the War of 1812-14.

George Bailey

During the War of 1812-14, Drummond Hill, the kame on top of the Lundys Lane Ridge of the Niagara Falls Moraine, was strategically important to military forces, because it was the highest point of land in the district.

The Battle of Lundys Lane took place in the evening hours of July 25, 1814, much of it along the northern slope of the ridge. In the beginning, the British artillery was on the top of Drummond Hill, Americans charged up the slope and overran the British guns. In turn, the British charged up the same slope, to regain control of the heights. There was fierce fighting, with many casualties, and the dead were later buried on the slope where they fell. Digging of graves was easy, in the glacial drift of the Lundys Lane Ridge. Coronation Park, a baseball playing field located on Summer Street, now occupies the area where some of the soldiers were buried.

After the War of 1812-14, as the nearby village of Drummondville grew, there was a need for building materials such as cement, mortar and foundation stone, as well as sand and gravel for roads. Early entrepreneurs dug a pit into the glacial drift here, a site convenient to the community, to supply the sand and gravel needs.

In 1856, the gravel pit was operated by one of the Morse family. He had a contract to fill the potholes on Portage Road (Main Street). Criticism of his work was reported in the local newspaper; there were too many human bones in the loads of gravel which he dumped in the potholes.

What happened was that, as the gravel pit progressed further into the bank, the soldiers' graves were undermined. When gravel was taken out from under the graves, the remains (bones) of the soldiers slipped into the pit and were picked up and loaded, along with the sand and gravel, for spreading on the roads.

An old resident has recounted how, in the 1890's, after the Niagara Falls Park and River Railway was built from Queenston to Chippawa, people came from Toronto to visit the Lundys Lane Battlefield. They travelled by boat to Queenston, then by the electric railway to Niagara Falls. On the battlefield site, they enjoyed their picnic lunches, then spent the day picking through the sand and gravel, even disturbing some graves, to retrieve military buttons and regimental badges.

This callous disregard for the remains of the soldiers who died on the Lundys Lane Battlefield, is in direct contrast to the care and consideration shown for the remains found in 1987, west of Fort Erie. They were the remains of soldiers, thought to be American, also from the War of 1812-14. They were carefully removed from the site of construction where they were discovered. After historical, archeological and forensic studies, they are to be reinterred with suitable military honours, in the United States.

Our Romantic Niagara in the News

146

Harper's Weekly

This woodcut illustration, from Harper's Weekly, 1883, depicts the voyage of the "Maid of the Mist" through the Whirlpool Rapids in 1861. This view is from the Railway Suspension Bridge, which had been operating for six years when the "Maid of the Mist" made that trip. Forty to fifty trains a day crossed over the bridge. The talus at the lower right of the picture is in the same place where a rock fall in 1935 caused the end of the Niagara Gorge Railway's operation

along the Whirlpool Rapids. Albert Tiplin observed in 1938, while standing at this location, that there was an occasional sprinkle of loose particles of shale which turned to a shower whenever a train went over the nearby bridge. This led him to conclude that the vibrations of the bridge, under the weight of a train, were communicated to the rock layers, causing the release of shale from the cliff face.

Hennepin's Falls

Perhaps the first white man to see the Falls of Niagara was some unknown "coureur de bois". He, doubtless being illiterate, did not leave any description other than that of word of mouth. But the fame of this mighty cataract grew among the Indians and the first white men until it became a point for all explorers and adventurers to visit at least once. Many, more gifted in language than in the physical abilities needed by anyone who wished to visit this wild country in those early days, merely wrote about the cataract from the reports they heard. Then in 1678 Father Louis Hennepin, part missionary and part explorer, actually saw the cataract and also wrote about it.

Here are some of his words: "Betwixt the Lake Ontario and Erie there is a vast and prodigious column of water, which falls down after a surprising and astonishing manner, inasmuch as the Universe does not afford a parallel. 'Tis true Italy and Swedenland boast of some such things; but we may well say that they are sorry patterns when compared to this of which we now speak.

"At the foot of this horrible precipice we meet the Niagara River which is not above one-quarter league broad, but is wonderfully deep in places. It is so rapid above the descent that it violently hurries down the wild beasts while endeavouring to pass it to feed on the other side, they not being able to withstand the force of its current, which invariably casts them headlong about 183 metres (600 feet) high. When the wind blows out of the south their dismal roaring may be heard more than 15 leagues off."

Now the reader will notice for himself the surprising tendency to exaggerate distances. The French league at this time was practically equal to the present one – that is about 4.8 kilometres (three modern miles). Father Hennepin certainly did not measure the height of the Falls for himself in the first instance. In the second error, he obviously has taken the word of some Indians who managed to misunderstand French – 72.4 kilometres (45 miles) is a long way to hear any falls, even with a favourable wind.

Such considerations led Peter Kalm of Sweden, the first professional naturalist to visit Niagara Falls, to write to a friend in Philadelphia in 1750: "Hennepin has gained little credit in Canada; the name of honour they give him there is 'un grand menteur' (a great liar). He writes of what he saw in places he never was."

It is obvious that Father Hennepin allowed his literary sense to run away with his scientific awareness. He wrote at different times of the Falls and there is a curious difference between the accuracy of his first and last accounts. However that may be, we should be grateful that the earliest print of the Falls, made in 1697, was based on his description in which he definitely states that there are two main falls and a cross-falls. Looking at the print it is evident that the cataract must have changed its shape and position a great deal since then.

As one gazes toward Table Rock House from Goat Island, he may readily observe how the rock bed dips between Table Rock House and the battery of lights which is to the north of Table Rock. The Ontario Power Generating Station is directly below. He may notice, too, that near Table Rock House there is a slight elevation of 1.8 to 2 metres (six or seven feet) above the lowest bed of the old river margin back of the House near the bluff. In 1799 there was still a pond north of Table Rock House with cedar and ash swamps between it and the bluff. This pond was the remnant of the stream which fed the cross-falls.

The Hall survey of 1842 shows the cliff at Table Rock 31 metres (100 feet) farther out than in 1905. As we know, Table Rock has receded naturally, and also mechanically with the help of dynamite. It has been estimated that the perimeter of the Horseshoe Falls in 1678, when Hennepin saw it, was about 457 to 549 metres (1,500 to 1,800 feet). Now (1938) it is over 914 metres (3,000 feet).

As the river cut back it would naturally drain the side falls, because the river would recede into a narrower channel from which it could not send forth stray water to sweep back of Table Rock and fall over the lower land just above the power house. In spite of road grading which has been done, this depression, the former channel of the cross-falls, is very obvious today.

It is remarkable that the fame of Niagara Falls preceded any sighting of them by Europeans. This fact is perhaps the best proof there is of the great esteem and awe in which the Indians held our cataract. Champlain was one of the first to mention the Falls in writing in 1604. At that time he had been carefully exploring Lake Ontario and heard of the Falls even though he had not seen them. Thus the Falls of Niagara were known before Plymouth Rock where the Pilgrims landed in 1620, or Jamestown, Virginia. Unless we are reminded, we are not accustomed to think of our inland falls as being known to white men before these famous places on the Atlantic Coast. This is a tribute to the daring and alertness of the early explorers.

Niagara Falls ranks close to the top of any list of natural wonders of the world. Interest among Europeans began over 300 years ago when this engraving appeared in the 1697 Dutch edition of Father Louis Hennepin's book Nouvelle Découverte. It was based on his written description of the Falls and was engraved by J. van Vienan. As Europeans could not conceive of a waterfall without mountains nearby, the engraver included distant mountains.

Niagara Falls Ontario Public Library

The Day Niagara Falls Went Dry

It happened during a south-west gale beginning before midnight on the night of March 29, 1848. The water level of the Niagara River dropped, until by early morning of March 30, the flow over the cataracts was reduced to a small stream in the centre.

A newspaper clipping from the Archives of Ontario, preserves a letter to the editor of the Evening Mirror, dated March 30, 8 p.m, 1848. A correspondent named "Spray", wrote: "Suddenly the water fell to a considerable extent so that the Termination Rock (the large rock which blocked the path along the ledge "Behind the Sheet of Falling Water" of the Horseshoe Falls) was left dry, sufficiently to enable those who were fortunate enough to be in the vicinity, to go far enough across the river bed to be directly over this tremendous rock. This feat was accomplished among others, by ladies... The villagers of Chippawa thought they had entirely lost their creek. Off the old Chippawa Fort, about 100 feet (30 metres) beyond low water mark, was discovered a burning spring in the bed of the Niagara River, which some had the curiosity to enclose with an old potash kettle, and a gun-barrel knitted therein, and succeeded in producing flames and a loud explosion. Several bayonets, muskets, swords etc., have been picked up. The water has since returned to its usual level."

An old resident who saw the dried off Falls recalled later: "It was so remarkable as to be noticed by the Buffalo papers". The Buffalo Times reported on March 31: "All the people of the neighbourhood were abroad exploring recesses and cavities that had never before been exposed to mortal eyes". The Iris, published in the village of Niagara Falls, New York, reported: "Judge Porter (owner of Goat Island) with his troop of blasters was early in the canals leading to the water-powered mills and factories, and the thunder of the blasts was heard all day from spots where never before stepped the foot of man; and where heretofore the reeking waters forbade too near approach, they now worked with safety on dry land".

From the American side, George W. Holley drove out from near the head of Goat Island to a point about 201 metres (660 feet) from shore along the Cascades to a point where a length of pine timber 30.5 centimetres (12 inches) square and 12.2 metres (40 feet) long was lodged. With the aid of four horses and a log cart, he removed the timber and brought it to Goat Island. Returning on a second trip that took him even farther out into the river, he salvaged a larger timber 18.3 metres (60 feet) long.

Thomas C. Street, the owner of Street's Mills, located at the present day site of the Toronto Power

Generating Station, was awakened by a knock on his door at 5 a.m. It was his miller, who told him that there was no water in the mill race and no water in the river alongside the millrace. After a hurried breakfast Thomas Street and his youngest daughter left their home, the present location of Oak Hall, and went on horseback to investigate.

They rode about 1.2 kilometres (three quarters of a mile) down the dry river bed alongside Cedar Island, to the precipice of the Horseshoe Falls. Here they dismounted and walked near the brink of the Horseshoe, about one third of the way toward Goat Island. At this point Mr. Street's daughter tied a handkerchief to a pole and stuck the pole in a crevice of the rock.

Mr. Street's account of the phenomenon appeared in the <u>New York Times,</u> from an interview Bishop Fuller, of Hamilton, granted the newspaper. "I did not see the occurrence myself, but I was told of it the next day by my brother-in-law Thomas C. Street M.P."

Those who witnessed the strange spectacle of a dried off Falls speculated as to the cause. Thomas Street gave a logical explanation, which Bishop Fuller related to the <u>New York Times</u> reporter. "The winds had been blowing down Lake Erie which is only about eighty feet (24 metres) deep, and had been rushing a great deal of water from it over the Falls. Then, suddenly changing, the wind blew this little water (comparatively speaking) up to the western portion of the lake. At this juncture the ice on Lake Erie, which had been broken up by these high winds, got jammed in the river between Buffalo and the Canadian side, and formed a dam which kept back the waters of Lake Erie a whole day."

It was not until 1953-54, when coffer dams were installed on both flanks of the Horseshoe Falls, that the river bed at the crest of the Horseshoe Falls was dried off again. The first time it happened, it was Nature's handiwork, the second time, man's.

This photo taken in 1954 shows the crest of the Horseshoe Falls dry, as Thomas C. Street saw it in 1848. When Thomas Street and his daughter walked out along the brink of the Falls to place a flag in a crevice above Termination Rock, there were few buildings on the Canadian shore. Today, the bank has

Table Rock House at the left, and the Scenic Tunnel Observation Plaza at the base of the gorge wall. The Ontario Power Generating Station is at the right, along the river's shore. The Illumination Battery and the Victoria Park Restaurant are on the upper gorge bank, directly above the power house.

Ontario Hydro

Table Rock

Captain Enys of the 29th British Regiment, visited the Falls of Niagara in 1787. In an entry in his Journal, he left an account of his visit to Table Rock. He received permission from Francis Ellsworth, whose Crown Grant abutted the Falls on the Canadian side, to cross his property and descend the upper bank on the way to the crest of the Horseshoe Falls.

"Not far from the house we came to the edge of a very steep bank, which we descended through a very deep ravine or gully", he wrote. "...not without some dread of rattlesnakes... After going some distance we got to the bottom of this nasty place and found ourselves again on level ground, which took us to the brink of the Falls at a place, from its appearance, called the Table Rock, over a part of which the water still rolls. The Table Rock is a very large flat rock projecting from the bank and overhanging its base very much. This being the nearest part of the Great Fall, you are of course almost stunned with its noise and perfectly wet with the continual spray arising from the bottom in the form of a pillar... many people think this is the best view in which you can place the Falls".

Charles Dickens, the British novelist, visited Canada and the Falls of Niagara in 1841 and wrote of his impressions in his American Notes (1842).

"It was not until I came on Table Rock, and looked – Great Heaven, on what a fall of bright-green water – that it came upon me in its full might and majesty. Then when I felt how near to my Creator I was standing, the first effect, and the enduring one – instant and lasting – of the tremendous spectacle, was Peace... Peace of Mind... Nature was at once stamped upon my heart, an Image of Beauty; to remain there, changeless and indelible, until its pulses cease to beat, for ever.

"Oh how the strife and trouble of our daily life receded from my view, and lessened in the distance, during the ten memorable days we passed on that Enchanted Ground! To stand upon the edge of the Great Horse Shoe Falls, marking the hurried water gathering strength as it approached the verge, yet seeming, too, to pause before it shot into the gulf below; watching the river as, stirred by no visible cause, it heaved and eddied and awoke the echoes being troubled yet, far down beneath the surface, by the giant leap."

All this, and much more, Charles Dickens saw from Table Rock. Dickens was famous for his novels, which appeared in serial form in British newspapers; they were much like our present day television soap operas. Dickens' excess verbiage is understandable when we remember that he was paid by the number of words he wrote.

Table Rock as Ferdinand Richardt saw it in 1856, after major rockfalls in 1818, 1829, 1850 and 1853 had considerably reduced its size. It was here in 1791 that Chateaubriand the French nobleman nearly lost his life. "Niagara eclipses everything" he wrote. Then: "While holding my horse's bridle twisted around my arm (on Table Rock), a rattlesnake came and rustled in the bushes. The startled horse reared and backed toward the falls. I was unable to release my grip from the reins; the horse still more terrified was dragging me after it. Already his fore-feet were off the ground; cowering over the edge of the abyss, it maintained its position only by the strength of its loins. It was all up with me, when the animal astonished at its fresh peril, gave a sudden turn and vaulted inwards."

Frances Wright, an Englishwoman travelling in Canada in 1819, wrote: "a part of the Table Rock fell last year (1818), and in that still remaining, the eye traces an alarming fissure, from the very summit of the projecting edge over which the water rolls; so that the ceiling of this dark cavern seems rent from the precipice, and whatever be its hold, it is evidently fast yielding to the pressure of the water."

In 1833, Major Thomas Hamilton wrote: "From the Table Rock, which projected upwards of 15 metres (50 feet) before its fall (in part) a few years ago, similar ideas of the grandeur of the Cataract are excited. In looking over this tremendous precipice, horror seizes the inmost feeling. The point of projection extends, shelving over the frightful gulph, by a thin layer of rock, at the top about two feet (0.60 metres) in thickness; under which it is completely hollowed out. Few persons dare look over without extending themselves flat. The appearance of anyone on the rock in an erect posture, when looking down, will thrill the stoutest heart."

Charles Dickens spent ten days in 1842 at Niagara Falls coming each day to Table Rock. He wrote: "It was not until I came on Table Rock, and looked – Great Heaven, on what a fall of bright green water! – that it came upon me in its full might and majesty."

Danger lurked there. On August 23, 1844, Miss Martha K. Rugg was walking to Table Rock with a friend. Seeing a bunch of cedar-berries on a low tree, which grew out from the edge of the rock, she left her companion, reached out to pick it, lost her footing, and fell 46 metres (150 feet) upon the rocks below. She survived about three hours. For years a painted board was set on the Rock with these words:

"Ladies fair, most beauteous of the race
Beware and shun a dangerous place.
Miss Martha Rugg here lost a life
Who might now have been a happy wife." Anon

George Borret wrote after visiting Table Rock: "I cannot tell you what we saw; you could not depicture it to yourself if you would. I will only say that one view from Table Rock would repay anyone a journey

from the farthest corner of the world. All landscapes I have ever seen – all the snow pictures of the Alps – all the coast scenery of the Mediterranean – all the lochs and moors of the Scotch Highlands – sink into insignificance when compared with the incomparable grandeur of Niagara... The setting is worthy of a gem.''

People viewing the Horseshoe Falls from Table Rock had a variety of views. A landscape architect commented: *''Nowhere, accessible to ordinary man, does so much water descend so far, providing a sight, a sound and a splashing whose effect on normal and* properly constituted people is beyond description and superior to adjectives.''

A tailor, once looking down on the Falls, and seeing the huge cloud of spray rising up to heaven, exclaimed; *''What a place to sponge a coat!''* Another, a farmer, cried out. *''It is just the spot for washing sheep.''*

An engineer, a practical man, has the final say: *''It seems strange to me that in all this discussion (on the preservation of the Falls) we hear nothing whatever of the good to come for humanity from allowing this immense falls to work out its board and lodging.''*

This view of the Falls of Niagara was engraved in 1804 by Frederick C. Lewis, based on a now lost oil painting done by John Vanderlyn in 1801. It is entitled <u>A View of the Western Branch of the Falls of Niagara Taken from the Table Rock, Looking Up the River Over the Rapids.</u> In the right foreground a small stream of water is flowing where the Hennepin side falls once cascaded into the gorge. Large pieces of rock are missing from the gorge bank, between the edge of this Hennepin Falls and Table Rock, which projects into the gorge just to the left of the crest of the Horseshoe Falls.

<u>The Horseshoe Falls with The Tower</u> by W.H. Bartlett, engraved by R. Branard, published in <u>American Scenery</u>, Vol. 1, 1838. Bartlett has captured both the awesome might of the falling water, and the precarious position of the lone observer on Table Rock. A solitary figure is shown on hands and knees, nervously peering over the edge of the rock ledge, at the churning water below. On the left flank of the Horseshoe Falls, dwarfed by the immensity of the Falls itself, is Terrapin Tower, built in 1833. A Jesuit priest, Pierre François de Charlevoix, in letters written in May, 1721, to the Duchess of Lesdiguières, first used the term ''horseshoe'' to describe the shape of the fall.

Niagara Falls, the Horseshoe was engraved by Salathe from an oil painting done by Hippolyte Sebron in 1852. Table Rock is shown level with the brink of the Falls. Note the undulations in the bare rock of the dried off former river bed in the area where the people are standing, and the horses and carriage are parked. The large timbers at the river's edge were washed down during a period of high water. They came from the lumber mills near Tonawanda on the American side. Sebron's conception of the first "Maid of the Mist" is seen in the river below.

Niagara Falls Ontario Public Library

This stereo view, 1862, by George Barker, shows Table Rock after the major rockfalls of 1828, 1829, and 1850. The circular frame structure to the left of the flagpole is a Camera Obscura. The lattice-work observation tower, top right, is Street's Pagoda, on Cedar Island.

Niagara Falls New York Public Library

Laurel Campbell-Stark

On January 19, 1887, the Niagara Falls Gazette reported: "Wednesday night last a large section of rock on the Canadian side, close to the Horseshoe Fall, fell with a deafening crash and jarring the earth for some distance away. The exact position of the break, which was 150 feet (46 metres) long and 60 feet (18 metres) wide, was the point visitors will recall. It was close to the Horseshoe Falls and protected by an iron railing.

"So little now remains of the once famous Table Rock that it can hardly retain its name. It originally extended out so far that a person on the edge stood directly in front of a portion of the Horseshoe Falls. In 1818 a mass 160 feet (49 metres) by 30 or 40 feet (9 to 12 metres) in width fell. In the winter of 1828 and 1829 several large masses fell leaving the table-shaped ledge without support on the North and South sides. About mid-day on June 26th, 1850, this table fell with a terrible crash which startled the inhabitants in the vicinity, the first impression being that an earthquake had occurred. It is said that a solitary stableman who was washing an omnibus on the rock escaped with his life, the vehicle, of which no traces were ever found, falling into the abyss. In 1862 several pieces of rock were blasted off as a prevention of accident."

In 1897 other pieces broke off, leaving Table Rock as only a slight projection. Finally in 1935 what was left of the overhang was blasted off as a safety precaution. Table Rock remains today in name only.

George A. Seibel

The projection on the left at the top of the gorge is what remains of Table Rock. The large boulders on the talus slope and at the shore are pieces of the rock which fell over the years from 1818 to 1897. The cemented portion of the top of the gorge bank, just below the Skylon Tower and above the end of the Ontario Power Generating Station, is where the side falls, shown in Hennepin's 1679 sketch, dropped over the gorge.

Ice Bridge

Water flowing in our Romantic River is the dynamic force which has changed our landscape, by creating the Niagara Gorge. We have already explained how the erosive power of falling water undermines the top layer of limestone and causes it to fall into the deep river below. Water turned to ice contributes further to this erosion, by finding its way into cracks and crevices, where it freezes. As the water freezes solid, it expands, spreading ever so slightly the crack in which it lies. This action, repeated year after year, eventually splits off the rock at the crack, separating it from the main gorge wall, so that it falls into the gorge below as talus.

Another form of ice, that which forms on the surface of Lake Erie and on the Niagara River, is also an erosive force. Lake Erie is the major producer of ice sent down the Niagara River. It is capable of producing 16,093 square kilometres (10,000 square miles) of ice. It is fortunate that most of the ice formed in Lake Erie melts in the Lake; only a fraction of the ice produced there flows, or is pushed, into the Niagara River. Sometimes, in past years, ice jammed in the river below the Falls in glacier-like quantities. Now, since the Ice Boom was installed at the entrance to the Niagara River, annual ice runs from the Lake may vary from virtually none in mild weather, to as much as 528 square kilometres (330 square miles).

Ice jams in the River are caused when ice on Lake Erie is affected by specific conditions. First, the lake ice is weakened by a period of mild weather; then it is broken up by a strong west or south-west wind and is driven by the wind into the Niagara River; the temperature drops. This wind-broken Lake Erie ice flows down the Niagara River and is broken into smaller pieces as it passes through the upper rapids and then drops over the Horseshoe Falls. Along with the river ice, frazil, slush and snow, it forms a well-wetted mixture, which freezes into an agglomerate mass when it is tossed out of the water below the Horseshoe Falls.

These floes of agglomerate ice are pushed downriver by the following ice. The river is narrower at the downriver end of the American Falls, opposite the Canadian Maid of the Mist Landing. This point is the beginning of a back eddy along the Canadian shore, which directs some of the ice floes back upriver, where they ground and stick along the shallow shore, gradually building up so that they extend out into the river. There they collide with the oncoming ice. An ice jam occurs. Depending on weather conditions, the jam gets larger and larger as more and more ice is brought over the Falls. The pushing, grinding action of this ice as it moves along the shore, and grounds on the river bed, moves large rocks about, and so contours the river shore line.

When the wind dies down, a seiche occurs in the Lake. A seiche resembles the effect of rocking or tilting a shallow saucer of water and then allowing it to stand and settle, so that an even water level returns. When the wind is no longer forcing water out of the Lake, a lower lake level results, that is, the lake level subsides to a lower level than before the wind began to push extra amounts of water into the Niagara River. Lake Erie has to fill up again before normal out-flow of water to the Niagara River can resume.

When the flow of water coming into the Niagara River is reduced, the water-level under the ice bridge drops, and the frozen mass is suspended between the shores of the river, with the river flowing underneath. The ice mass becomes an ice bridge. There is no erosion because the ice bridge is suspended over the water, and it will remain in this position until warmer weather causes it to collapse, or until another south-west wind drives more water than usual over the Falls. More water would, in turn, raise the river level under the ice bridge. This would cause the ice to break up and float downriver in large floes. This happened in 1912, with dramatic suddenness, when many sightseers were on the ice bridge. Three people who were unable to reach shore were carried on ice floes into the Whirlpool Rapids. It was impossible to rescue them and they lost their lives.

There may be only one major ice run that jams, and stays in the river below the Falls for the whole winter, depending on the severity of the weather; or there may be several, if the weather is alternately cold, then mild.

In 1964, the International Joint Commission approved the installation of an Ice Boom, each winter, at the entrance to the Niagara River. Since then, severe ice jams no longer occur. This boom holds back Lake Erie ice, preventing it from entering the Niagara River in the tremendous quantities which, in past years, damaged power facilities, businesses and property along the river and caused the collapse of the Upper Steel Arch Bridge in 1938.

The Ice Bridge and the American Falls, 1890. This romantic view of the Niagara River ice bridge is from an oil painting by Edward Lowe. People are shown climbing and sliding on the ice mountain in front of the American Falls. Evergreen trees are stuck in crevices and crevasses to warn of danger.

Wunderlich and Company Inc.

This view in the 1890's shows the composition of the ice bridge, with millions of small pieces of broken lake ice frozen together in an agglomerate mass. The huts on the ice bridge sold food and other refreshments, even whiskey.

On January 25, 1938 at 9:30 p.m. there was very little ice in the river below the Falls. Weather conditions, ideal for the formation of an ice bridge, that is, mild weather followed by a south-west wind of gale force, drove ice down the Niagara River with such force and in such quantities that before 8 a.m. the next morning, the Niagara River was jammed with ice, up to 18 metres (60 feet) thick, from the base of the Horseshoe Falls to Niagara-on-the-Lake, 26.4 kilometres (16.5 miles) downriver. The Ontario Power Generating Station was flooded and filled with ice, and a killing blow was dealt to the Upper Steel Arch Bridge. This photograph taken on January 26, shows ice piled up at the abutments of the Upper Steel Arch Bridge.

Niagara Falls Historical Society

Frank O. Seed

The Ontario Power Generating Station was flooded and almost filled with ice in both the 1909 and 1938 ice jams. This view of 1909 ice conditions inside the power house, shows the generators half covered by ice.

January 26, 1938. Workmen are shown in a futile attempt to clear ice away from the hinge bolts, which attached the arch to the abutments of the Upper Steel Arch Bridge.

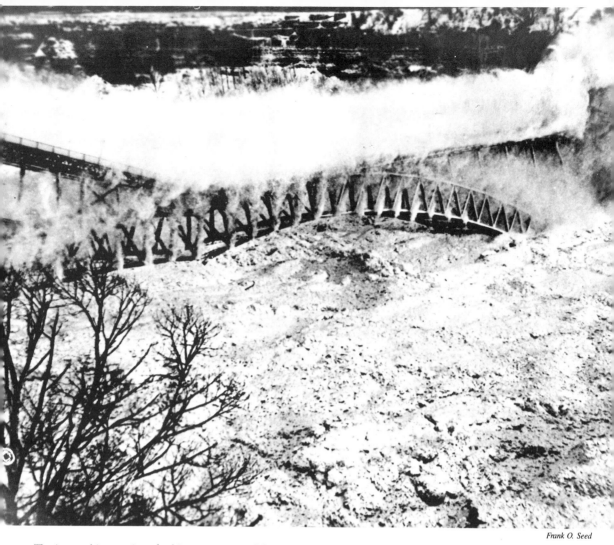

The ice pushing against the hinge supports of the arch, where they were fastened to the abutments, bent the girders of the Upper Steel Arch Bridge. It was only a matter of time before the bridge would fall. Traffic was stopped on the bridge about 4 a.m. on January 27, and a death watch began. Newspapers from all over Ontario and New York State sent photographers to record the expected collapse. When the end came, with dramatic suddenness, at 4:20 p.m. on January 27, Frank O. Seed of Niagara Falls, New York was the only photographer to take the picture. The others, who expected more forewarning of the collapse, were in nearby restaurants, getting warm – and waiting.

January 29, 1938. The point of pressure at the hinge bolts, after the collapse.

January 28, 1938. The Upper Steel Arch Bridge sprawled in tangled disarray on the ice bridge.

This is a view of the 1956 ice jam, looking downriver from the Horseshoe Falls. This was the last major ice bridge before the installation of the Ice Boom in 1964. Notice the three small patches of open water, and above two of them, the sheer walls of agglomerate ice, more than 12 metres (40 feet) thick. What began as an ice bridge, has now become a broken configuration of jumbled ice, caused by mild weather which allowed the ice in the centre of the ice bridge to drop into the river. This 1956 ice jam extended to Niagara-on-the-Lake as did the 1938 ice jam.

Ken James

Fall of Prospect Point

The year 1954 was a momentous one in the geological history of Niagara Falls. It was made noteworthy by one natural occurrence, the fall of Prospect Point, and two man-made undertakings, the construction of the International Control Structure, upriver from the Horseshoe Falls, and the remedial works which filled in part of the river at Terrapin Point, and deepened the flanks of the river on the Canadian side of the Horseshoe Falls.

At Prospect Point there was ample warning that something was about to happen, when water began to seep, then to flow, into the elevator shaft adjacent to the Point (This elevator carried sightseers down to the Maid of the Mist landing). In late July an ominous crack, which extended right across the Point, appeared in the pavement of the viewing area. The area was roped off and a death watch began.

Among the crowd of photographers who had gathered to wait the outcome, was Frank O. Seed, the same patient photographer who had captured on film the collapse of the Honeymoon Bridge, some 16 years before. Frank Seed's patience was again rewarded and at 4:05 p.m., on July 28, he took his first picture of the Point beginning to break away, followed by his spectacular photo of the 182,040 tonnes (185,000 tons) of rock which made up the Point, in mid flight as it toppled into the gorge below.

Water had found its way into fractures in the rock behind the Point. Hydrostatic pressure became so great that the weakened rock projection broke away from the main cliff and fell into the gorge. Prospect Point exists no longer as a point, but is now only a viewing area, in line with the rest of the gorge.

The shower of small pieces of rock falling into the gorge occurred just as Prospect Point began to collapse at 4:05 p.m., July 28, 1954. Such an advance shower of rock heralded the collapse of the gorge wall on the Schoellkopf Power Plant two years later.

Frank O. Seed

Frank Seed just had time to advance his film before he took this picture of the second stage of the collapse of Prospect Point.

Prospect Point at the precise moment it separated from the gorge wall. Notice that water is draining off the edge. By the time the rockfall was complete, some 182,040 tonnes (185,000 tons) of rock had been separated from the upper gorge wall and had fallen into the gorge below.

Preserving the Falls

Until the establishment of public parks on both sides of the Niagara River at the Falls in 1885, the public concept of "preservation of the Falls" was construed to mean the retention of the scenic beauty of the area adjacent to the Falls and the restriction of rampant commercialism.

The first commercial use of the water of the Niagara River for electric power generation, in 1881, led to a new public concern. That concern was to preserve the beauty of the Falls themselves, while at the same time, to divert as much water as possible before it fell over the Falls, into water intakes and the penstocks of the power houses.

Power houses above and below the Falls on both sides of the Niagara River, used the height of the gorge to get the maximum head of water possible, as it dropped through their penstocks to the turbine runners of their generators, located at the lower river level. As more and more power houses were built along the Canadian shore, using the river's flow which was greater along that bank, the tendency was

for the remaining flow to become more and more concentrated in the centre of the Horseshoe Falls. This caused the centre to erode at a much faster rate than the flanks.

Many schemes designed to spread out the flow of water over the Horseshoe Falls, were proposed over the years. All would require the construction of a series of underwater weirs, but nothing was done until 1942. At that time during World War II, additional power was needed for wartime industries. A Special International Niagara Control Board authorized the construction of a submerged weir, designed to raise the level of the water surface 30 centimetres (one foot) in the Grass Island Pool, in the upper river. This would provide more water for the power generating station intakes adjacent to the pool, on both sides of the river.

This weir was composed of large blocks of limestone, dropped into position from cables which were suspended from two temporary steel towers, built for the occasion. The weir was built about 1.6

kilometres (one mile) above the Horseshoe Falls, from a point 91 metres (300 feet) from the Canadian bank. It extended 443 metres (1435 feet) across the Canadian channel. This weir was in use until the present International Control Structure was built in 1953-54.

The construction of the International Control Structure and the accompanying remedial work car-ried out on the flanks of the Horseshoe Falls, were designed to spread out the flow of water over the crest of the Horseshoe. While a more or less even flow of water would be maintained for scenic purposes, at the same time the maximum amount of water could be diverted for electric power generation.

No. 1 is the weir which diverts water towards the twin 13.7 metre (45 foot) diameter tunnels whose entrances are controlled by gates, No. 2, and No. 3. The International Control Structure, No. 4, was built in 1953-54 after the 1950 Niagara Diversion Treaty between Canada and the United States. It holds back the river's flow in order to maintain a sufficient supply of water for diversion through the tunnels upstream, on both sides of the river, for electric power generation at Queenston and Lewiston. As well, operators opening and closing gates in the structure can control the flow of water so that it is distributed more or less evenly along the crest of the Horseshoe Falls. No. 5, Goat Island; No. 6, Horseshoe Falls; No. 7, Toronto Power Generating Station; No. 8, Ontario Power Generating Station intake structure.

Ontario Hydro

This photo, taken before work began in 1955 on the remedial work on the Canadian flank of the Horseshoe Falls, shows the work to be done. The dotted line out in the river denotes the boundary of the coffer dam which was to be laid down, to dry off the river bed inside the dammed-off area. The broad white dotted line, with the word "fill" inscribed, denotes the area to be filled in. This is now part of the Table Rock viewing area.

This photo, taken in August 1954, shows that remedial work has already begun on the American side of the Horseshoe Falls. The coffer dam dried off the river bed so that the area around Terrapin Point could be filled in. Terrapin Point shows as the rounded projection of rock, at the far left of the dried off crest of the Horseshoe Falls. The build up of talus at the base of the Falls is evident, and rocks are visible at the base of the Falls at the right end of the dried off area. This is an indication that subsequent falls of rock from the crest in this area will come to rest on top of this talus, piling up much as it has done at the base of the American Falls. The glacial boulders which abound in the river bed inside the coffer dam, were not completely cleared out, but were left to provide natural rapids.

Ontario Hydro

This air view, taken August 1954, shows the remedial work being carried out on the Canadian flank of the Horseshoe Falls. The area being filled in at the very edge of the crest of the Falls, is shown, with the new retaining wall already in place. The river bed has been cleared of the glacial boulders which caused turbulence and white water rapids. The undulating surface of the Lockport Limestone layer which comprises the river bed, is visible at the right hand end of the dewatered crest. The small island on the curved area at the edge of the coffer dam has since increased in size, and is a favourite nesting area for the myriads of gulls and terns that inhabit the area.

This photo shows work being carried on inside the six-sided coffer dam during 1963. The area dried off was a shoal, which caught ice, and caused it to jam and back up, so that it obstructed the entrances to the Robert Moses tunnels which carry water from above the Falls to the Robert Moses Generating Station at Lewiston. Rock was blasted from the river bed here, to make the bed lower inside the coffer dam. This in turn made the river deeper.

Niagara Falls New York Historical Society

Collapse of the Gorge Wall on the Schoellkopf Power Plant

The most dramatic rockfall in the recorded history of the Niagara gorge occurred on June 7, 1956, when the gorge wall collapsed and destroyed the Schoellkopf Power Plant, in a series of rockfalls that claimed the life of one man.

The Schoellkopf Power Plant was built in four stages, over a period from 1897 to 1925, at the former site of what was known as the Mill District. It was located on the gorge bank in Niagara Falls, New York, about 0.8 kilometres (0.5 miles) downstream from the American Falls. Here were located a number of water-powered mills, producing flour, and paper and doing silver-plating. They used water-power to drive grinding wheels, belts and pulleys, which in turn operated their machinery. Their water courses and wheelpits were cut through solid rock and they were unlined, allowing water under pressure to penetrate the surrounding rock.

When the first unit of the Schoellkopf Power Plant was constructed in 1897, the penstocks were enclosed in a rough masonry wall, which can be seen today. The second plant was constructed as soon as number one was completed and its penstocks were also encased in a masonry wall. The third and fourth plants were built between 1913 and 1925 adjoining the other plants, and below the former mill sites,

without the precaution of shoring up the gorge wall. This was to be a costly error, for when this section's penstocks, which carried the water to the generators, began to leak, the water penetrated the already honeycombed gorge wall. This built up hydrostatic pressure, which resulted in progressively more and more leakage within the power plant. Then, on June 7, 1956, 30 years after the last section of the plant was completed, the weakened gorge wall gave way and demolished that half of the power plant.

L.S. Bernstein, Senior Engineer of the Schoellkopf Power Company, was present during the events of June 7, 1956 and he wrote a graphic account of the progressive deterioration of the situation: "On June 7, at about 9:30 a.m. a large leak was reported by the Station Operators, which was located south of the Power Station... I arrived at 11:20 a.m. and observed that the leak came from the cliff near the top of the talus about 61 metres (200 feet) south of the Power Station... The stream was about 2.4 metres (8 feet) wide and about 15 centimetres (6 inches) deep and its velocity was about 1.8 metres (6 feet) per second".

Mr. Bernstein then proceeded to make an inspection of the inside of the Power Plant, where: "cliff seepage from the wall has always existed and was

The Mill District along the gorge bank in Niagara Falls, New York, circa 1886. After falling down shafts cut through the rock of the gorge wall, the water is pouring out of the wheel pits of numerous mills built along the gorge. The shafts and pits were not lined and so water seeped into the surrounding layers of rock. This began the honeycombing process which resulted in the collapse of the gorge wall on the Schoellkopf Power Plant in 1956. This picture was taken from the deck of the third ''Maid of the Mist'', launched in 1885.

drained through floor drains''. The wall to which he referred was constructed across the wheelpit of one of the old flour mills and as he watched, the seepage became a stream and the stream gradually became larger. As the afternoon wore on, a slight bulging of the Power House floor was noticed in one location. Then at about 5:15 p.m. he was advised that the glass in some windows was cracking in the Station House. He, along with men by the name of Draper and Chapman, went outside to the south side of the building, to the foot of the talus.

Mr. Bernstein reports: "I then observed a large leak of muddy water in the cliff near the top of the talus, about 30 feet (9 metres) south of the Power House. We climbed up the talus towards the leak. I then observed that the leak had cut out a trench about 8 feet (2.4 metres) wide and about 4 feet (1.2 metres) deep at the top of the talus, and that it was flowing with high velocity out of the rock seam near the top of the talus.

"By the time we descended down the talus, the stream from the junction of the original leak, with the new leak, was now about 25 feet (7.6 metres) wide by about 8 feet (2.4 metres) deep and flowed at a rate of about 8 feet (2.4 metres) a second.

"We then started toward the Power Station. By the time we reached the middle of the stream about 40 feet (12 metres) south of the Station House and about 5 feet (1.5 metres) west of the west wall, pieces of stone from the south wall of the Power House began to break out and fly out. This prevented us from entering the Station. The south-west corner of the stone wall fell toward the river.

"In a short space of time the south wall collapsed and fell to the south. The flow in the stream in which we were standing immediately increased to a depth of about 2 feet (0.6 metres). I could not observe where this additional flow came from. Draper and I were washed toward the river at the same time. I was able to cross the stream to the south. Chapman was to the south of us and had no trouble. Draper was about 6 feet (1.8 metres) west and a few feet (0.06 metres) north of me. He was washed into the river.

"I then observed several rocks in varying size from about 4 inches (10 centimetres) to possibly 12 inches (30 centimetres) in size, falling from the cliff in the region of the north end of the Power Station (Station Number 3). A portion of the cliff about 60 feet (18 metres) long, extending from the leak 30 feet (9 metres) south of the Station to about 30 feet (9

The Mill District, Niagara Falls, New York, circa 1897. The industries obtaining water-power here included three flour mills, three pulp mills, and a silverplating works. No. 1 is the Pittsburgh Reduction Company, later the Aluminum Company of America, which chose this location to be close to the source of electric power; No. 2, Joseph Schoellkopf's Niagara Falls Hydraulic Power and Manufacturing plant, with an addition under construction. The black steel penstocks visible on the gorge bank, are being encased in a rough masonry wall; No. 3, the Cliff Paper

Company, formerly Quigley's Mill, is where, in 1881, hydraulic electric power was first generated at Niagara Falls. Here water-wheels operated under a head of 26 metres (85 feet). These water-wheels ran the machinery of the paper mill, several other small industries and an arclight machine owned by the Brush Electric Light & Power Company, which supplied electric power for lighting to adjoining mills and several businesses in the Village of Niagara Falls, New York.

metres) north of the south wall of the Power Station collapsed.

"As Chapman and I retreated south along the bank of the river, a series of rockslides took place, extending progressively from south to north. In each case it started with small pieces of rock falling from the face of the cliff. Then a portion of the cliff collapsed. Each slide appeared to have a length of 60 feet (18 metres). The rock slides terminated at the south crane pit wall".

As a result of the collapse, Plants Numbers 1 and 2 were buried in the rubble; Plant Number 3 was damaged beyond repair, and Plant Number 4 was salvageable. This section was reactivated and resumed production, with a capacity of 95,000 kw,

a decrease from 385,000 kw when all four sections were in operation before the collapse. On September 30, 1961, when the new Robert Moses Generating Station was capable of utilizing all of the water allotted to the United States under the 1950 Treaty, Plant Number 4 was retired from operation, and was subsequently razed.

The Schoellkopf Geology Museum is now located on the Schoellkopf Power Company's former property at the top of the gorge. It is an educational facility with geological displays and films, and a staff of naturalists who conduct nature walks along the American side of the gorge. This Museum is under the jurisdiction of the New York State Department of Parks and Recreation.

The Schoellkopf Power Plant when using the full head of 64 metres (210 feet) available, had a capacity of 425,000 hp. The section on the far left, Plant No. 1, was built in 1895-96; No. 2, next to it, was built in 1896-99. The penstocks of these two sections were encased in a rough cast masonry wall at the back of the plant, which also served to support the gorge wall. Plant No. 3 was built in 1913, and Plant No. 4, at the far right, was completed in 1925. The gorge wall above the last two sections was not supported by masonry. While the most modern technology was used in generating equipment, the tunnels which supplied this plant with water were cut through the rock and left unlined. Consequently the water flowing through the tunnels forced itself into the crevices in the surrounding rock, weakening it. The gorge wall, which was already honeycombed with the tailraces of the old water-powered mills of the Mill District, weakened and collapsed on the power plant in 1956, when a major leak developed between the tunnels and the entrance to the power house.

The destruction of the south end of Plant No. 4, at 5:15 p.m., June 7, 1956. A part of the gorge wall has collapsed on the plant. The small leak of water, which began at the back of the power plant, grew larger throughout the day, and by 5:00 p.m. became a raging torrent.

Schoellkopf Geology Museum

The torrent of water has eroded the gorge wall at the rear of the plant, and a section of the gorge wall is falling towards the centre of the building. The section of the gorge to the right is also beginning to fall; notice the dust just above the roof level. The generators in the old plant, left of the photo, are running wild and shorting. Notice the arcing showing through the windows and the wisp of smoke just above them.

The aftermath, with Plants No. 3 and No. 4 completely destroyed and Plant No. 2 badly damaged. June 7, 1956.

Niagara Falls Ontario Public Library

Schoellkopf Geology Museum

Looking down on the devastated power plant, June 7, 1956.

Over thirty years later, October 1987. More of the gorge wall has collapsed on the ruins of the power plant. Nature is trying to cover the remains with foliage.

George A. Seibel

Dewatering of the American Falls

In 1965, Mayor E. Dent Lackey of Niagara Falls, New York, and the *Niagara Falls Gazette* launched a campaign to win state and federal support for a program to remove the "unsightly" rock debris at the base of the American Falls. Erosion at the top of the Falls had caused the pile up of talus that had crept halfway up to the lip of the 55 metre (185 foot) cataract. The Niagara Falls, New York, City Council asked for "remedial action to prevent further erosion and rock slides which were endangering tourists and sending them to Canada to view the already stabilized Horseshoe Falls."

Preliminary studies by the United States Army Corps of Engineers were carried out and the International Joint Commission was asked to approve an inspection project which would require the dewatering of the American Falls. Canadian agreement was forthcoming in March, 1969. The New York State Power Authority and Ontario Hydro agreed to contribute $385,000 towards the $445,412 estimated cost of the inspection project. These funds were to be raised from sale of the additional power generated. All of the water that previously went over the American Falls was to be diverted to the Horseshoe Falls channel and used for increased power generation.

A coffer dam, constructed of rock and fill, was built, extending from the mainland to the head of Goat Island. When the dam was completed on June 12, 1969, the water leading to the American Falls was cut off and diverted to the Horseshoe Falls channel. The huge mound of talus piled up at the base of the Falls astounded engineers and visitors alike.

While the flow of the river was cut off, pipes were laid down the river bed to the precipice, providing a continuous spray of water on the face of the Falls to prevent the rock from deteriorating and crumbling. Shortly after the dewatering, the river bed was cleaned by air-water jetting, and sandblasting where needed, for a distance of some 122 metres (400 feet) upstream from the crest of the Falls. Rock joints and fractures were mapped. Instruments called piezometers were placed in holes which had been bored upstream from the crest of the Falls, to measure water pressure in the rock joints. Rock samples taken from the bored holes were sent to the United States Army Corps of Engineers laboratories for testing.

Work began on November 25, on the removal of the coffer dam. At 10 a.m. that morning the first flow started over the Falls and by midnight on November 26, 1969, the Falls was in full flow again.

The studies and deliberations as to what forms any proposed remedial work would take lasted until 1974.

During 1973 the International Joint Commission – created by the Niagara Diversion Treaty of 1950 to act as trustees to preserve and enhance the beauty of the Falls and the River – issued a booklet summarizing a number of physical changes that might enhance the beauty of the American Falls. A coupon-ballot was enclosed with every booklet, giving interested readers an opportunity to vote on the options, one of which was to make no physical changes in the American Falls' appearance. The public was invited to: "Join us in making the best decision for the American Falls and for our future generations".

On October 1, 1974, seven years of study and deliberation came to an end when the American Falls International Board reported. This Board was appointed by the International Joint Commission and included an engineer representative and a landscape architect from each country. They said that: "... the 214,200 m³ (280,000 cubic yards) of talus at the base of the American Falls were a dynamic part of the natural condition of the Falls and the process of erosion and recession should not be interrupted". They felt that it was "wrong to make the Falls static and unnatural, like an artificial waterfall in a garden or a park, however grand the scale". The growing environmental movements of the late 1960's and 1970's influenced this decision, to allow nature to take its course.

The dried-off American Falls, showing the ragged contour of its crest. The pipeline, which provided a continuous spray of water on the face of the Falls, is seen just back of the crest. The talus at the base, 214,200 m³ (280,000 cubic yards), reaches more than halfway up the face of the Falls. It was thought that when the dewatering was reported in newspapers across the United States, tourists would come to Niagara Falls in increased numbers to see the dried-off Falls. What really happened was that many who were planning to come that year (1969), postponed their trip, because they thought that both Falls were dry. The result was a below average tourist season.

New York Power Authority

The dewatered cascades above the American Falls,
July 1969, showing the ridges of rock which form the
sides of the ancient Falls-Chippawa, or St. Davids
River.

Herbert C. Force

This profile of an Indian head was revealed silhouet-
ted against the illuminated American Falls, on June
11, 1969. The profile was discovered when the
dewatering of the Falls began. It remained in view for
167 days, until the U.S. Corps of Engineers removed
the coffer dam and allowed water to flow once again
over the American Falls.

New York Power Authority

This air view of the Horseshoe Falls and the
dewatered American Falls, taken in August, 1969,
shows: No. 1, Goat Island; No. 2, upper cascades
above the Horseshoe Falls; No. 3, Terrapin Point;
No. 4, Prospect Point; No. 5, New York State Park
Observation Tower; No. 6, Maid of the Mist Canadian
landing; No. 7, Table Rock viewing area in Canada.

Helga Studio

Niagara Falls, an oil painting by John P. Beaumont,
circa 1820, shows the American and Horseshoe Falls
in misty perspective. This sylvan scene is just north of
Prospect Point, giving us a view of the wild, natural
state of the area around the Falls before the advent of
European settlement.

178

Whirlpool Reversal Phenomenon

In March 1965, Robert B. MacMullin of Lewiston, N.Y. was showing the sights around Niagara Falls to Mr. Tashiro, a visiting Japanese friend. Mr. MacMullin, without looking at the water, was giving his usual discourse on the geology of the Whirlpool. He told how the current circulates in a counter-clockwise rotation, how the river loops-the-loop. "Mac San", said Mr. Tashiro who was looking at the water, "Please explain counter-clockwise". Mr. MacMullin explained and Mr. Tashiro immediately remarked "Honourable river going wrong way"!

Three years after the latest diversion of water for electric power generation in 1962, a diversion which was the contributing cause of this reversal phenomenon, it was a Japanese visitor who first recognized and commented on the change in direction! The Whirlpool had been flowing in a counter-clockwise rotation for almost 4700 years, until 1962, when the water level of the river was lowered by the diversion for the Robert Moses Generating Station.

During normal flow the rush of water enters the pool and is carried past the river outlet on the right. It then circulates in a counter-clockwise direction, from 6 o'clock, past 12 to 9 o'clock, then it dives under the incoming stream and emerges at the outlet in dark, boiling, slugs of water and then flows downriver.

At times of low water when the Niagara River flow goes below 17,500 m³/sec (62,000 cfs), the direction of flow in the Whirlpool becomes clockwise. This usually occurs each winter between November first and April first when there is an increase in the amount of water diverted through the tunnels above the Falls, for electric power generation. The water coming into the Whirlpool is directed to the Canadian side, influenced by the sandstone ridge which lies under the entrance. At these times it shows a clockwise rotation.

Diagram of normal Whirlpool rotation.

Erna Jahnke

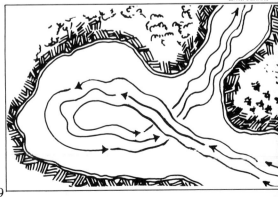

The Whirlpool, June 6, 1968 with slightly more than 2832 m³/sec (100,000 cfs) flowing in a counter-clockwise rotation. Note the shrunken shoreline and the narrow throat at the inlet to the Whirlpool.

This photo from the American Falls International Board Report, December, 1971, shows the Whirlpool on December 18, 1964 with 1444 m³/sec (51,000 cfs) flowing in a clockwise rotation. This represents minimum flow and water level under the 1950 joint treaty between Canada and the United States, which guarantees 1416 m³/sec (50,000 cfs) in the non-tourist season, or during non-viewing hours in the tourist season.

Terrapin Point

Terrapin Point, the rock projection on the American flank of the Horseshoe Falls, was almost as famous as Table Rock on the Canadian side, as a viewing point for the Horseshoe Falls. It was named Terrapin because the exposed rocks in the river there were rounded, resembling half-submerged tortoises.

Erosion in the area of Terrapin Point was not as dramatic as that at Table Rock. As more and more water flowed toward and over the centre of the Horseshoe Falls, there was less flowing over the American flank of the Horseshoe, where the Point was situated. In 1969 cracks were first noticed in the pavement at the viewing area at Terrapin Point. On September 9, 1972, the U.S. Army Corps of Engineers closed the Point to sightseers and installed seismic sensors to monitor changes in water pressure in the rock.

From that time on, any movement recorded by the sensors was reported to the newspapers. Seven years later, in 1979, after one such report, the Point came into national prominence, when a self-proclaimed psychic predicted its collapse. The collapse was to be on Sunday afternoon, July 22, 1979, at 4:56 p.m. Terrapin Point would collapse into the gorge. The onrush of water that would result when the rock fell into the river, would capsize a nearby "Maid of the Mist" boat, which would be carrying a group of deaf children. The prediction gained some credibility when, just a few days before the predicted rockfall, the seismic sensors set off an alarm, warning of rock movement on Terrapin Point.

On the day of the predicted fall, the banks on both sides of the river were lined with sightseers, gathered to see whether the Point would collapse as predicted. Just before the announced time, one "Maid of the Mist" left the American dock with dignitaries and officials from both the Canadian and the American sides of the border. The boat arrived opposite the Point precisely at the appointed time, and stayed for a time in the "shoe" of the Horseshoe near the Point, as is usual on such boat trips. Nothing happened as the appointed time, 4:56 p.m., passed and the vast crowds of people, disappointed not to have witnessed a tragedy, began to leave for home. As they tried to leave the Parks, and cross the bridges for home, all at the same time, they created one of the worst traffic jams ever experienced in the cities of Niagara Falls on both sides of the border!

In the meantime the Point was still closed off to sightseers. In 1983, after much investigation, it was decided that Terrapin Point would be blasted off. A fifteen week project carried out by Acres International, under the direction of the U.S. Army

Corps of Engineers, prepared the way for the blasting off, which occurred on July 8, at 12:19 p.m. There was no "onrush of water" because the 25,046 tonnes (25,000 tons) of rock fell on the accumulated talus below. Only a few small pieces of rock reached the water.

In 1833, the Porters built a sturdy, stone tower just back from the brink of the Horseshoe Falls, on Terrapin Point. The walkway to the brink was still in use, but the 3 metre (10 foot) overhanging viewpoint was eliminated. The rounded tortoise-like rocks in the water, which gave the point its name, are shown in this oil on canvas by G. Lotti, circa 1840.

This view of Terrapin Point is from a water colour painted in 1832 by Lieutenant-Colonel J.P. Cockburn, a British military officer. The sketch from which it was painted was done in 1828, the year following the construction of a sightseeing walkway over the shallow water at Terrapin Point to the crest of the Horseshoe Falls. The walkway was 61 metres (200 feet) long and extended 3 metres (10 feet) into space over the brink of the Horseshoe Falls. Judge Porter, who owned Goat Island, "had the bridge built to give sightseers an American attraction equal to Canadian Table Rock" (Theodora Vinal, 1948). The original water colour of 1832 is hanging in Oak Hall, The Niagara Parks Administration Headquarters.

This is a stereo view of Terrapin Tower, circa early 1860's by George Barker. William H.G. Kingston is quoted in Dr. H.G. Dow, vol. 1, p. 1085: "Descending a winding path, we reached the south end of the Horseshoe Falls, where a wooden bridge, some forty yards (22 metres) long, or more, resting on a succession of small rocks parallel with the very brink of the Fall but three or four feet (0.90 to 1.2 metres) from it carried us to the foot of a little tower, whence we ascended a spiral stair to a platform at its summit, surrounded by a light iron railing, literally overhanging the great cataract itself. Here the sight is grand and awe-inspiring". The buildings visible are across the River, on the Canadian side. Thomas Barnett's new Museum, built in 1859-60, is at the far right. Next to the Museum is the Museum Hotel, then the Prospect House, built in 1844. The building just to the right of Terrapin Tower contains a Camera Obscura. The arrow to the left of the tower points to the location of Table Rock.

On July 8, 1983, at 12:19 p.m., in a cloud of smoke and rock dust, followed a few micro-seconds later by a thundering boom, Terrapin Point collapsed and crashed into the gorge below. The detonation of 3629 kilograms (8,000 pounds) of dynamite separated the 25410 tonnes (25,000 tons) of unstable rock from the main cliff. The thousands of seagulls who make this area of the Niagara Gorge their home were seen flying in all directions, in a state of confusion because of the noise.

Terrapin Point's new look as seen from the deck of the "Maid of the Mist". The Point is now a jumble of smaller rocks on the talus slope. Care was taken when the explosion was set off to have the rocks fall directly onto the talus below, and not into Canadian territory as the International Boundary crosses the talus in this area. The large slabs of rock in the foreground are from rockfalls which occurred in 1885.

Niagara Falls New York Public Library

The Land Our Servant

This 1895 charcoal drawing portrays one of the Scottish stone masons with a 6 to 7 tonne (6 to 7 ton) block of limestone which he has selected from the quarry blocks at Queenston Quarry. He is taking it to his working area where he will fashion it into building stones.

The Duke de la Rochefoucault Liancourt visited the Falls of Niagara in 1799 and wrote in his Travels through the United States of North America… and Upper Canada in the years 1795, 1796, and 1797: "… an iron mine, too, has lately been discovered near Chippeway Creek. A company has associated for the working of this mine and resolved on erecting an iron-forge in the vicinity of the falls". The man who intended to establish an iron works near the Falls of Niagara was Robert Randall, a native of Maryland, who emigrated to Upper Canada about 1799. When he couldn't obtain permission to erect new mills, he made a working agreement with Phelps and Ramsay, who owned the Bridgewater Mills at present day Dufferin Islands.

Randall added an iron works with clay furnaces, to the saw and grist mills. Randall obtained his "iron" ore from the source about which Liancourt wrote, the marshy banks of the Welland River (Chippawa Creek). It was actually "limonite", a mineral described as "hydrated oxide of iron". Using this material he made what he claimed to be the first iron bars and the first wrought iron products in Canada.

Natural Gas

It is in this same Bridgewater Mills area, at present day Dufferin Islands, that a natural gas spring was discovered during the excavation for the foundation of one of the mills. The natural gas which bubbled up through the water at Bridgewater Mills was not used for heating or lighting, but it became Niagara's first tourist attraction.

An early entrepreneur built a shelter over it. He then enclosed the spring by putting a barrel over it, with a pipe protruding from the top. When a cork stopper was placed in the pipe, it allowed the gas to build up pressure in the barrel. When an audience had been assembled, the cork was removed, the gas was lit, and a "Burning Spring" resulted. This natural gas spring was exhausted during the early 1880's just prior to the expropriation of the property around the islands by the Queen Victoria Niagara Falls Park Commission.

The gas came from the layer of Red Medina Shale, also known as Queenston Shale, which is exposed along the lower Niagara River. It is about 183 metres (600 feet) below the surface of the ground a little south of Chippawa, and even deeper towards Lake Erie. Natural gas is one of a group of hydrocarbons produced from rotting vegetable and animal matter which has encountered high pressure, and possibly great heat, in some earlier formative period of the earth when Nature's processes were, perhaps more quick than they are today.

There were many other such natural gas springs bubbling up along the river shore, for many years after settlement began. It was not long before the early settlers found that, by drilling they could tap the reserves of natural gas which lay underground all through the townships above the escarpment in the Niagara District. It was a common sight well into the 1940's for travellers along the roads in Willoughby, Crowland, and Bertie Townships, to see stand pipes protruding above ground level, with a pipe laid along the top of the ground, leading to the farm house, or to a storage tank. The stand pipes were the tops of natural gas wells, which reached hundreds of feet below ground. They were convenient for the lucky farmers who had them, for they didn't have to chop wood for winter heating or cooking.

The Burning Spring from a guide book of the 1860's.
Carol Breton

This gas, as is also true of petroleum and asphalt, is usually found under some dome of impervious rock that is, on a grand scale, usually within an upward slope of rock. Such slopes are characteristic of our Niagara District, and were formed during the Silurian Period, over 400 million years ago. The dome of impervious rock in this district is in the deep layer of Clinton Shale and Limestone capping, along the Medina Red Shale (Queenston Shale) which underlies Lake Ontario to a depth of more than 396 metres (300 feet). Sometimes, while in the early stages of drilling a well, a supply of sulphur gas is struck not far down. This has an unpleasant sulphurous odour. Usually the order of substance produced by drilling is as follows: water, sulphur or mineral water, sulphur gas, a minor flow of natural gas, and then, finally, the expected flow of high pressure natural gas.

In th Niagara District, the deepest gas well, according to my information (1938) is on the Morningstar farm, not far from the Sauer farm, about 8 kilometres (5 miles) along the Sodom Road south of Chippawa. Here 51 years ago (1887), a well was put through to 960 metres (3,150 feet) and has been producing since that time. Wells drilled through to the top layer of Red Medina Shale, about 183 metres (600 feet) down, have been known to produce 49.6 cubic metres (1,750 cubic feet) of gas a day, while those drilled further into the Red Medina Shale produced 396.4 cubic metres (14,000 cubic feet) per day.

N.B. The Provincial Natural Gas Company supplied natural gas to domestic and commercial customers from wells drilled in the Bertie Township area near Sherkston, and other wells in Crowland, until Alberta gas was brought into the area by pipeline in the mid 1950's. These wells were almost depleted when Alberta gas arrived. For a number of years during the late 1940's and early 1950's the company augmented its supply of natural gas with manufactured gas, purchased from the Iroquois Gas Company in Buffalo, New York.

The Consumers Gas Company, successor to the Provincial Natural Gas Company, through a subsidiary company, Underwater Gas Developers, carries on a continuing program of drilling for gas. The drillers are looking for new supplies of natural gas along and in Lake Erie, and for new storage space, in the domes of the Silurian reef, where Alberta gas can be stored, ready for periods of high demand.

There are hundreds of private gas wells still providing natural gas to farms and homes in our district, and all along the north shore of Lake Erie. The standpipes are set close to the ground and are unobtrusive. This gas comes with a natural sulphurous odour, whereas the Alberta gas has no discernible odour and a "stinker", a few drops per hundreds of thousands of cubic metres (millions of cubic feet), has to be added at one of the district pumping stations before the gas is distributed to homes, business and industry throughout our district. Possible gas leaks can then be detected by smell.

The river channel at the entrance to the Dufferin Islands embayment. The two bridges are the pedestrian bridge, Castor, and the Niagara Park and River Railway Bridge. The building between the bridges housed the Burning Spring, until 1885, when the Queen Victoria Niagara Falls Park Commission

expropriated the property. A private company erected a new Burning Spring building, on the top of the bank, at the right, and had gas piped in. The former Burning Spring, located at the river level, was a gas spring emanating from the rock below.

Stone Quarrying

The early settlers quarried limestone from at least three known locations in present day Niagara Falls: the Thompson quarry at Thompson Point, opposite present day Niagara Parks Whirlpool Golf Course Club House; the Bender quarry at the foot of Bender Hill, where the Niagara Falls Museum is now located; the McMicking quarry, a rectangular excavation which is now a pond, visible from the Niagara Parkway north of the Glen.

The largest quarrying operation was carried on by John Thompson at Thompson Point, where he cut into the exposed rock face adjacent to the edge of the gorge, to quarry limestone. He built two lime kilns in which he burned the limestone, to produce agricultural lime. He bartered his agricultural lime with merchants in the area, for food, clothing and other household necessities. As well, he had a thriving business selling this product to merchants in York (now Toronto) and Kingston.

The Bender quarry appears in the foreground in stereo views of the Upper Suspension Bridge. There were many stone masons among the early settlers and the stone quarried here was used for foundations and walls of houses.

The McMicking quarry, now filled with water, is at the 14th hole of the Whirlpool Golf Course. It is about 3 metres (10 feet) deep in the centre, with a layer of silt at least 1.5 metres (5 feet) deep at the bottom. Because Thomas McMicking was a stone mason, the stone quarried from this excavation was probably used for building stone. The Niagara Parks Commission is presently arranging to make it a storage pond for the irrigation system which waters

In 1806 John Thompson built this stone barn, using limestone from his quarry. The slits in the walls are for ventilation. The barn, located near what is now the 13th fairway of the Whirlpool Golf Course, was torn down during the construction of the Queenston-Chippawa Power Canal in the early 1920's.

the golf course. For years it has been a watery grave for errant golf balls.

When settlers arrived in this area, they built their first houses of logs. Then as soon as they were able, many of them had stone houses built. John Thompson, of Whirlpool Farm, had a stone house built in 1802 and a stone barn in 1806, using stone from his own quarry. The farm occupied much of the land on which the Whirlpool Golf Course is now laid out, and there are remains of stone foundations to be seen today in the left rough of the 13th fairway. In 1825, Old St. John's Anglican Church on the Portage Road was built of slabs of limestone, rough laid and covered with stucco. Some stone houses from this era are still standing today. The home of John Thompson's son is on the Portage Road just north of Valley Way, the Samuel Pew house is on Portage Road South, and there is a stone house of this era at Cloverhill Farm on the Mountain Road.

These three early quarries were very modest operations compared with some of those which began later. Queenston Quarries, established in 1837, and Walker Brokers Quarries, established in 1887, are still in existence today.

Queenston Quarry

I am sure that many readers have wondered from what far-away place came the attractive grey building stone used in Niagara's new gem, Oakes Garden Theatre. With quite a self satisfied air, we show some renewed faith in our district, when we learn that this stone, called Lockport Dolomite, came from the Queenston Quarry, about 11.3 kilometres (seven miles) away. It is often asked to take longer journeys, though – Oak Hall, Harry Oakes mansion; the Hamilton Post Office; and Canada House, in Hyde Park, London, England – all are of this same material.

This Lockport Dolomite rock is so named because it occurs prominently along the course of the Erie Canal at Lockport, New York. At Queenston Quarry there is a unique deposit, 3.7 metres (12 feet) thick, within the Lockport Dolomite stratum. It is the Gasport layer, Crinoidal Calcite Dolomite, which is quarried to provide the special blue dolomite which is sought after for prestigious stone buildings.

The Court House, Niagara-on-the-Lake, Ontario (1837) is constructed of Queenston Limestone, as was Brock's Monument of 1840 and the present monument of 1856; the culverts, tunnels and bridges of the Great Western and Grand Trunk Railways are of Queenston Limestone; as are the gate entrances

This romantic sketch of Queenston Quarry during Wm. H. Hendershot's tenure, appeared in Page's Atlas of Lincoln and Welland County, published in 1876. It was a very busy operation. The Hendershot Company was one of ten which together employed as many as 600 men at one time. The Great Western Railway spur line is shown, with a train standing by, while large blocks of stone are loaded onto the flat

cars by the guy derrick, at the top right. Various quarrying operations are shown, including several that involved hand chipping the stone. The horse and carriage and dozens of blocks of stone, as well as other features, are drawn out of proportion to the artist's depiction of the quarry face in the centre of the picture, to the left of the railway track.

Page's Atlas

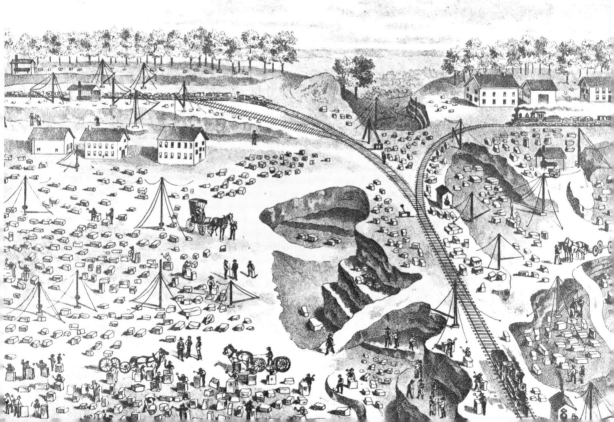

Queenston Quarries

This 1970's air view of Queenston Quarry shows the 101 hectares (100 acres) of the quarry property and the surrounding countryside. No. 1, the location of the very old quarry workings where stone was cut from the face of the escarpment and tumbled down the bank to the lower level, where it was cut into smaller building stone; No. 2, the underground mines where the 1.8 metre (6 foot) layer of Decew dolomite was mined, to be processed into hydraulic cement; No. 3, the four brick-lined kilns where the limestone was burned and processed by the Usher family of St. Davids, from 1885 to 1905, to produce rock cement; No. 4, where quarrying began about 1837; No. 5, location of the "Settlement" of fourteen workers' houses and the company general store which was open from 1928 to 1938; Nos. 6, 7, 8, the areas where building stone was quarried until late 1979; No. 9, the Bruce Trail which runs along the escarpment and winds through quarry property; No. 10, former Braas Brothers sand-pit, part of the Barre Moraine; No. 11, St. Davids (Ravine Hill) sand-pit, at the end of the Whirlpool-St. Davids Buried Gorge; No. 12, the indentation in the escarpment marking the eastern edge of the Whirlpool-St. Davids Buried Gorge; No. 13, St. Davids, one of the earliest settlements in the area; No. 14, York Road, formerly Kings Highway No. 8A, running along the ridge of glacial Lake Iroquois beach; No. 15, Kings Highway No. 406, joining the Queen Elizabeth Way on the west, and the Lewiston-Queenston Bridge (out of the picture at the right); No. 16, Ontario Hydro Pump Storage Reservoir.

and fence at the Governor-General's residence in Ottawa (1878). Stone was supplied for the East Block of the Parliament Buildings, Ottawa; Table Rock House and the Administration Building, Queen Victoria Park; Post Office and adjoining Royal Bank building, Queen Street, Niagara Falls, Ontario; buildings at McMaster University, Hamilton and Queen's University, Kingston, Ontario.

The most attractive feature of this stone is that it tends to become whiter as it weathers. Indiana Limestone, a competitive stone mined in Indiana, was used by the builders of the Toronto Power Generating Station in Queen Victoria Park, Niagara Falls. It is not as hard as the local product; moreover, it tends to weather darker with time, and it is subject to a peculiar surface softening. This is caused by the usual weathering agencies, as well as by sulphuric acid diluted in the atmospheric moisture from coal burning fires, and in more modern days, from automobile exhaust, and chemical factory smoke – in short, acid rain. This darkening can be seen in the stonework of the Toronto Power Generating Station.

Building stone quarried at Queenston Quarry is selected for even texture by the quarry foreman. Even so, these blocks may contain "goodes", which do not materially affect the strength of any blocks used in building, but which detract from the beauty and symmetry of the stone face of the block. Goodes are small pockets composed of pure, pink dolomite found in the limestone. Only the smooth goode-free blocks are used for building stone; the others are broken up, or used as barriers along lake shores and river banks to prevent erosion. Most limestones are more or less pure forms of calcium carbonate. A dolomite is the same sort of limestone, changed into a more marble-like rock by the magnesium salts in the salt water seas, of which it was once the sea bottom; or else by magnesium vapours given off by the lower rock beds; or, more likely, by decomposing organisms in its own structure, as the limestone slowly hardens and crystallizes over millions of years. It is perhaps significant that in dolomite beds, fossils are comparatively rare. It is likely that their constituent chemicals were used up in dolomitizing of the limestone deposit. Corals are fairly abundant however, but as is well known, these are really rock themselves.

This 1938 photograph shows quarrymen pounding steel wedges, called pegs and feathers, into holes that have been partially bored into the huge blocks of Lockport Dolomite, to split them into the required block size. A drill operated by compressed air is in the left foreground.

A.H. Tiplin

Blocks of limestone from the Gasport formation in Queenston Quarry, awaiting shipment to stone fabricators, who fashioned the stone into building blocks.

The quarry has been in continuous operation for almost 150 years, making it one of the oldest quarrying operations in Canada. The operation was begun by John Brown, a Scottish stone-cutter and masonry contractor, who emigrated to the Niagara frontier on the U.S. side in the 1830's. In 1838 he emigrated to Upper Canada, where he began quarrying building stone at the present Queenston Quarry site, and incorporating it into the many building projects of which he was the masonry contractor. These projects included the locks of the Second Welland Canal, built 1841-42; the stone towers and retaining walls of the Railway Suspension Bridge – the retaining walls are still standing today at the foot of Bridge Street in Niagara Falls, Ontario, opposite the entrance to the Whirlpool Rapids Bridge; the stone towers of the Lewiston-Queenston Suspension Bridge – they are still in existence today, on the U.S. side, at New York State Artpark, where they support the elevated viewing platform which overhangs the Niagara River at this point.

Queenston Quarry, where this superb Lockport Limestone building stone was quarried, is located on the Niagara Escarpment, adjoining Queenston Heights Park and 3.2 kilometres (2 miles) west of Brock's Monument. From the beginning the quarry has operated as a building stone quarry. The quarry was "high-graded", that is mined selectively for the best stone – in this case, the Gasport layer.

Queenston Quarry building stone was quarried in large blocks and shipped to independent cut stone fabricators in Ontario, Quebec and the Maritimes. Sawn slabs were also supplied to fabricators. In late 1978 the supply of building stone from the Gasport layer dwindled to the point where further quarrying of this stone was uneconomical. From then on, the quarrying operations concentrated on producing crushed stone aggregate for construction and road building. Current production is 344,400 tonnes (350,000 tons) annually. Quarry reserves at the present rate of production (1987) are estimated to be sufficient for 25 years.

From 1871 to 1878 some ten companies, employing up to 600 men at one time operated independently in the quarry, on a royalty basis. In 1876, William Hendershot of Thorold was the major operator. After 1878 Johnson and Murray operated the quarry. When Mr. Murray died, P.A. Johnson and Company carried on until 1897 when a joint stock company was formed. From 1905 until 1924, the Lowreys of St. Davids operated the quarry, during which time the stone crusher was rebuilt twice and power-driven saws for cutting stone replaced hand-operated stone cutting saws. In the spring of 1925, the Canada Crushed Stone Company Limited of Hamilton, purchased the operation, named it Queenston Quarries, and carried on the operation until Steetley Industries Limited, from England, purchased the facilities in 1952. Steetley Industries Limited are the current owners and operators.

Rehabilitation of the quarry property is an ongoing program, while quarrying operations for aggregate are still being carried on. In 1982, Queenston Quarries received the Annual Design Award of the Ontario Association of Landscape Architects, for their final site rehabilitation plan. The original 101 hectares (250 acres) of quarry property was reduced in size in 1987 when 40.15 hectares (100 acres) of land bordering the Niagara Escarpment were transferred, through the Ontario Heritage Foundation, to the Niagara Parks Commission. In February, 1988, the Ontario Heritage Foundation recognized Steetley Industries Limited as a "Friend of the Escarpment", for this significant contribution to the protection of the Niagara Escarpment.

This photograph, circa 1938, shows work in progress on the stone wall, composed of Queenston Limestone, hand cut on the site, at Niagara Glen. This work was done during the Depression of the 1930's when skilled masons were paid 60 cents an hour.

A.H. Tiplin

This serpent-like cavity was discovered when a slab of limestone was cut with a saw. It is a solution channel where a mixture of minerals, including salt, once flowed, dissolving the limestone. If the source of the solution had not dried up, and the flow had persisted, the channel would have enlarged until it formed an underground cave.

An interior view of Milk Cave on the U.S. side, showing the erosive power of water running underground through fractures in the Lockport Limestone. Milk Cave was described in an 1857 guidebook to Niagara Falls as "an opening 20 feet (6 metres) high, 40 feet (12 metres) wide, and having a stream running from it. When it rains, the stream is kind of foamy. The cave is also known as Buttermilk Cave" (Ensminger 1987).

New York Power Authority

A.H. Tiplin

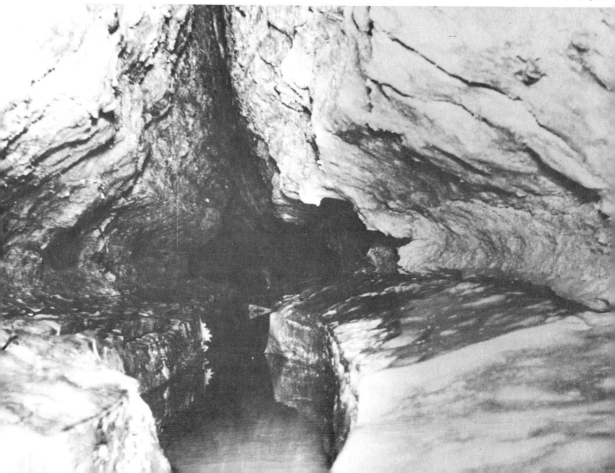

Old Cement Quarry

A few weeks ago, while getting samples of rock-wool shale for my classes at Stamford (1938), I ran across an inviting opening in the Lockport rock layer on the brow of the escarpment at Queenston Quarries. As soon as good photograph-taking weather allowed, I returned with a small party of students. We wore old clothes, had a flashlight each, about three cameras among us, and a supply of flash bulbs.

We found that the main portal (one of four) which is pictured here, allowed entry into a pool of water. A smaller opening next to it which gave enough clearance for our bodies, led to a shelving of rock and a pile of what seemed at the time to be like crushed stone for road-surfacing. We followed this pile, which was long and narrow. It led in about 30 metres (100 feet) and formed an isthmus in the water. We soon realized that this flat-roofed cave, with its many dark, water-filled passages, around large supporting pillars, was not natural.

Protruding from the water, just out of reach, and seemingly in 1.2 to 1.5 metres (4 or 5 feet) of water, but actually only about 45.7 centimetres (18 inches) there was a stout post of wood jammed against the roof as a too-slender support. From this isthmus of small rocks, the cave seemed never ending and just as mysterious as the large caverns found elsewhere, where one may swim in underground lakes and become lost for days, or for an eternity. Actually the extent of the underground quarry area is about 0.40 hectares (one acre).

After some scouting around, we found another entrance under a ledge of rock about 45 centimetres (18 inches) from a fairly dry mud floor. This was well hidden in a gully without a valley, which I consider I was either lucky, or stubborn enough, to explore thoroughly and so find the opening. The mud floor was fairly dry until one got in about 6 metres (20 feet). Then, slowly, the distance between one's back and the flat ceiling began to increase. On looking down, it was invariably seen that the feet were sinking. There seemed to be a yellowish crust which was easy to break through and which was harder than the blue-grey, slimy, layer beneath that. It would be quite possible to get caught as in quicksand, especially when an attempt was made to go around the edge of the water which cut off, with one long indentation, a particularly inviting expanse of dark passages.

It was very uncomfortable in there, for the reason that we could not proceed even on hands and knees, and so we squirmed about on thighs and elbows. Every once in a while, one of the party would forget the "ceiling zero" and bang his head, or would try to hurry with the crawl method and find himself brought up short with his back trying to lift the ceiling. One of the remarkable features of the cave was the flat roof, which was merely the petrified mud floor of an ancient shallow sea, with the previously formed rock layers below it removed by the quarry men in the olden days.

There were plenty of timbers lying about; whether these were brought in by the spring floods or were the original material of the workmen, I did not know. They are not smoothly shaped. We found an old sledge hammer which seemed unlike those of the present day.

Studding the roof were the tiny icicle-like formations of stone called stalactites, formed of calcium carbonate. I did not see any which were over an inch long. So tough were they that one of the students had to use some solid instrument to break off some for souvenirs. I am not sure, but I think he used the end of my flashlight. Experts on caves say that such stalactites take one hundred years on the average to form a cubic centimetre. Of course the amount of the deposit would depend on the quantity of carbon dioxide dissolved in the percolating waters. When such water flows through limestone layers, it is enabled, because of this "dissolved" gas, to eat away at the rock. Whenever it drips from the roof of any cavity slowly, or runs slowly over a surface, the carbon dioxide disappears into the air and the limestone or calcium carbonate is deposited again from the water as it drips or oozes.

I questioned a workman, who happened to be passing, about the old kilns which seemed well-preserved but long-unused, farther down the side of the hill. Then he surprised me by telling me that the rock taken from the cave we were just in was burned in those kilns to make cement for the second Welland Ship Canal, about one hundred years ago.

And then I realized that the rock layer which had been so carefully taken out was the same hydraulic natural cement rock which nature had dissolved to form the Devil's Hole cave, downriver from the Niagara Glen on the American side.

N.B. According to Francis Petrie, 1972, Isaac Usher emigrated to Upper Canada from Kansas in 1882 and purchased 404.7 hectares (1000 acres) along the escarpment from Queenston Heights to St. Davids. In 1885, a short distance from his home, he started the first natural rock cement plant in Ontario. Four entrances were cut into the face of the escarpment and limestone (Decew dolostone) was tunnel-mined, using steam-powered drilling equipment. The raw rock was hauled to brick-lined kilns, in mine cars running on iron tracks, and drawn by mules or horses. The rock was burned in the 18 metre (60 foot) deep kilns to produce rock cement, also known as hydraulic cement, which was sold under the brand name "Red Star". The limestone mined here was found to have a very high content of magnesia salts, and was suitable for making hydraulic rock cement only. The increasing use of a much superior type of cement, Portland cement, led to the abandonment of this rock cement works in 1905.

A.H. Tiplin

This 1938 photo shows the Stamford Collegiate students who accompanied Albert Tiplin on an exploration of the old cement works. They are standing in front of one of the four entrances made in the face of the escarpment near St. Davids, where a 1.8 metre (6 foot) layer of Decew dolomite limestone was tunnel-mined as a natural source of hydraulic, or rock, cement.

Spun Rock-Wool

In the 1930's, an American researcher, looking for an insulating material that was fire-proof, and flexible so that it could be wrapped around pipes, discovered that such an insulation could be made from a certain type of shale. This shale had a high proportion of silicate of alumina (kalonite) and is known under at least three names: shaley dolomite; argillaceous dolomite or limestone; and argillaceous shale.

When this shale is heated in a high-intensity furnace, it melts at 1482 degrees Centigrade (2,700 degrees Fahrenheit). When the stream of molten rock is poured from the furnace, it is struck by a stream of live steam at about 689.5 kilopascals (100 pounds) pressure. This blows the heated material into a chamber already preheated. Here it turns into a greenish cotton-batting-like material having special insulating properties, vermin-proof, and fire-resistant. It is called spun rock-wool insulation.

The Federal Department of Mines, Ottawa, was given the task of finding where this material existed in Canada, so that a Canadian plant could be established close to a source of supply of this special shale. An 18 metre (60 foot) layer of this argillaceous shale was found on Queenston Quarry property directly under the hydraulic cement layer, in what

was an abandoned part of the quarry.

In 1932, Spun Rock Wool opened their Canadian plant in the town of Thorold. After a period of experimentation, during which time the plant was often closed down for furnace cleaning or other necessary repairs, it produced spun rock-wool for insulation.

Queenston Quarry shale was used in the process for many years, before similar shale was purchased from Walker Brothers Quarry because it was closer to the Spun Rock Wool plant in Thorold. It was dark grey, having been the ancient mud bottom of seas which once partially covered our continent in this district, at a period when vegetable matter flourished. When this vegetable matter decayed, it built up on the sea bottom, giving the dark carbonaceous colour to these rocks.

Spun rock-wool, or rock-wool, became very popular as an insulating material, and in the mid-1950's, over 80 per cent of the insulation sold in Canada was rock-wool insulation. Spun Rock Wool went out of business in 1978, partly as a result of competition from fibre-glass insulation which came on the market in the 1960's. Rock-wool is still used as insulation, mainly blown into attics and walls.

Walker Brothers Quarry

In 1887, John Walker, a marble carver, opened a quarry on leased land on the brow of the Niagara Escarpment. Shortly thereafter he transferred this business to his three sons and it became known as Walker Brothers Quarry. Since that time, for over 100 years, the Walker family, including three generations of brothers, has been quarrying limestone on the same site, in the north-east corner of what is now the City of Niagara Falls, Ontario.

From this central location, close to markets in the Niagara Peninsula and adjacent to the third Welland Ship Canal, building stone was transported by way of the Welland Canal to Hamilton, Toronto, and to the Province of Quebec. During this time building stone was quarried and shipped to provide stone for Armouries in Hamilton, Toronto and Chatham; for the Adams Power House in Niagara Falls, New York, and for the Canadian Niagara Power House in Niagara Falls, Ontario, both owned by the Niagara Falls Power Company. The last building stone quarried by Walker Brothers was in 1927, and was used for an addition to St. Andrews Presbyterian Church in Thorold.

There was waste from the quarrying of blocks of limestone building stone, and a use was found for this waste in the development of two apparently unrelated fields. One was paper making, the other was road building.

The St. Catharines, Thorold and Suspension Bridge Toll Road Company received its charter in 1852. The road we now know as Thorold Stone Road, was part of this Toll Road, which ran from St. Catharines, through Thorold, down the present Thorold Stone Road to Stanley Street, then to present day Bridge Street in Niagara Falls, and to the Railway Suspension Bridge.

When the portion known as Thorold Stone Road was macadamized – that is, surfaced with successive layers of broken stone, each layer subjected to pressure before the next was laid – Walker Brothers Quarry was close by and probably supplied stone at that time and for subsequent additions to the road surface.

Walker Brothers Quarry

Wayne Farrar

This 1901 photograph shows work in progress in the quarry. A steam-powered drill is in the foreground, with two operators who are boring holes in the stone bed, in preparation for the placing of dynamite charges. The guy derrick, in the centre right, lifts the blocks of blasted rock away from the quarry face where the men are standing, centre left of the photo, and piles them ready for loading on the railway flat cars. An engine and tender stand ready to pull out with the loaded flat cars, to transport them to stone fabricators at building sites throughout the Province of Ontario. The black smoke at the top right, is from the coal-fired steam generating plant, and the wisps of white, seen at the base of the guy derrick, are steam escaping from the steam piping system.

Operating areas of Walker Brothers Quarries are shown in this mid-1980's air view. No. 1, the active quarry face; No. 2, active landfill site, started in 1982; No. 3, construction of the new landfill cell; No. 4, tailings pond from quarry washing operation; No. 5, crushed stone plant; No. 6, screening plant; No. 7, crushed stone stock piles; No. 8, the third Welland Canal lands, with abandoned filling ponds and locks.

In 1864 Thomas Riordan established the first sulphite process paper mill in Canada, at Merritton. Limestone was required for the sulphite process. Limestone for paper mills was called "one man rubble" because it was hand broken into pieces weighing about 22.7 to 27.2 kilograms (50 to 60 pounds), the weight one man could carry.

Stone quarrying, stone cutting and transportation were all labour intensive in those days. Ships carrying Walker Brothers building stone would be unloaded at dockside in Toronto by a gang of stone hookers, where it sold for $9.00 a toise – a toise was the equivalent of 7.87 tonnes (8 tons). Building stone for the Adams Power house was transported across the Railway Suspension Bridge to the United States in horse-drawn wagons, each carrying 2.9 tonnes (3 tons).

To release the rock in the quarry, the stone face was blasted with dynamite, producing a few tonnes (tons) of broken rock. Then the large rock would be drilled and blasted again, producing smaller rocks, some of which had to be broken by manual labour, using rock hammers. The pieces were then picked up and loaded into three-sided dinkey cars which ran on tracks throughout the quarry, each car holding about 2 tonnes (2 tons) of stone. Workmen pushed the dinkey cars along the narrow gauge tracks to a guy derrick, which lifted the cars to the level of the steam-powered stone crusher, where they were unloaded by hand and the rock fed into the crusher. The crushed stone chip was then loaded into rail cars for shipment. By this manual process, it took 19 man hours to produce 12.5 cubic metres (19 cubic yards), that is, one rail car load. Stone chips sold at 18 cents for 0.984 tonnes (one ton). Production was 197 tonnes (200 tons) a day.

As the use of automobiles increased, there came a need for better roads, which required stone. Walker Brothers Quarry supplied stone for many roads and highways in the Niagara District, including the first multi-lane, divided highway in Canada, the Queen Elizabeth Way. In return for the stone business from the Ontario Department of Highways, Walker Brothers and other quarries were required to contribute 5 cents a ton, as a "voluntary" contribution to the ruling political party. Walker Brothers supplied 39,360 tonnes (40,000 tons) of stone for the Queen Elizabeth Way during 1938-39 and contributed $2,000 to the Provincial Liberal Party of the day.

In 1929 a new crusher, which was still hand loaded, went into production. This produced primary stone that was 19 centimetres (7.5 inches) in size, then 10 centimetre (4 inch) secondary stone. In 1941 the use of dinkey cars was discontinued and the crusher was moved to the quarry floor. Hand loading had been replaced gradually by steam-powered, then diesel-powered shovels. Production of crushed stone aggregate rose to 590 tonnes (600 tons) a day. With the installation of the current mechanized plant in 1947, production increased to 246 tonnes (250 tons) an hour, for a nine hour day.

Walker Brothers continues to be a family business. One of the second generation, David Walker, designed both the first stone crushing plant in 1905, and the second improved plant in 1929. John Greenhill Walker, of the third generation, designed and had built the first fully mechanized plant, in 1947. After transferring ownership and management of Walker Brothers Quarries to his sons, John and Norris, in 1967, John Greenhill Walker remained active. For the newly acquired quarry in Vineland, he designed and built the most advanced crushed stone plant in the Niagara Peninsula, complete with remote controls for product conveyor stacking, and electrically controlled product mixing.

Although limestone for construction and road building is still the main business of Walker Brothers Quarries, a natural outgrowth of the quarrying business is to provide landfill space for community and industrial waste. The company is now providing scientifically prepared landfill facilities, with carefully laid down clay beds impervious to leaking, so that liquid waste cannot leach into the surrounding water table. These facilities are now being used by Niagara District communities and industries.

Walker Brothers Quarries carry out a continuing program of rehabilitation and quarry beautification, with tree plantings and grassy berms surrounding the quarry property. In 1987, Walker Brothers Quarries, currently operated by John and Norris Walker, celebrated the 100th Anniversary of the business by sponsoring several conservation projects: restoration of the gardens of Rodman Hall in St. Catharines to their former splendour; beautification of a community park in Thorold; creation of a hiking and biking path along the old Welland Canal.

Power

<u>Six Million Wild Horses</u>, *an allegorical oil painting by an unknown artist, portrays the great horsepower which men of vision have long dreamed of harnessing from the Falls. The upsurge from the falling water waiting to be harnessed, is depicted in the herd of wild horses surging forward and plunging through the rapids below the Falls. When this painting was commissioned in 1924, electric energy generated from dropping the water of the Niagara River over the gorge, and through the power houses, was rated in horsepower. Today's production of electricity from the Niagara River is rated in less romantic kilowatts.*

This 1875 photograph shows the Gaskill Flouring Mill, the first industry to use the energy from dropping water over the gorge bank at Niagara Falls. In 1847 Augustus Porter and Peter B. Porter who called themselves "proprietors of the lands which embrace the Rapids and Falls, on the American side of the Niagara..." issued an "Invitation to Eastern Capitalists and Manufacturers" to develop the power at Niagara Falls. It was not until 1853 that work began on a canal, which was to be 3 metres (10 feet) deep and 21.3 metres (70 feet) wide, cut through the solid rock, leading from the upper rapids above the American Falls, 1372 metres (4500 feet) diagonally through the village of Niagara Falls, to a point on the gorge bank, about 0.8 kilometres (a half mile) downriver from the American Falls.

Water first flowed through this canal in 1857, to drop over the gorge bank, unutilized. It was not until 1875 that the first utilization of this water, from the Hydraulic Canal, falling over the high bank began. The Gaskill Flouring Mill, used only one eighth of the potential energy available from the 64 metre (210 foot) head available when it dropped its allotment of water onto a water wheel located 7.6 metres (25 feet) below the top of the cliff. A system of belts and pulleys transferred the energy generated by the spinning water wheel, to run the machinery in the mill.

F.H. Leslie

Niagara Falls Park and River Railway Power House

The first diversion of water for electric power generation on the Canadian side of the Niagara River took place when the Niagara Falls Park and River Railway Company built this power house, in 1892, to provide direct electric current for their scenic railway. This hydraulic power plant shared its intake with the City of Niagara Falls waterworks. The intake led water into a forebay, then through a screen house where floating debris was screened out. From there it entered the penstocks through two 2.1 metre (7 foot) diameter iron gates, which could be hand operated to shut off the flow of water to the turbines in case of an emergency. The penstocks were constructed of 0.95 centimetre (3/8 inch) steel plate. They were 2.3 metres (7.5 feet) in diameter and 13.4 metres (44 feet) long, and led to the turbines in the wheelpit.

The wheel pit was 18.3 metres (60 feet) deep, 4.9 metres (16 feet) wide and 9.1 metres (30 feet) long. At the bottom of the wheelpit, operating under a head of 18.9 metres (62 feet), were located two, 1000 horsepower reduction turbines, built by W. Kennedy and Sons of Owen Sound, Ontario. They were 1.1 metres (3 feet 9 inches) in diameter, American type wheels, operating at a speed of 200 revolutions per minute.

From each turbine, a vertical shaft 19 centimetres (7.5 inches) in diameter, ran through the penstocks and continued up to drive a bevel gear 1.9 metres (6 feet 3 inches) in diameter. This gear in turn meshed into two pinions, each with a diameter of 1.7 metres (5

feet 8 inches). This system was used to change the rotation of the vertical turbine shaft into the rotation of horizontal line shafts. These latter shafts ran along the plant just parallel to the screen house wall. Each gear and pinion set weighed 5.9 tonnes (6 tons). Upon the line shafts were placed driving pulleys 2 metres (6 feet 6 inches) in diameter, one for each generator. Leather belts operating at a speed of 1341 metres (4,400 feet) per second, were used to connect the line shaft pulleys to the direct current generators.

The generators were 200 kilowatt Thomson-Houston multipolar machines manufactured by Canadian General Electric. When they were installed in 1892 they were the largest units made by Canadian General Electric. Originally three machines were placed in the power house, but by 1904 three more generators had been installed to keep pace with the increased amount of traffic on the railway. Five were connected as ordinary direct current generators, with the sixth being used as a booster to maintain the voltage of distant lines. The tailrace of this plant was regarded as a notable engineering achievement at the time. it was a 183 metre (600 foot), 2.4 metre by 3 metre (8 by 10 foot) tunnel cut in the rock just below the Lockport limestone layer. The plant was re-equipped in 1903 with new 2000 horsepower turbines and generators. The forebay and screen house were extended in anticipation of adding three more units. They were never installed. The railway ceased operating after its charter expired in 1932. The Niagara Parks Commission used the building as a works storehouse, then a retail merchandise storehouse, until 1984, when the building was razed.

Canadian Niagara Power Co.

Canadian Niagara Power Generating Station

As early as 1889, negotiations began between the Queen Victoria Niagara Falls Park Commissioners and a group of American investors, for the right to generate electric power from the waters of the Niagara River above the Falls. They withdrew their application when they could not arrange financing. They were succeeded by a group of English financiers whose option expired on March 1, 1892, and was not renewed.

The Park Commissioners then signed an agreement with the original group, incorporated as the Canadian Niagara Power Company. It was given monopoly rights to use the water from the Niagara River on the Canadian side, to generate electric power, on condition that the generating station be in operation by May 1, 1897. This franchise lapsed by default after the promised completion date passed. It was renewed in 1899, without the monopoly provision previously granted. Work began on May 23, 1901, on the Canadian Niagara Power House.

The powerhouse is located in Queen Victoria Park about 0.80 kilometres (a half mile) above the Horseshoe Falls, where it takes advantage of the natural flow of the river which used to run around Cedar Island there. A weir which is submerged during the summer months, diverts the river water into the outer forebay. Then by a short canal, which was the

river's former south channel around Cedar Island, it enters the inner forebay which is located on the old Cedar Island channel. (Cedar Island disappeared when this power house project was built).

The water then enters the power house through steel penstocks, which lead to the turbines, located near the bottom of the wheel pit, 39.6 metres (130 feet) underground. After the water passes through the turbines it is discharged to the lower river level, through a 61 metre (200 foot) tunnel, cut through solid rock. This tailrace tunnel outlet can be seen just to the right of the Table Rock Observation Plaza.

Power was first produced in 1905. The eleven 10,000 hp (7500 kilowatt) generators, were the largest ever constructed up to that time. The generators have vertical shafts, wound for three-phase current, 11,000 volts of 25 cycle power at 250 revolutions per minute. The power house has an effective head of 39.6 metres (130 feet) and uses 283 cubic metres (10,000 cubic feet) of water per second to generate 82,500 kilowatts of electricity.

This was the first power house to produce electric power for transmission and sale outside of Niagara Falls. At times this power house is shut down while Ontario Hydro uses its allotment of water in its Sir Adam Beck facilities, to take advantage of the higher head there. At such times the Canadian Niagara Power Company receives an allotment of electric power from Ontario Hydro to compensate for their lost production.

Ontario Power Generating Station

The Ontario Power Generating Station was built in the early 1900's by the Ontario Power Company, an American company. Water for the generating station is drawn from the intake structure opposite Dufferin Islands, about 1.6 kilometres (one mile) above the Horseshoe Falls. To gather the water, the intake structure was built out into the Niagara River, directing the water required into an inner forebay, where the entrances to three 5.5 metre (18 foot) diameter conduits, or tubes, are located. More than twice the volume of water required is diverted; some of the excess water is then diverted through controlled gates into the Dufferin Islands channel, the rest passes into the river, by means of an overflow dam.

The conduits, two of steel and one made of wood bound with iron hoops and encased in concrete, run underground for 1884 metres (6,180 feet), along the edge of the glacial drift bank, to the top of the cliff above the Ontario Power Generating Station, which is located below the Horseshoe Falls. There, each conduit connects with six penstocks, 1.8 metres (6 feet) in diameter; each penstock delivers 110.4 cubic metres (3900 cubic feet) of water per second when its connected generators are fully loaded.

At the point where the conduits and the penstocks are connected each has a section which turns upwards into a spillway, called a surge tank. These surge tanks serve to reduce fluctuations in head and pressure during both the increase and decrease of loads. The spillways, being open, and provided with overflow pipes, send any excess water to the river when the load is suddenly reduced and this prevents any dangerous rise in pressure. Only two of these surge tanks, located south of the Victoria Park Restaurant in Queen Victoria Park, exist today. The Illumination Battery is on top of one of them. The third surge tank, connected with what was to be a temporary wooden pipe line, built to supply power for wartime production during the Great War, 1914-18, was dismantled in 1967. Tail water from this generating station discharges directly into the river.

The fifteen generators, using 226.4 cubic metres (8,000 cubic feet) of water per second, with an effective head of 54.8 metres (180 feet), produce 203,000 hp (132,500 kilowatts) of 25 cycle electric power. This plant has twice been flooded by ice and water, in 1909 and 1938, putting it out of service each time for many months.

Toronto Power
Generating Station

This Italian Renaissance style power house, constructed of Indiana limestone, was built by a syndicate of Canadian investors which included Henry M. Pellatt, the builder of Casa Loma in Toronto. The syndicate was known as the Electrical Development Company. It received a franchise to develop 125,000 hp, using the water of the Niagara River above the Horseshoe Falls.

The power house, 141.7 metres (467 feet) long, 27.7 metres (91 feet) wide, was built on land reclaimed from the river bed, where the water was formerly from 2.4 to 7.3 metres (8 to 24 feet) deep. The wheel pit, 126.7 metres (416 feet) long, 6.7 metres (22 feet) wide, and 45.7 metres (150 feet) deep, is brick lined.

Water was collected from the river by a wing dam which extends 224 metres (735 feet) into the river, and is from 3 to 8.2 metres (10 to 27 feet) high. The water passed through submerged arches into the inner forebay and then dropped down steel penstocks, 3.15 metres (10 feet 6 inches) in diameter, to the turbines. From the turbines the water flowed into tunnels paralleling the wheel pit on either side, and converg-

ing, beneath the down river end of the power house, into the main tailrace tunnel. This 9.6 metre (32 foot) horseshoe-shaped tunnel carried the tailrace water 609.6 metres (2000 feet) to its outlet behind the centre of the Horseshoe Falls. The tunnel is lined with concrete, formed in slab like sections designed to break off cleanly whenever the eroding Horseshoe Falls reached a break-off section.

Power from the 11 generators of 11,000 hp each, was first delivered in November, 1906. The installed capacity of the power house was 110,000 hp or 98,000 kilowatts. The Hydro Electric Power Commission of Ontario (now Ontario Hydro) purchased the facilities in 1920. Improvements to the generators increased the generating station's capacity, and when the power house was removed from service in 1974, the generators produced 12,500 hp each, making the total capacity 137,500 hp. The water formerly used at this power plant is now being used at the Sir Adam Beck Generating Stations at Queenston, where, because of the greater drop, more power can be generated from the same amount of water. The effective head at the Toronto Power Generating Station was 41 metres (135 feet), while it is 89.6 metres (294 feet) at the Sir Adam Beck plants.

Sir Adam Beck
Generating Stations

This 1963 air view shows Ontario Hydro's Queenston power complex. No. 1, Sir Adam Beck Generating Station No. 1, formerly the Queenston Generating Station, was for many years the largest hydro-electric plant in the world. To utilize the maximum drop over the gorge, water had to be diverted from an intake 3.2 kilometres (2 miles) above the Horseshoe Falls at Chippawa, to the generating station here at Queenston. To accomplish this, the Welland River was reversed from its former mouth at the Niagara River to enter a canal, 13.6 kilometres (8.5 miles) long, cut through solid rock through the city of Niagara Falls, Ontario, leading to the forebay, or head pond, at the power house. From the forebay penstocks carry the water to the turbines of the generators in the power house below at the river's edge. The power house itself is 55 metres (180 feet) above its foundation, and is 171 metres (560 feet) long. If it were placed in front of the American Falls it would almost hide it. Using a head of 89.6 metres (294 feet) of water, its ten generators have a capacity of 403,900 kilowatts. The first generator went into production in January 1922; No. 2, Sir Adam Beck Generating Station No. 2. This generating station is supplied with 68 million litres (12 million gallons) of water drawn from the river above the Horseshoe Falls through two 14 metre (46 foot)

diameter, concrete lined tunnels, which run directly under the City of Niagara Falls, Ontario, at a depth of up to 100 metres (330 feet). The tunnels surface at the edge of the Whirlpool-St. Davids Buried Gorge. Water is carried across this Gorge on a concrete flume, then in a canal cut through rock, to the forebay. Power was first produced in 1954. The 16 generating units are housed in a building almost twice as long as the adjoining plant, and have an installed capacity of 1,223,600 kilowatts. The two Sir Adam Beck Generating power plants use 1839.5 m³ (65,000 cubic feet) of water per second; No. 3, the forebay of the Robert Moses Niagara Power Plant of the Power Authority of the State of New York; No. 4 is the 300 hectare (750 acre) Ontario Hydro Pump Storage Reservoir, where 182,000,000 m³ (650,000,000 cubic feet) of water is stored to be passed through the generators of No. 5, the pump generating plant. The water is pumped up into the reservoir during the night, when power demand is low and the water would otherwise not be used for electric power generation, and then released through the pump generating plant during periods of high demand. This pump generating plant went into production in 1958. It is capable of producing 176,700 kilowatts of electric energy; No. 6, the Lewiston-Queenston Bridge; No. 7, Smeaton Ravine; No. 8, Queenston Heights Park; No. 9, Queenston Quarries.

Dorothy Gordon

The outer forebay of the Toronto Power Generating Station circa 1900, with the wing dam and the stone arches leading to the inner forebay. The contour of the dried off river bed is visible.

The Falls from the British Side by James P. Cockburn, 1832. It shows the river channel around Cedar Island. The Canadian Niagara Power Generating Station is now located on the bank of the river below, in the centre of the picture. The channel was filled in when the power plant was built.

Niagara Parks Archives

Robert Moses Niagara Power Plant

The fireworks display over the Robert Moses Niagara Power Plant, on July 31, 1986, celebrated the 25th anniversary of the Plant.

Water for this Power Plant is drawn from the Niagara River four kilometres (two and a half miles) above the Falls on the American side, through two 213 metre (700 foot) long harmonica-like structures. Each contains 48 slotted openings, located below water level. Twin conduits, 14 metres (46 feet) wide by 20 metres (66 feet) high – each conduit is equivalent in size to six double-track railroad tunnels – lead from the intake and run 7.2 kilometres (four miles) to the forebay. Each conduit has a 394 tonne (400 ton) vertical lift gate, and each gate is housed in a structure approximately 15 metres (49 feet) wide and 20 metres (66 feet) high.

From the forebay, water enters the turbines through 141 metre (460 foot) long penstocks, which are 8.7 metres (28.5 feet) in diameter at the top, narrowing to 6.4 metres (21 feet) where they enter the turbines. Tailrace water discharges directly into the lower Niagara River.

The thirteen generators are rated at 200,000 hp (150,000 kilowatts) each, at 91.40 metres (300 feet) net, of head. The first power was produced on January 28, 1961. There is a 760 hectare (1900 acre) pump storage reservoir and there is also a pump storage generating plant with a capacity of 240,000 kilowatts.

The Robert Moses Niagara Power Plant is one of the largest hydro-electric plants in the world. It is owned by the people of New York State, through the New York State Power Authority.

Bibliography

American Falls International Board.
*Preservation and Enhancement of the
American Falls at Niagara Falls. Final report
to The International Joint Commission.* 1974.

Colossal Cataract. Irving H. Tesmer, editor;
by Jerold C. Bastedo, and others. Albany:
State University of New York Press, 1981.

Dow, Charles M. *Anthology and Bibliography of
Niagara Falls.* Albany: State of New York,
1921.

Drescher, Nuala. *Engineers for the Public
Good.* Buffalo: United States Army Corps of
Engineers (n.d.)

Ensminger, Scott A. *Canadian Caves of the
Niagara Gorge.* North Tonawanda:
Ensminger, 1983.

Forrester, Glenn C. *Niagara Falls and the
Glacier.* Hicksville: Exposition Press, 1976.

Gillard, William and Tooke, Thomas. *The
Niagara Escarpment.* Toronto: University of
Toronto Press, 1975.

Hobson, George D. and Terasmae, Jaan.
*Pleistocene Geology of the Buried St. Davids
Gorge, Niagara Falls, Ontario; Geophysical
and Palynological Studies.* Ottawa:
Geological Survey of Canada, 1969.

Hydro-Electric Power Commission of Ontario.
*The Hydro-Electric Power Commission of
Ontario: Its Origin, Administration and
Achievements.* Toronto: HEPC, 1928.

Hydro-Electric Power Commission of Ontario.
*Report on 2nd Queenston Development;
Preliminary Geological Report.* Toronto:
HEPC Generation Department, 1950.

MacMullin, Robert B. *The Niagara Whirlpool
Reversal Phenomenon.* Niagara Falls, N.Y.:
Schoellkopf Geology Museum, 1973.

Prest, V.K. *Canada's Heritage of Glacial
Features.* Ottawa: Geological Survey of
Canada, 1983.

Special International Niagara Board. *The
Preservation of Niagara Falls: Final Report of
the Special International Niagara Board.*
Ottawa: King's Printer, 1930.

Spencer, J.W.W. "Discovery of the Preglacial
Outlet of the Basin of Lake Erie Into That of
Lake Ontario; with Notes on the Origin of
the Lower Great Lakes." *Quarterly Journal of
the Geological Society,* 46, 1890.

Spencer, J.W.W. "The Duration of Niagara
Falls". *American Journal of Science,* 18:3,
1894.

Spencer, J.W.W. "The Iroquois Beach: A Chapter
in the Geological History of Lake Ontario".
*Proceedings and Transactions of the Royal
Geological Society of Canada,* 1881.

Tovell, Walter M. *The Niagara Escarpment.*
Toronto: Royal Ontario Museum, 1965.

Tovell, Walter, M. *The Niagara River.* Toronto:
Royal Ontario Museum, 1979.

Index

Page numbers in italics are for illustrations